T0291253

Reimagining India–Thailand Relations

A Multilateral and Bilateral Perspective

Reena Marwah

Delhi University, India

Reimagining India–Thailand Relations

A Multilateral and Bilateral Perspective

 **World Scientific**

NEW JERSEY · LONDON · SINGAPORE · BEIJING · SHANGHAI · HONG KONG · TAIPEI · CHENNAI · TOKYO

Published by

World Scientific Publishing Co. Pte. Ltd.

5 Toh Tuck Link, Singapore 596224

USA office: 27 Warren Street, Suite 401-402, Hackensack, NJ 07601

UK office: 57 Shelton Street, Covent Garden, London WC2H 9HE

Library of Congress Cataloging-in-Publication Data

Names: Marwah, Reena, 1960–   author.
Title: Reimagining India-Thailand relations : a multilateral and bilateral
    perspective / Reena Marwah (Delhi University, India).
Description: USA : World Scientific, 2020. | Includes bibliographical references and index.
Identifiers: LCCN 2019053437 | ISBN 9789811212031 (hardcover) |
    ISBN 9789811212048 (ebook)
Subjects: LCSH: Economic development--Asia. | India--Foreign relations--Thailand. |
    Thailand--Foreign relations--India. | Asia--Economic conditions--21st century.
Classification: LCC HC412 .M3547 2020 | DDC 337.540593--dc23
LC record available at https://lccn.loc.gov/2019053437

British Library Cataloguing-in-Publication Data
A catalogue record for this book is available from the British Library.

For any available supplementary material, please visit
https://www.worldscientific.com/worldscibooks/10.1142/11601#t=suppl

Desk Editors: Anthony Alexander/Sandhya Venkatesh

Typeset by Stallion Press
Email: enquiries@stallionpress.com

Dedicated with Affection and Gratitude
to Daddyji — My father-in-Law
and
In Loving memory of my Parents

Preface

India has decisively shifted its policy stance for Southeast Asia from Looking East in the 1990s to Acting East, since 2014. This re-articulation, after a gap of more than two decades, brings an expectation from India for enhancing and deepening its engagement both with ASEAN and bilaterally with each of the member countries. While India has its own *raison d'être* to Act East, ASEAN too seeks India as a balance to an aggressive China.

This book focuses on India's relations especially with Thailand, bringing to the fore our historical and cultural linkages not only through the Sanskrit language but through Brahmanism and Buddhism as well. Economic and commercial engagement coupled with strategic and security engagements have brought India–Thailand closer.

While USA has had a sustained interest in Southeast Asia and especially in Thailand, a rising China is not only posing a threat here to American foreign policy interests but also changing the dynamics of India's relations with ASEAN countries. The political change within Thailand after 2014 and the changing dynamics of USA–China–ASEAN–Thailand relations for India need to be well articulated.

India must demonstrate that its Act East Policy is not just a new term. For India, the Act East Policy must become one of the most important cornerstones of its foreign policy. Possibly then, this would further encourage and embolden Thailand's Look West Policy, even as the visits of General Prayut Chan-o-Cha to India during June 2016 followed by January 2018 seek. The two countries could engage in newer areas of convergence to compel greater cooperation in all aspects from the cultural and social to the economic and strategic.

Whether India has been able to leverage its historical and cultural linkages for enhanced economic and strategic cooperation will be examined both through primary and secondary sources and include interviews of members of Indian diaspora, academics, diplomats, industrialists, and policymakers.

The literature examined for writing this book compelled a contextual study of India–ASEAN relations, as foregrounding the research on India–Thailand relations, articulating the following:

Rise of Asia: Narratives of colonialism and regionalism: Narratives focusing on the rise of Asia, an ascendant Asia, have brought within the ambit the rise of China and India as well as the importance of ASEAN. Hence, reviewing this literature provided the context for the study. Here, Basu (2017), Acharya (2013), Mason 2000, Kristoff and WuDunn (2001), and Hopkins (1952) provide interesting insights into the rise of Asia. Hopkins (1952) provides a journalistic account of Asian countries after his own travels to many of them. Butwell's (1964) work on Southeast Asia emerged out of concern for newly independent countries. His work discusses issues of political development and the dynamics of state conflicts in Southeast Asia. A more recent work by Wang (2010), which is underpinned on the historical situation in Asia, especially Southeast Asia, discusses the contours of party and nation-making in the context of some countries including Thailand. While Mason (2000) provides a historical perspective, blaming the colonizers of Asian nations for many of their present problems, he also underlines how the exploitation of resources by their colonizers undermined the colonies. Kristoff and WuDunn (2001) provide a more contemporary analysis by viewing the 1997 economic crisis in Asia as a game changer for the countries as it helped them emerge out of protectionism, and government regulation that had been crippling business for decades. Stronger nations emerged with the capabilities to challenge the West. This reiterates the growing importance of Asian countries in the East. Acharya (2013) investigates the origins and evolution of Southeast Asian regionalism and international relations and underlines the importance of regionalism elsewhere in the world. His work gives a very thorough account from pre-history up to the 13th century, as well as the post-13th century to the coming of European influence. That Thailand could avoid colonialism is well discussed. Rachman (2016) discusses rising Asia and Easternization, but he does not fail to warn nations of the political ambitions of states such as India and China. His narrative on prospects of war or peace hinges on the dynamics of big power rivalry. This is because America has come to see China as a threat to its global primacy and China has begun to seek an enhanced role in East Asia. Hence, this book could not afford to neglect the fact that ASEAN countries including Thailand are in the center of the ambitions of big powers, India included.

Basu (2017) weaves together a compelling account of how Asia's nations overcame European domination in the 20th century — and its legacies of war and famine — to initiate economic dynamism within their nations. The India connection with Southeast Asia is also discussed. In contrast to aspects of mainly strategic power calculations, Hoontrakul, Balding, and Marwah (2014) discuss aspects of Asia's economic transformation in the 21st century.

India's relations with Southeast Asia: Thailand–India relations cannot be studied in a vacuum. This has been highlighted by several studies of significance on India's relations with Southeast Asia. These underline the historical, cultural, and religious exchanges that took place for several centuries and continue to present the imprint of India on them. Brahmanism and Buddhism continue to impact people's lives in all these countries.

Chakraborti and Chakraborty (2018) elucidate India's engagement with Southeast Asia since India initiated the Look East policy. Grare and Mattoo (2001) have focused on the *raison d'être* for India to look East and the politics that underpinned this. Their writings are on India's foreign policy at the turn of the century and examine the forging of new partnerships in Southeast Asia. Devare (2005) brings forth aspects of Security Convergence between India and ASEAN and takes forward the logic presented by Grare and Mattoo (2001). Devare (2005) reiterates the significance of India's presence in Southeast Asia leveraging on its centuries old linkages. Sundaraman (2016) also discusses the dynamics of change in India–Southeast Asia relations. She underlines the importance of building strategic partnerships, in the wake of China's deep inroads in SEA. The importance of India in Southeast Asia, with a vision for enhanced geopolitical and geostrategic engagement, has been explained by C. Raja Mohan (2008) and GVC Naidu (2000). Grare (2017) discusses the rationale for India's gaze toward the East. The author asserts that viewing China as a security threat, India has stepped up its cooperation and engagement with the United States. Although India's policy has generated a number of joint declarations, the engagement has been modest in the defense and strategic areas. But India's attempts to strengthen ties with Myanmar and other countries in Southeast Asia have been hampered by countries' reluctance to antagonize China. Indeed, India itself does not want to confront China. The China factor looms large on India's relations with SEA as well as with Thailand.

The strategic to the cultural and religious aspects of India's engagement with ASEAN countries have been documented. It is these historical and cultural linkages that India seeks to leverage in its engagement with Thailand. Coedes (1996) and Majumdar (1927) have provided a detailed account of the Indianized States of Southeast Asia. While Majumdar goes as far to refer to them as Indian colonies in the Far East, Coedes presents a more cogent and balanced view of the transplantation of Indianness in Southeast Asia. Sastri's (1949) seminal work on South Indian influence in the Far East underlines the fact that China and India were the two main sources from which higher cultural influences kept flowing into Southeastern Asia in pre-historic as well as historic times. He also discusses the role of the missionaries of Indian civilization and the route they traveled. Sastri (1949) reveals that people from India could have come through Burma or by sea (possibly after crossing the Isthmus of Kra). Wherever they went, their culture prevailed.

Shastri (1982), one of the most renowned and revered scholars of the *Ramayana*, mastered the Thai version of *Ramayana* and published a book entitled *Ramakirtimahakavyam* (A Sanskrit Mahakavya on Thai *Ramakien*), which was published in 1990. His writings inspired Her Royal Highness Maha Chakri Sirindhorn, the princess of Thailand. Hence, she developed keen interest in Indian culture, India's cultural imprint in Southeast Asian countries, and the various versions of Ramayana. Given the fact that Indian influence and culture is visible in all Southeast Asian countries,

Suryanarayan (2019) has written about the cultural indebtedness of all Southeast Asian countries to India. Singh and Dhar (2014) provide a comprehensive account of Asian cultural interactions during the pre-modern and early modern periods through the prism of politics, art, religion, and trade. Their articulation underlines the importance of undergirding research on India–Thailand cultural relations through the historical context in which they took place. Chandra and Ghoshal (2011) also emphasize on the traditions of connectivity and mutual reconciliation between various cultures, a tradition of the countries of the region which was strengthened by close contacts with India, both in the ancient and medieval periods.

Kumar, Sen, and Asher (2006) through their research on India–ASEAN economic relations focused on the challenges of globalization, primarily focusing on China's rise. The authors assert that India is clearly at a serious disadvantage in trade relations with ASEAN. A policy brief by Nanda (2018), mainly to highlight 25 years of India–ASEAN relations, is a compilation of events, declarations, as well as issues confronting the region. Another commemorative study by De and Singh (2018), focusing on the imperative for India to Act East, brings into discussion the connectivity challenges to India's Northeast region. Manguin, Mani, and Wade (2011) have also documented archaeological research carried out on both sides of the Bay of Bengal, in combination with renewed approaches to textual sources and to art history.

Thailand — History, religion, and culture: Pollock (1996), writes about the "Sanskrit cosmopolis", which he dates approximately between the years 300 and 1300. He interrogates the reasons for the spread of Sanskrit from the Indian subcontinent to Southeast Asia and concludes that Sanskrit became the primary expression of the polities of Southeast Asia. The importance of Indianization through language is underlined. Wales (1931) has made a great contribution to the understanding of Hindu rituals and the presence of Brahmanas in the royal palaces. Wales himself had moved to Siam in 1924 and served as an adviser to the courts of King Rama VI and King Rama VII until 1928. His experiences provided the basis for his writings on the ceremonies and rituals followed by the monarchs, all of whom who took the title of Rama.

Baker and Phongpaichit (2005) track Thailand's economic changes through an economic boom, globalization, and the evolution of mass society. Their historical work provides an analysis of Thailand's recent political, social, and economic developments, covering the coup of 2006, the violent street politics of May 2010, and the landmark election of 2011 and its aftermath. It shows how in Thailand today, the monarchy, the military, business, and new mass movements are players in a complex conflict over the nature and future of the country's democracy. This has implications for India's relations with Thailand. Kusalasaya (2013) writes of the Thailand–India connection through Buddhism. Owing to the tremendous influence Buddhism exerts on the lives of its people, Thailand is called by many foreigners "The Land of Yellow Robes", for yellow robes are the garments of Buddhist monks. The Thai people are forever grateful to India for enriching their culture. Phillips (2018) writes about Thailand's position during the Cold War. At this time, India–Thailand relations were at a low ebb. Thailand, though never formally a client state of the United States, was very closely embedded in the Western camp through the commitment of Thailand's cosmopolitan urban communities to developing a modern, consumerist lifestyle. Considering popular culture, including film, literature, fashion, tourism, and attitudes toward Buddhism, the book shows how an ideology of consumerism and integration into a "free world" culture centered in the United States gradually took hold and became firmly established, and how this popular culture and ideology was fundamental in determining Thailand's international political alignment.

India's historical and cultural relations with Thailand: On issues of ethnicity, culture, and religious engagement through Buddhism, authors such as Ghosh (2004) provided interesting perspectives. Srichampa has articulated the possibilities of cooperation through harnessing of the soft power of India and Thailand. Ghosh *et al.* (2006) have also written about the issues of identity among women across Asian countries and in this context explored some of the historical and cultural aspects of Thai society.

There are other important studies on soft power, religion, and culture that merit attention. These include the following:

Chitrabongs (2015) discusses the omnipresence of the *Ramayana* in Thai arts and culture. It is well known that the *Ramayana* has also greatly molded the art and architectural works of India throughout the centuries. Srichampa (2015) describes the long-standing relationship between India and Thailand since ancient times. This relationship commenced through trade, and later, Indian religion and culture followed. Thailand remains influenced by Indian elements, which mixed with the local beliefs and culture. There was no hard power used directly from India toward Southeast Asia or Thailand in particular. Rather, it was soft power that India used to forge ties with Thailand. Poolthupya (2008) has written about rising India and Indian communities in East Asia. She is a well-known scholar on India and has written about the multidimensional contribution of the Indian diaspora to Thailand.

Contemporary aspects of India–Thailand economic relations — bilateral and multilateral: Ram (2007) discusses the imperative for enhanced India–Thailand relations, in the ambit of new partnerships and alliances that India must orient itself to. This will enable it to be better prepared for both new challenges and opportunities — strategic, security, political, social, ecological, economic, and commercial — that are being presented in the 21st century. He also underlines the importance of this time-tested relationship. A perspective from Thailand to forge economic links with India's Northeast has been provided by Chirathivat (2010). Although India's Northeast region and its association through ethnic communities with Thailand has been discussed in literature on the subject by Phukan (1990), it is well known that India's Northeast region had been neglected for a long time. Hence, aspects of infrastructure development in recent years assume importance for a meaningful discussion. Moreover, connectivity corridors and linkages through Myanmar are of great significance. The importance of connectivity corridors as an integral component of India's economic diplomacy with India's Eastern neighbors has been articulated and discussed by Bhatt (2016) as well as De (2018). De (2018) has undertaken a detailed empirical assessment of connectivity through corridors. Both studies point to the importance of improving the security conditions in Manipur and Mizoram for enhancing border trade with Myanmar.

A recent study by Mukherjee and Goyal (2018) discusses the case of India and Thailand within the framework of a possible integration of

South and Southeast Asia through services value chain. A more comprehensive analysis of India's relations with Thailand since 1990 has been provided by Kumar (2014), in which he discusses trade relations over the period 1990–2011 and delineates aspects of bilateral cooperation in some multilateral forums.

About the Book

Thailand's importance for India cannot be ignored for several reasons — economic, cultural, and strategic and as an important neighbor. Moreover, it was the coordinator country for India–ASEAN relations in 2019. The study draws extensively from several interviews of experts, diplomats, journalists, businesspersons, and members of the Indian community based in different cities in Thailand.

This book brings into focus India's relations with ASEAN and Thailand in particular. In the 1990s, India revived its relations with Southeast Asia. Yet, in comparison to China, India continued to be a distant neighbor. Hence, India has once again, through its 'Look and Act East' policies, become intertwined with its immediate neighbors in the East, especially with Thailand. The objective of this work is to contextualize India's relations and influence in Southeast Asia over a period of nearly 2000 years, through culture and religion. The scope extends beyond bilateral issues to include the multilateral, bringing in issues of trade negotiations under the Regional Comprehensive Economic Partnership (RCEP) and the Indo-Pacific construct. As ASEAN's and Thailand's (one of the Big Five Countries) importance grows in the regional and global landscape, there are ramifications for its relations with its traditional partners. A rising India seeks a united and strong ASEAN both as a natural partner and in a bid to balance China's growing assertiveness and deep pockets. It also brings into discussion the importance of India's Northeast and Myanmar. This book encompasses a wide range of aspects that pertain to the historical, cultural, economic, and strategic international relations of Thailand with India.

The book is composed of three sections; viz. the first section includes chapters on India–ASEAN and India–Thailand cultural connect through historical times. An understanding of the colonial influence in

Southeast Asia and Thailand provides the basis of comprehending the contemporary aspects of Thailand's foreign relations.

The second section focuses on ASEAN's centrality and the multilateral architecture to situate India–ASEAN relations.

The third section includes chapters on Thailand as well as chapters on India's relations with Thailand in terms of the economic, cultural, and strategic linkages as well as India and Thailand in sub-regional groupings.

In all, the book is composed of nine chapters, through which the author seeks to answer questions such as the following:

1. Do the historical and cultural links between Southeast Asia, particularly Thailand and India, have the potential to transform/enrich the scope of bilateral relations and further enhance people-to-people contacts?
2. Can Thailand be a significant and strategic partner of India both on the continental shelf (linkages through Northeast and cooperation in anti-smuggling, anti-money laundering activities, etc.) and in India's maritime space (Bay of Bengal, Indian Ocean, Malacca Straits, and beyond)?
3. What are the pathways for India to build on existing commercial, economic, and strategic engagement with Thailand so that India can truly engage and Act East?

About the Author

Reena Marwah, M.Phil, PhD, International Business, is Associate Professor, Jesus and Mary College, Delhi University. She was an ICSSR Senior Fellow, MHRD, Government of India, affiliated with the Centre for the Study of Developing Societies, New Delhi, from June 2017 to May, 2019, during which her study was on *Reimagining India–Thailand Relations*. She has also been on deputation as Senior Academic Consultant, ICSSR, Ministry of Human Resource Development, Government of India for 3 years (2012–2015) and continued, on behalf of ICSSR, to coordinate/lead the India–Europe Research Platform (EqUIP) till July 2017.

She has been teaching Indian economy, financial markets and institutions, macroeconomics, and politics of globalization. She is the recipient of several prestigious fellowships including the McNamara Fellowship of the World Bank, 1999–2000, and the Asia Fellowship of the Asian Scholarship Foundation 2002–2003, during which she undertook research in Thailand and Nepal. She has undertaken short-term consultancy assignments of the World Bank and UN Women. She is also a Senior Fellow of the Institute of National Security Studies Sri Lanka (INSSSL).

During her teaching and research experience, she has worked closely with several think tanks, international donors, embassies, ministries of the Government of India, and research councils in Asia. Among her research interests are international relations issues of China, Philippines, Thailand, and India and development issues of gender, globalization, and poverty in South and Southeast Asia. In addition to several chapters and articles published in books/journals, she is co-author/co-editor of 12 books and monographs including *Contemporary India: Economy, Society and Polity* (Pinnacle, 2009, 2011), co-edited volumes including *Economic and Environmental Sustainability of the Asian Region* (Routledge, 2010); *Emerging China: Prospects for Partnership in Asia* (Routledge, 2011); *On China by India: From a Civilization to a Nation State* (Cambria Press, USA); *Transforming South Asia: Imperatives for Action* (Knowledge World, India) 2014; and *The Global Rise of Asian Transformation* (Palgrave Macmillan, 2014). Her latest co-edited book is *China Studies in South and Southeast Asia: Pro-China, Objectivism, and Balance* (2018; editors: Chih-yu Shih, Prapin Manomaiviboo, and Reena Marwah; World Scientific Publishing Company, Singapore). She is the founding editor of *Millennial Asia*, a biannual journal on Asian Studies of the Association of Asia Scholars, published by Sage Publishers.

Acknowledgments

This study has been completed in fulfillment of the research project, *Reimagining India–Thailand Relations*, sanctioned by the Indian Council of Social Science Research (ICSSR), Ministry of Human Resource Development, Government of India. My sincere thanks are due to ICSSR former Chairman, Professor Sukhadeo Thorat, late Professor B.B. Kumar, as well as Member Secretary, Professor V.K. Malhotra for reposing faith in my ability to merit this prestigious fellowship. Without the kind cooperation of Professor Sanjay Kumar, Director, Center for Study of Developing Societies (CSDS), for affiliation with the Center, this study would not have been possible. I am truly indebted to the members of the Governing Body of my parent institution, Jesus and Mary College, University of Delhi, and in particular to Sister Rosily RJM for her invaluable encouragement and blessings.

I have been fortunate to have received kind guidance, mentoring, and knowledge from several senior experts, policymakers, officials, members of the Indian diaspora, and friends in Thailand, Myanmar, and India. I am particularly thankful to the Indian Embassy in Thailand and Thai Embassy in India for their generous cooperation. Mentors became good friends, especially in Chiang Mai University, Chulalongkorn University, and Thammasat University. Discussions and formal interviews helped to enrich my understanding of the subject. I am grateful to each of them mentioned in the book.

My family has been my constant strength, through my frequent trips and travel in India and abroad. My husband Rajeev has been a true partner in my academic pursuit. I am grateful to my children for their valuable support. I am truly blessed to have been in the midst of people who have believed in me and invited me for several conferences, seminars, and discussions as well as published my writings. This work acknowledges the seminal contribution of several authors, who have contributed to enriching my knowledge and understanding of the subject.

This book would not have been possible without the kind cooperation of the production and editorial team of World Scientific. Each one deserves my sincere appreciation for their cooperation.

Contents

List of Abbreviations

ACMECS	Ayeyawady-Chao Phraya-Mekong Economic Cooperation Strategy
ADB	Asian Development Bank
ADMM	ASEAN Defence Ministers' Meeting
AEC	ASEAN Economic Community
AEP	Act East Policy
AIC	ASEAN–India Centre
AIFTA	ASEAN India Free Trade Agreement
ASEAN	Association of South East Asian Nations
APEC	Asia–Pacific Economic Cooperation
ARF	ASEAN Regional Forum
APT	ASEAN Plus Three
BSA	Bilateral Swap Arrangements
BIMSTEC	Bay of Bengal Initiative for Multisectoral Technical and Economic Co-operation
CECA	Comprehensive Economic Cooperation Agreement
CLMV	Cambodia Lao PDR Myanmar Vietnam
CMIM	Chiang Mai Initiative Multilateralization
CORPATs	Coordinated Patrols
CSOs	Civil Society Organizations
DONER	Ministry of Development of North Eastern Region
EAS	East Asia Summit
GCI	Global Competitiveness Index

GAME	Guidelines for Air Military Encounters
GMS	Great Mekong Subregion
HADR	Humanitarian Assistance and Disaster Relief
IMT MVA	India–Myanmar–Thailand Motor Vehicle Agreement
ITEC	Indian Technical and Economic Cooperation
IWT	Inland Water Transport
KMMTTP	Kaladan Multi Modal Transit Transport Project
LEP	Look East Policy
LoC	Lines of Credit
MAI	Market Access Initiative
MDA	Market Development Assistance
MEA	Ministry of External Affairs
MFN	Most Favored Nation
MGC	Mekong Ganga Cooperation
MIEC	Mekong India Economic Corridor
MPAC	Master Plan of ASEAN Connectivity
NER	North Eastern Region
PPP	Public-Private Partnership
ReCAAP	Regional Cooperation Agreement on Combating Piracy and Armed Robbery against Ships in Asia
RIMPAC	Rim of the Asia Pacific
RCEP	Regional Comprehensive Economic Partnership
RIS	Research and Information System for Developing Countries
SEA	Southeast Asia
SEATO	South East Asia Treaty Organization
SEZ	Special Economic Zone
SIPI	State Investment Potential Index
TPP	Trans-Pacific Partnership
UNCLOS	United Nations Convention on Law of the Seas
WTO	World Trade Organization

List of Figures

List of Tables

Chapter 1

Southeast Asia: An Indian Imprint

Southeast Asia has been referred to by several names since the pre-Christian era. Sanskrit sources indicate that SEA was referred to as *Suvarnabhumi* (the Land of Gold) or *Suvarnadvipa* (the Golden Island or Peninsula). The 10 countries of ASEAN, viz. countries of maritime Southeast Asia, include Indonesia, Malaysia, East Timor, Philippines, and Singapore, while mainland Southeast Asia is composed of Cambodia, Laos, Myanmar, Vietnam, and Thailand.

The Southeastern sub-region of Asia is located in the South of China, East of India, and North of Australia. Brunei and Singapore are two of the smallest countries of Southeast Asia, with Brunei measuring 5,765 km^2 and Singapore, 724 km^2.

The geographically (in terms of area covered) largest Southeast Asian countries are Myanmar and Indonesia. Myanmar covers a massive area of 676,000 km^2, and Indonesia measures square 1,904,569 km. Indonesia is the most populous among the SEA countries. In 2018, the Indonesian population was 267 million people. The top 10 largest cities of Southeast Asia are Bandung, Bangkok, Cebu, Hanoi, Ho Chi Minh City, Jakarta, Kuala Lumpur, Manila, Medan, and Quezon City.

A study of India's relations with Thailand, positioned in the Southeast Asian context, cannot be commenced without a discussion of the historical and cultural underpinnings of these two countries.

This chapter attempts to provide insights from both geography and history, discussing at length the process of "Indianization" in Southeast

Asia. It also shows the influence of Hindu religion, specifically through mythological figures, literature, and epics — the *Ramayana* — and how it was embedded in the cultural fabric of these societies and continues to influence their contemporary art, architecture, literature, and sculpture, to the present day.

1.1 Introduction: Geography and Culture as the Context

Southeast Asian history shows that there has been a churning of people replete with people from different countries of Asia, resulting in an intermingling of cultures. The people of maritime SEA — present-day Malaysia, Indonesia, and the Philippines — are believed to have migrated Southwards from South China, possibly between 2500 and 1500 BC. They continued to be in contact with the Chinese civilization (well established in the second millennium BC). However, it was the civilization of India whose influence, in comparison, was far deeper and wider.

Mainland SEA comprising Myanmar, Thailand, Laos, Cambodia, and Vietnam has three distinctive features. First, lowland plains are extremely suitable for rice cultivation. Second, it has a distinctively long coastline facing the South China Sea and the Gulf of Thailand. Third, it is drained by three major river systems — from the West to the East, which includes the Chao Phraya River, the Red River, and the Mekong River.

Despite the proximity in terms of distance and accessibility, that is, land and sea routes, in most of these countries, there are several differences in the geography of these countries. A significant aspect of mainland geography is the long rivers that have their sources in the highlands that separate Southeast Asia from China and Northeast India.

According to Amitav Acharya:

> Region naming is different from region building. While the naming of SEA may have been accomplished by Allied Powers and Cold War geopolitics, the fact that SEA is a region with shared features and continuous interactions has its basis in a cultural and historical matrix (Acharya, 1997).

Southeast Asia was at the hub of land and sea routes connecting Han China (206 BCE to 220 CE) and the Roman Empire (27 BCE to 476 CE), in the early times. The seaports on India's Western coasts used to be landmarks in the processes of assimilation and exchange. Mainland SEA's long coastline enabled the region to become an integral part of the maritime trading network that linked Southeast Asia to India and to China. As Kaplan has articulated:

> The Indian Ocean and its tributary waters bear the imprint of that great, proselytizing wave of Islam that spread from its Red Sea base across the longitudes to India and as far as Indonesia and Malaysia, so a map of these seas is central to a historical understanding of the faith (Kaplan, 2010).

Monsoon winds which regularly blow from the Northwest, and then in reverse — blowing from the Southeast, affect the region and its activities. These wind systems bring fairly predictable rainy seasons. It is interesting to note that it was these wind systems which enabled traders from foreign places to come and go with ease, at regular intervals. Because of this reliable wind pattern, Southeast Asia became a meeting place for trade between India and China — the two greatest markets of early Asia.

In the words of Kaplan:

> Thanks to monsoon winds that shift direction at regular six-month intervals the waters connecting these far-flung shores have long been readily navigable, even by relatively primitive sailing vessels. Linked first by Muslim merchants, the Greater Indian Ocean was later dominated by Portugal, then by the British and most recently by the United States (*Ibid.*).

From the winds to the seas themselves, Southeast Asia is blessed with shallow ocean parts and warm waters that provide a congenial home to the breeding of fish, corals, seaweeds, and other flora and fauna of the sea. Though the seas in some areas are rough, the region as a whole, except for the Philippines, is usually free of hurricanes and typhoons. However, most have active volcanoes and are extremely vulnerable to earthquake activity (Andaya, 1994).

A distinctive feature of Southeast Asia is its cultural diversity. There are ~1,000 languages spoken in the SEA countries. It is well known that migration into the region had been dictated by proximity to river systems, especially the movement of tribal groups from Southern China to the interior areas of the mainland. Linguistically, the mainland is divided into three important families — the Austro-Asiatic (Cambodian and Vietnamese), Tai (Thai and Lao), and the Tibeto-Burmese (including highland languages as well as Burmese). Languages belonging to these families can also be found in the Northeastern parts of India and Southwestern China. The language of the Tai people who live in different parts of Northeast India, including in parts of Arunachal Pradesh and Assam, has some similarities with the language spoken in Thailand and Laos. They are all various branches of the Tai–Kadai language family.

Southeast Asia is also unique in the way in which people have adapted to their local environments. In pre-modern times, many itinerant groups lived in boats and were called "sea people". The deep jungles provided shelter to numerous small wandering groups, and tribes that survived in the further interior regions also included headhunters. On the fertile plains of Java and mainland Southeast Asia, sedentary communities grew rice; along the coasts, the principal occupations were fishing and trade.

Harry Hopkins describes Southeast Asia as having emerged in 1945 as a warm, brightly colored jungle-girt world, then-inhabited by 150 million people of many languages, skin shades, and levels of culture. It is through his words we learn that:

> These people were not arranged neatly, race by race within political boundaries ... but overflowed through the entire peninsula, which — with its front door in China and its back door opening down on India, stretched through a mountainous neck two thousand miles from the borders of Tibet to Singapore, the navel of the East and then through the great arc of the Indonesian islands and spanning the equator to the threshold of Australia (Hopkins, 1952, pp. 3–4).

It was more than 2,000 years ago when cultural changes first began to affect Southeast Asia. These came mainly from the Chinese expansion

South of the Yangtze River, which consequently led to the colonization of Vietnam. Although China's control ended in 1427, it was not without the influence of Confucian philosophy. Vietnam was also greatly influenced by both Buddhism and Taoism. For the rest of mainland Southeast Asia, as well as in the Western areas of the Malay–Indonesian archipelago, the role of traders adopting Indian influences and cultural practices was more prominent. Elements of both Hinduism and Buddhism had a profound influence on the way kings ruled over the people. This will be discussed in detail in a subsequent chapter.

1.2 Indigenization and Cross-Cultural Borrowings

The process of Indigenization underpins cross-cultural borrowings, further reinforced by cross-cultural contacts. It is to the credit of the mariners, before the coming of the European colonizers, that cultural intercourse took place. With goods traveled artifacts of culture including literature, philosophy, belief systems, as well as art and sculpture.

That the seas connected ancient civilizations is well known. Several historians have written about the importance of ancient trading routes. During those times, the world's maritime trading routes, called the world system, linked Eastern Europe and India and also linked Southeast Asia and Southern China via the seas. One such route started from the West coast of Thailand on the shore of the Andaman Sea and ended on a Southern part of the Gulf of Thailand, in Surat Thani. The communities near the Andaman Sea in Southeast Asia, including those in the South of Thailand, were included in the system. These areas became port cities, or trading stations, that facilitated the exchange of local and foreign goods and cultures between India, China, the Middle East, and the Roman Empire (Szczepanski, 2019).

Hence, it is important to understand India's geographical proximity to this region. It is obvious that this proximity facilitated the movement of people from India to the lands lying eastward. This can be gauged from the fact that the island of Pu Breush, located in the Northwest of Sumatra, is only 92 nautical miles from the Indira Point (which is less than the distance between Chennai and Tirupati). Similarly, Phuket, in Thailand, is only 273 nautical miles away from Indira Point (which is less than the distance between Chennai and Madurai).[1]

1.2.1 *Locating India's Historical Influence in Southeast Asia*

This section discusses India's historical impact in Southeast Asia, including the scholars' perspectives of historical idioms of Indianization or colonization by India, of Southeast Asia.

The history of Southeast Asia by Coedes (1966, pp. 220–221) describes it as a history of events of wars, conquests, and internal insurgencies. Robert R. Jay, in his review of Coedes's book, observes that Coedes contrasts the intrusion(s) — first, by the Chinese, and then, of Indian civilization — into SEA. Although Chinese influence preceded that of the Indians by a few centuries, it apparently traversed at a far greater pace and was absorbed into the Northern part of what is now Vietnam, instituting a form of cultural imperialism. Chinese influences were unleashed in waves of more direct political encounters. Hence, there was an area in this region from which subsequent Indian influences were almost entirely excluded. This was entirely unlike the process by which Indian influences were absorbed into Southeast Asia.

Miriam T. Stark and S. Jane Allen have explained that the Han Empire's Southward expansion into what is now Southern China and Northern Vietnam culminated in the administrative control of the region by the 2nd century BC. At the Western end, overland trade networks linked Southeast Asia to Northeastern India and Bangladesh, and maritime trade networks linked Southeast Asia with India, China, and possibly further to the Middle East. The region was influenced by political domination of the East and commerce and religious ideologies (see, e.g., Hall, 1985) of the West. By middle of the 1st millennium AD, many of Southeast Asia's coasts and major river valleys housed huge populations (Stark *et al.*, 1998).

According to Wheatley, during the earliest times, Southeast Asia was occupied by a mosaic of societies and cultures [... within a common,

---

[1] Interview of Prof. Suryanarayan to the author in Chennai, February 4, 2019.

identifiable path of cultural evolution]. Moreover, "… These communities ran the whole gamut from bands to chiefdoms … hereditary hierarchical statuses and discernibly redistributive elements of economic integration not different from those of true States".

What is of great importance here is what he summarized, "… it is these pre- and proto-historic paramountcy that much of the so-called Hinduization process should be sought" (Wheatley, 1982, p. 18).

1.3 Indianization: Relevant Literature

Southeast Asian kingdoms benefited through vibrant commercial connections with traders from East Asia, South Asia, and West Asia (the "Middle East") for centuries. These Asian travelers and traders influenced the locals of the region, with religious intercourse as well as exchanging customs and traditions. Several of these became embedded in the psyche and were adopted in the daily lives of these people. Hence, their relationship became closer with both strands of economic and cultural interplay. Southeast Asian rulers were enamored by the indigenized practices of kingship institutions or Raja dharma from South Asia.

Hermann Kulke, writing on the concept of cultural convergence, provides an overview of India's strong impact on the emergence of the early kingdoms in the first millennium CE, during the second stage of the early state formation in Southeast Asia. According to Westerners, India was one of the most attractive pursuits for the West, since Alexander's campaign more than 2,000 years ago. Claudius Prolemy used the term "Trans-Gangetic India" for SEA; other names such as "Further India" and "East Indies" were also used (Wheatley, 1982, p. 13).

According to Jacq-Hergoualc'h, the process of "Indianization" may have begun as early as the 2nd century AD in Peninsular Thailand. Qualitative changes occurred, however, in the 5th century AD when Indic writing and architecture began to appear across the Malay Peninsula (Jacq-Hergoualc'h, 2002). The Indocentric (mis)interpretation of Southeast Asian history and culture reached a peak in the 1920s and 1930s when Indian nationalist historians brought in the concepts of "a Greater India" and Hindu colonies. The most famous proponent of this school was R.C. Majumdar, who addressed this in a series of monographs. The title of the monograph was 'The Indian Colonies in the Far East' (Kulke cited in Singh and Dhar, 2014, p. 4). Majumdar's treatise has been criticized by Van Leur and others, and the former's research encompassed a study of different theories of Indianization. It refuted the two hypotheses of Kshatriya or warrior and the Vaisya or trader and concluded that it was the Brahmanas who were the major agents of Indianization. Mabbett (1977) wrote a well-sourced article on this, emphasizing the role of traders and trade in India's early contacts with SEA.

Coedes famous work "The Indianized states of SEA", writes of the transplantation of the Indian civilization into SEA (Coedes, 1968, p. 16). De Casparis (1983, p. 7) called attention to some of the weaknesses of the theories about Indianization. It is important to mention here that while Southeast Asian countries adopted ideas from India, they did not emulate them in entirety. The SEA countries adapted them according to their local context and contemporary setting. Brown, for example, has explained the extent to which Indian art and culture did influence the indigenous Southeast Asian cultures. "It was like a thin flaking crust", he writes, and there is little evidence to suggest that identical sculptures would be produced in India and in Thailand (Brown, 1999, p. 5). Although it is to be verified how the Indian art styles are manifested in Thai art without there being any copies, it is notable how archaeological, linguistic, and historical art-research has been undertaken and now continues to discover ancient cultures of Siam (dating back to a time before Indian concepts and influences were introduced in the land). However, the role of India in premodern Southeast Asian society and culture cannot be downplayed. According to Kulke (cited in Singh and Dhar, 2014, p. 6), new archaeological findings require an understanding of the acceptance of India's influence, and the later Indianization, as the culmination of SEA indigenous pre-history and proto-history.

1.4 Empires, Kings, and Early Exchanges

It is known that around 400 AD, Asvavarman's son, Mulavarman assumed the foreign Indian royal title of "raja" (or king), defeated neighboring chiefs, and made them tribute-givers. He invited Brahmanas to perform grand rituals at a sacred place near his town (Kutei in East Kalimantan,

Indonesia) and produced the series of Yupa inscriptions. The Brahmanas were further showered with land and cows as gifts of deference. It was at this stage of the emergence of early kingdoms in SEA that Indian influence was very well received. Brahmanas were welcome administrators and provided additional credibility and recognition for the rajas.

Kulke further examined the possible causes of early local state formation in SEA under Indian influence in the 4th and 5th centuries. He observed that on the other side of the Bay of Bengal, similar evolutionary processes were functional. Samudragupta's inscription in Allahabad provides insights into processes of state formation in Eastern and Southern India. It is also known that India produced very well-crafted Buddhist art and stupa architecture after the age of the Mauryas. However, the Buddhist centers on India's eastern coast such as Amravati and Nagarjunakonda did not have much influence on the emergence of SEA art and architecture.

This changed from the late 7th century as Java's earliest temples on the Dieng Plateau are contemporaries of the Shore temple at Mahabalipuram and the Kailashnath temple at Kanchipuram in South India. These were probably the most fascinating for the sea-faring visitors from SEA. Kulke concludes that the early temples of SEA are contemporary to the Hindu temples in Central, Eastern, and Southern parts of India. He further added that the early temples of SEA developed unique regional styles in various parts of India and the spread of the Hindu temple architecture was directly linked with the emergence of the early regional kingdoms (Singh and Dhar, 2014, p. 9).

The Brahmanas who brought the so-called Pallava Gnantha script to Indonesia in about 400 CE were not emissaries of powerful Hindu rulers of South India, but came from the courts of early kingdoms such as the Pallavas, who had only then established their own authority with the help of Brahmanas and were able to successfully solve problems (coincidentally similar to those being faced by such chieftains in SEA). Thus, India's culture did not reach SEA through an act of transplantation but a complicated network of relations. It can be inferred then that there was a process of Indianization and cultural convergence, the former a result of social distance and the latter due to social nearness.

Smith (1999, p. 15) also confirms the above as she writes "... prior to 4th century AD Indian trade activities appear to have been relatively infrequent, as the level of open water sea-faring technology in the subcontinent seems to be rather limited".

The depictions of boats from the early centuries are riverboats and not seagoing craft. She also highlights that the adoption of Indian traditions in SEA is visible only after the 4th century and it too was undertaken by dynastic leaders who were not only increasing their dominance over local groups but also building contacts with other cultures. According to her, it was the fame of the Gupta Empire who ruled much of India (3rd to 6th century) and its technological innovations and culture, which is linked to the development of SEA.

Jordaan claims that the classical monuments of Central Java, particularly the Borobudur, are the creation of the Sailendra dynasty of India, who brought craftsmen and their Shilpa Shastra manuals (design manuals of art and culture). Although this is not well corroborated by other historians, it is generally agreed that the style of art of the Sailendras was influenced by the art of the Pala dynasty of Bihar and Bengal (best known for the great monastic Buddhist university of Nalanda).

According to Sheldon Pollock, Sanskrit, as a language used by the people, does not make its appearance in inscriptions until the early centuries of the Common era. Its usage and application(s) took over very gradually and then for almost a thousand years Sanskrit "ruled" in this enormous domain. He locates a date for what he calls the "Sanskrit Cosmopolis", between 300 and 1300 AD, and asserts that there was an almost concurrent spread of Sanskrit in South India and Southeast Asia in the 1st century. Sanskrit, according to him, spread through traditional intellectuals and religious professionals. He dismisses all aspects of Indian colonization of Southeast Asia as a reason dictating the spread of Sanskrit; it is from the 5th century onward that Sanskrit inscriptions appear around the same time in present-day Southeast Asia nations, especially in Java and in Angkor. It was in Angkor that Sanskrit became the pluralistic language for self-presentation of the elite (Pollock, 1996).

According to Wheatley, Southeast Asian nations came to realize the value of Indian concepts as a means of legitimizing their political status and possibly, stratifying their subjects. It was mainly for this reason that they invited Brahmanas to their court as they were skilled in protocol and ritual(s) (Wheatley, 1961, p. 161)

According to Stark and Allen, an explanation for the paucity in the availability of archaeological information on the early historic period in Southeast Asia could be due to the focus of historians on studying, and often reconstructing, the same sites such as exclusively Buddhist and Hindu. This has resulted in the belief of historians that state development in Southeast Asia was a result of foreign influences. They further state that early Southeast Asian texts were recorded on palm leaves and other decomposable material(s), which is why they could not last long in the tropical climate.

The adoption of Indian political and religious concepts enabled the chieftains of Southeast Asian countries to forge cosmopolitan polities based on universal moral principles represented in the Buddhist concepts of the dharmaraja and chakravartin (Pali cakkavatti). They also drew upon the epic traditions of the *Mahabharata* and the *Ramayana* to enhance their credibility. Shiva was worshipped and was invoked for the prosperity of the people and their lands. Spirit-worshipping traditions were amalgamated with rituals of Hinduism and practices of Buddhism in Southeast Asia. Chapter 2 provides details of the intersection of Brahmanism and Buddhism in Thailand.

As the Indian influences began to be felt, the local people adopted them as their own in order "to the lay of the land and the needs of the time".

To quote Noor,

> Indianisation was never a straightforward and direct process, but rather a selective endeavour where the agency and selectivity of the recipient communities were evident.

In the early period of Southeast Asian history, boundaries and political frontiers were fluid and, therefore there was no sense of political loyalty to the state (Suryanarayan, 2013).

It is also known that several communities like the Malays, Minangs, Javanese, Cantonese, Arabs, Tamils, and Eurasian Peranakans existed long before the advent of colonialists. There were differences in language, culture, art, as well as social customs among these groups. At the same time, however, there was cultural overlapping, cross-cultural fertilization, and cultural hybridization. With the advent of the colonial rule, ethnicity got entrenched.

As Prof. Charles Hirschmann has rightly pointed out:

> More than rubber and tin, the legacy of colonialism in Malaya was the racial ideology.

There was a development of categories, which were accentuated and viewed through political lenses, as far as Malaysia and Singapore were concerned.

Much later, it was the British who belittled those they subjugated by stating that the *"Malay is an idler, the Chinaman is a thief and the Indian is a drunkard", yet each, in his unique class of work is both cheap and efficient, when properly supervised (Ibid.).*

1.5 Diffusion of Indian Religion and Culture in Southeast Asia

India's religious and cultural influence is visible in Southeast Asia, from Myanmar to the Philippines. This section of the chapter focuses on the cultural give and take between India and SEA.

It was in 3rd century BC, during Ashoka's expression of missionary zeal that Buddhism quickly spread out through Asia, particularly to China, Japan, Myanmar, Laos, Kampuchea (Cambodia), Vietnam, and Thailand. Buddhist monks traveled from India to the East and from the East to India, the well-known of whom are the Chinese monks Fa Hein and Hiuen Tsang. The propagation of Buddhism promoted India's contacts with Sri Lanka, Myanmar, China, and Central Asia. Short inscriptions in Brahmi script relating to the second and first centuries BC have been found in Sri Lanka. Over time, Buddhism came to acquire a permanent stronghold in Sri Lanka. In the early centuries of the Christian era, Buddhism spread from India to Burma.

The Burmese developed the Theravada form of Buddhism and erected many temples and statues in honor of the Buddha. It is even more important to note that the Burmese and Sri Lankan Buddhists produced important Buddhist literary works, which cannot be found in India, exclusive to the former countries. During Kanishka's reign in the 2nd century, a large number of Indian missionaries went to China, Central Asia, and Afghanistan to preach their religion. China emerged as a great center of Buddhism. The Chinese records mention 162 visits made by the Chinese monks from 5 AD to 8 AD. However, the visit by only one Indian scholar, Bodhidharma, to China, is recorded in this period. From China, Buddhism spread to Korea and Japan, and it was in search of Buddhist texts and doctrines that several Chinese pilgrims, such as Fa Hein and Hiuen Tsang, came to India. Eventually, this contact proved fruitful for both the countries (Sharma, n.a.).

A Buddhist colony arose at Dun Huang and marked the first point of contact of the companies of merchants crossing the desert. It became a center of Buddhism on the Silk Road. Indians learned the art of growing silk from China, and the Chinese learned from India the art of Buddhist painting.

In the ancient canonical legends of Buddhism, Nalanda occupies a very important place. Lord Buddha himself visited this old seat of Buddhist learning later on. According to H.D. Sankalia, a renowned archaeologist, Nalanda as a residential university was set up by the Gupta dynasty in 425 AD. The royal patronage offered by the rulers subsequently enabled the university to emerge as the most prestigious institution of Buddhist learning and Mahayana doctrine between the 5th and 7th century AD. Students from Java and the Far East received their education at this place, who later on spread Mahayana teachings to other parts of the Buddhist world. However, in the late 12th and 13th centuries, mainly due to the advent of Muslims, Buddhism declined in India; with this, the importance of Nalanda was also adversely impacted (Sankalia, 1965).

From the 1st century AD onward, India established close trading relations with Java in Indonesia, which was called *Suvarnadvipa* or the "island of gold" by the ancient Indians. The earliest Indian settlements in Java were established in 56 AD. In the 2nd century of the Christian era, several small Indian principalities were set up.

The name *Suvarnabhumi* (present-day Thailand) was given to Pegu and Moulmein in Burma, and merchants from Broach, Banaras, and Bhagalpur traded with Burma (*Ibid.*). It is well known that when the Chinese pilgrim Fa-hien visited Java in the 5th century, he found the

Brahmanical religion prevalent there. In the early centuries of the Christian era, the Pallavas founded their colonies in Sumatra, resulting in the development of the kingdom of Srivijaya. It continued to be an important power and a center of Indian culture from 5th to 10th centuries. The Indian settlements in Java and Sumatra became centers for the spread of Indian culture.

In Indo-China, which in the modern day can be classified as parts of Vietnam, Cambodia, and Laos, the Indians set up two powerful kingdoms in Kamboja and Champa. The powerful kingdom of Kamboja, coterminous with modern Cambodia, was founded in 6 CE. Its rulers were devotees of Shiva and developed Kamboja into a center of Sanskrit learning, where numerous Hindu inscriptions can be found.

In Champa (in present-day Vietnam), it is believed that the traders set up colonies. The king of Champa was also a Shaiva, and the official language was Sanskrit. This country was considered to be a great center of education in the Vedas and Dharma Shastras. Indian settlements in the Indian Ocean continued to flourish until the 13th century, and during this period, people of different cultures intermingled — giving rise to diverse variations in the culture and the literary world (*Ibid.*).

There are several examples of the rich and robust blending of cultures and religion. The most famous Buddhist temple is to be found not in India but Borobudur in Java. Considered to be the largest Buddhist temple in the world, it was constructed in the 8th century, and 436 images of the Buddha engraved on it illustrate his life. The temple of Angkor Wat in Cambodia, built by the Khmer kings in the 12th century, is larger than the one in Borobudur. The stories of the *Ramayana* and *Mahabharata* are narrated through art on the walls of the temple. The story of the *Ramayana* is so popular in all of SEA, especially in Thailand, Cambodia, and Indonesia, that many folk plays based on the same are frequently performed. The languages of these countries contain numerous words that find their origin in Sanskrit linguistics.

1.5.1 *Ramayana in Southeast Asia*

According to Satya Vrat Shastri, who has written "Ramayana in Southeast Asia — A Comparative Analysis", the *Ramayana* is popular in SEA, but with different names. In Indonesia, the epic is known as *Ramayana Kakavain* or *Ramayana Kavya*; in Myanmar, it is called *Rama Thingyan* or *Rama Vatthu*; in Thailand, it is the *Ramakien*; in Laos, it is called *Phra Lak Phra Lam*, in Cambodia, it is the *Ramaker*; in Malaysia, it is *Hikayat Seri Rama*; in the Philippines, it is *Maharadia Lawana*. It is believed that each of these countries has different versions and interpretations of the *Ramayana* because the story went through a process of acculturation in every country where it was adopted (Shastri, 1982).

According to Francisco, the popularity of the *Ramayana* in present-day Myanmar (Burma was a part of India till 1937) is believed to have made its way through Thailand and reached its peak in the first half of the 18th century. This was when the story of Rama became the basis of a series of 347 stone relief sculptors at the pagoda of Mahalokmara-zein constructed in 1849, in honor of Maung Duang Sayadaw, the chief Buddhist primate of Amarpura. In contrast to Thailand, Cambodia, and Indonesia, the representations of the *Ramayana* are different in Malaysia. The epic may have reached Malaysia by way of Javanese traders who brought their shadow play, Wayang Kulit. Many changes were developed in the Malay version of the *Ramayana*, and those changes depended upon the local traditions and politics. The changes were also due to religious beliefs, as Malays were followers of Islam. The "*Hikayat Seri Rama*" exists in both written and oral form, and the "Wayang Kulit Siam" is a shadow play from Kelantan, a place which lies on the border of Malaysia and Thailand. According to Juan Francisco, the focus on Indonesia (Javanese) and Malay versions of the *Ramayana* becomes relevant to the introduction of the story into the Philippines and its subsequent indigenization. This can be understood because there were linguistic similarities between the Javanese and the Philippines (Francisco Juan, 1994).

Shastri opines that it was not the version of Valmiki alone that traveled to different countries — there were different versions of the *Ramayana* even within India. This was because as people moved to different countries, an amalgamation of versions with some local influence emerged. Hence, the story of Rama got retold in different ways. The death of Ravana, the killing of Maricha, abduction of Sita, the fight with Jatayu, the contact with Sugriva, and other events in the Rama story find their unique version in each of the Southeast Asian countries. For example, the death of Ravana as written by Valmiki was when Rama shot the Brahmastra at Ravana, thereby killing him (after several failed attempts on Rama's part). In another version of the *Ramayana*, it is the heads of Ravana which despite being severed keep returning to their original position; in the *Ramakien*, it is the limbs which keep getting severed and reunited with the body during the fight. Instead of the Brahma-shastra being the final weapon of assault on Ravana's navel, in the *Ramakien* it is Ravana's soul which is kept safely guarded in a cage away from his physical body that needs to be killed. The *Ramakien* also states that Hanuman, who is given the responsibility of locating Ravana's soul, not only locates it but crushes it as well, between big stones. It is after Ravana's soul is crushed that he is killed on being assaulted by Rama. There are other instances of differences between the two versions. Jatayu (the bird) intervenes when Sita is being carried away by Ravana to Lanka and tries to prevent Ravana by pulling on him with his claws. Ravana then severs the wings of Jatayu (*Ibid.*). Jatayu boasts that he cannot be killed unless the ring Sita is wearing is used to hurt him, and on hearing this, Ravana immediately removes the ring from Sita's finger and throws it at the bird. There are other differences as well in the Thai and Valmiki versions regarding the rebirth of Hanuman.

M.R. Chakrakot Chitrabongs in the "Omnipresence of the *Ramayana* in Thai Arts and Culture" states that in SEA, there are the Tai people who shared the same beliefs in ghosts, spirits, and supernatural beings. These Tai people also shared another belief, which is now known as Samsara. According to this belief, every living individual has to undergo an unavoidable "dukkha", and it is to alleviate a condition of suffering to escape from perpetual reincarnation. In India, philosophies turned into philosophizing, which turned into faith, and later developed into the Brahman religion, and this Tribhumi cosmography, according to the author, was created and consisted of heaven, hell, and earth. If one lived a good life to be born in heaven, one could escape from continuous suffering, whereas if one lived a sinful life, then one would go to hell. It was Brahman priests who offered their services (as they were considered the middlemen) to convey the people's wishes and appease the gods. It was Gautam Buddha who appealed to the subconscious minds of the people and provided insights to the path to *Nirvana* (*a state of perfect happiness*) (Chakrakot, 2015).

The ethnic groups of SEA adopted the teachings of the Indian Brahmanas, and these teachings arrived in *Suvarnabhumi* during the rise of the great Khmer empire, i.e., 8th to 15th century. It was at the height of their rule in the 12th century that unparalleled creativity was displayed. A manifestation of the same is the famous Angkor Wat, in Cambodia. It is a man-made mountain temple which depicts the Buddhist cosmology and has been recorded in the Tipitaka Pali texts. Angkor Wat is a tangible heritage bearing witness to the movement of the Brahmanic Hindu beliefs into SEA from India. It was the source of the power of the Hindu–Buddhist influences that ultimately was embedded throughout *Suvarnabhumi*. As vassal states of the Khmer empire, there was interest among the Tai ethnic groups in Indian culture. Although the Khmer rule gradually waned and lost control over the vassal states, the Indian cultural influences remained strong in the local cultures by choice.

It is the concept of "divine kingship", which needs to be explained here because it had become embedded with Indian cosmological ideas and became the basis of the state and kingship; the layout and structure of capital cities, temples and palaces, the titles of kings, queens, and officials and so on. The concept viewed the king as the living God, the incarnation of the Supreme, often attributed to Shiva or Vishnu on Earth. Politically, the concept implied ascribing a divine justification of the king's rule. Moreover, the monarch could use political credibility to engage and manage the economy, as well as society. Monuments such as Prambanan and Angkor Wat were erected to celebrate the king's divine rule on Earth.

The magnificence of Angkor Wat is multiplied by a confluence of paintings, miniatures that record both the epic gods of faith, and the more human aspects of contemporary life. In one such miniature, it has been shown that a group of Indian Brahmanas are the only ones who do not prostrate before the king: this was their exalted position in India, and this would be their position under Jayavarman II (9th century), Yasovarman, and their successors.

1.6 Intermingling of Cultures

The temples of Angkor Wat in Cambodia, Pagan in Myanmar, and Borobudur and Prambanan in Indonesia bear evidence to the deep penetration of Indian art and architectural forms in these famous Southeast Asian monuments. Some of these monuments in their carvings surpass the grandeur of Indian temples from the same period. Moreover, sculptors and artists copied and combined original Indian motifs with local artistic motifs to arrive at something distinctively Southeast Asian and produced stylized masterpieces of their own. Modeled after Gupta period icons, the Cambodian (Khmer) sculpture of 8th to 13th centuries though dissimilar in their form are an undoubtedly magnificent representation of gods, goddesses, Buddha, Apsaras, and demons with Southeast Asian features (Sengupta, 2017).

The fusion of Indian art with the local art traditions of Southeast Asia is reflected through some examples of sculptures including the head of the Buddha from Thailand, the head from Kamboja (synonymous with Kampuchea and Cambodia), and the magnificent bronze images from Java. Similarly, beautiful examples of painting, which are comparable to those of Ajanta, are found not only in Sri Lanka but also in the Dun Huang caves on the Chinese border.

Suchandra Ghosh, who discusses the circulation and transportation of votive tablets or sealings, states that art and sculpture played a major role in the exchange of ideas between India and Southeast Asian countries at the time. Since votive tablets could be easily mass-produced, they could also be used as souvenirs and gifts by traders for pilgrims and others. Ghosh also underlines the fact that it was Nalanda, and not Bodhgaya, which exerted greater influence in Peninsular Thailand, possibly due to its proximity to Srivijaya, and in turn, Nalanda. Although the votive tablets (in comparison to the rich tapestry and vast array of cultural manifestations of art, sculpture, dance, and religion) were minor objects, they do provide a greater understanding of the shared cultural practices. Amulets have also been recovered and these too signify their importance as totems which ward against danger or for protection and prosperity. It is evident then that the most popular image that was engraved on the tablets was that of Avalokitesvara, who is considered as both a savior and a protector (Ghosh, 2017).

It is not enough to attribute the spread of culture to Indians alone. Indians imbibed the craft of minting gold coins from the Greeks and Romans; they learned the art of growing silk from China; they learned to grow betel leaves from Indonesia; and more. It would not be inaccurate to state then that while India retained and developed its own identity in spite of foreign influences, Southeast Asian countries developed a unique culture of their own by imbibing Indian elements and indigenous elements.

While religion, both Buddhism and Brahmanism, helped in the spread of Indian culture, the role of traders and invaders cannot be denied. Trade and commerce played a vital part in establishing India's relations with SEA. The very names *Suvarnabhumi* and *Suvarnadvipa*, given to territories in Southeast Asia, suggest Indians' search for gold. Trade led not only to the exchange of goods but also to varied facets of culture. By the 13th century, the Indians were the in the forefront of businesses in the Arabian Sea and the Bay of Bengal. This was further provided a fillip by the economic recovery of Northern states of India, and several merchant families, especially in Gujarat. They took advantage of new trading opportunities caused by the decline of Srivijaya, which had previously controlled the Sunda Straits and the Strait of Malacca. In fact, the Mahayana Buddhist Empire of Srivijaya was perhaps Asia's and the world's greatest trading empire from the 8th to the 10th centuries and even till the 13th century. It extended through the Malay Peninsula up to Kedah and Patani (which is now a part of Thailand) (Basu, 2017, p. 44).

Thus, India's relationship with Southeast Asia has numerous components. Historically, trade between India's coastal kingdoms of Odisha and Southern India, and countries in Southeast Asia such as Thailand, Malaysia, and Cambodia are well documented. Also, Buddhism and Hinduism, both Indic religions, retain a strong influence in Southeast Asia, with epics like the *Mahabharata* and *Ramayana* being part of the cultural landscape.

The confluence of cultures was upset by the European colonizers, whose influence comprises the next chapter.

1.7 Conclusion

Southeast Asia has always been subjected to external influences. However, as stated above, in the early phase of its history, it was the Indian influences that were more dominant. While Southeast Asia traded extensively with China and the Far East, it was from India that much of Southeast

Asian religion, philosophy, and esthetics were drawn. As the Malaysian scholar Farish A. Noor has written, "[the] development of Southeast Asian civilization went hand in hand with that of the Indian sub-continent" (Noor, 2009, p. 99). V. Suryanarayan, an Indian expert on Southeast Asia in an interview to the author, stated that "Out of the ten Southeast Asian countries, nine and a half are indebted to India for the cultural richness. These countries realize this and are grateful to India. Hence, India must include culture as an instrument of its foreign policy when engaging with Southeast Asian countries, who are very important for India's aspirations as a global power".[2]

A significant phase in Indian and Southeast Asian history includes the fascinating encounter between the cultural exchange(s) in the two regions. Kingdoms of Funan, Sri Kshetra, Pagan, Champa, Srivijaya, Sailendra, and Majapahit, used Sanskritic vocabulary alongside Thai and Bahasa; architectural wonders including Lara Djonggrong and literary master-pieces such as Amramala, Arjuna Vivaha, Bharata Yuddha, and more, all bear testimony to the qualities that were easily assimilated by the people of Southeast Asia.

The debate by scholars questioning whether it was Indian merchants or Southeast Asian mariner–merchants who played the central role in bringing Indian religious conceptions to Southeast Asia continued till the 1960s. The dictum that India "colonized" Southeast Asia was rejected. With discoveries by archaeologists and greater reliance on primary sources, the early theories are being contested. The political cultures of Java, Cambodia, Burma, and Thailand continue to reflect the heritage of early kingdoms in which Indian religious concepts were welded to local traditions, and Brahman priests played a central role in royal rituals (Collins, 2013).

Thus, it would be pertinent to state that although the Indian influence spread to several countries in SEA, Indianization was never a straightfor-ward process. There was an intermingling of cultures, with influences being absorbed selectively. Merchants brought trade; from India, the Brahmanas brought something more valuable to the great elites of Southeast Asia — their philosophy, literature, and the vehicle of this

---

[2] Interview of Prof. Suryanarayan to the author in Chennai, February 4, 2019.

knowledge, Sanskrit. Sanskrit, one of the mother languages of world history, emerged from an Indo-Iranian dialect in the Swat region North of Taxila and spread by the turn of the millennium to the North of India. After that, in more rapid strides, it became the *lingua franca* of high learning. Sanskrit was, like all functioning thoroughfares, a two-way street.

The story of Indian Brahmanas in Southeast Asia is significant in the repertoire of culture, faith, trade, and perhaps most important, the language of Sanskrit, and its creation of so many exquisite bridges between India and Southeast Asia. Their great influence lay as much in the narratives they carried as the language that etched literature, philosophy, and faith into elite and then popular belief.

India's philosophy, which was essentially imbued with a vision of peace and harmony, not seeking invasion, conquest, or domination, was adapted by the local communities in different parts of SEA. It absorbed other ideas and faiths like Buddhism and shaped a syncretic whole — combining intellect, culture, and civilization. Sanskrit merged into intellectual systems and structures of Southeast Asia to create a new dynamic. The *Ramayana* story itself has rewritten itself, adapting to the local narratives. Rama, Krishna, and the Pandavas became household names in Southeast Asia more than 1,500 years ago, subsequently taking roots that produced the fruit of many varieties. More than 30 Cambodian kings between 514 and 1327 had "Varman", or Burman (meaning Lord Vishnu, in Tamil language), in their name. There is no doubt about the tremendous influence of Tamil in this region. Tamil inscriptions have been found in Sumatra and the Malay Peninsula.

The synthesis of culture and faith in the shared space between India and Southeast Asia is one of the great outcomes of this inclusive philosophy. In Cambodia, by the time of Jayavarman V (Khmer king in the 10th century), Mahanaya Buddhism had become part of court faith and culture, and there was a form of Brahman-Buddhism until the time Buddhism became prevalent by the 13th century.

The transition was slow and peaceful. Islam arrived from the Arabian Gulf and Gujarat, peacefully occupying its own space among other existing faiths. In Malaysia and Indonesia, conversions to Islam took place, and with time, it became the dominant religion. As a result, there was a marked decline in the Indian influence post 13th century. However, in

Bali, Indonesia, Hinduism continues to be practiced by the majority. The culture was resilient enough to adapt to religion, and religion created space for culture. This is an elemental part of our shared inheritance, not merely myriad forms of geographical proximity on display but social proximity too, i.e., similar social and political processes that became the significant factor in promoting the selection and adaptation of Indian cultural elements in SEA.

Chapter 2

Southeast Asia: The Colonial Capture (14th–20th Centuries)

The intermingling of cultures, ideas, and faith points to the role of traders, sailors, and the religious in India's relations with Southeast Asia. European colonizers entered Asian waters and lands as a result of their passion for overseas exploration. This chapter provides an overview of Southeast Asian (SEA) history, for which it is vital to elucidate the role and impact of the colonial powers who jostled for influence in these countries, leaving behind unresolved boundaries and destroyed habitats.

2.1 European Colonization of Asia: The Genesis

The discovery of America and that of the passage to the East Indies by the Cape of Good Hope are the two greatest events recorded in the history of a [human] kind — Adam Smith, in The Wealth of Nations (Smith, 2000).

Pre-colonial history informs us how the perspective of ancient and medieval Western civilization, whose limited concept of an essentially flat, *known world* stretched from Northern Europe to the Sahara Desert, from the Atlantic Ocean to India (and a distant China). The ancient Greeks and Romans traded with *distant Asian cultures* via intermediate states — goods were shipped overland or by combined land/sea routes. In the medieval period, the *Byzantine Empire* continued to utilize these trade links; *Western European* trade collapsed (with the fall of the Western Roman Empire), but then recovered in the later Middle Ages (European Colonialism, 2019).

The period which followed, i.e., from 1420 to 1520, was the age of Discovery and is also known as the age of European exploration, conquest, and colonization. Initially, the foremost motivation for these efforts was the search for trade routes with India and China. The initial years from 1420 to 1492 is regarded as the early age of Discovery, during which Portugal initiated the global naval era by exploring the coast of Africa (in hopes of finding a way round to India), colonizing several Atlantic islands, and establishing African trading posts. It was Henry the Navigator, a Portuguese prince who was the key patron of these voyages. The turning point in Portugal's quest for a sea route to India was the rounding of the Southern tip of Africa, achieved by Bartholomew Diaz. The Cape of Good Hope marks the point at which the African coastline begins to trend eastward instead of Southward, making it the critical turning point of Diaz's voyage (Nowell, 1936). Ian Morris alludes to the transforming power of geography when he states:

> Geography determined that it was Western Europeans, rather than the 15th century's finest sailors — the Chinese — who discovered, plundered, and colonized the Americas (Morris, 2010).

2.2 Southeast Asia: Before the Advent of the Europeans

Until the dawn of European colonialism, the Asian world order comprised the boundaries of several ancient civilizations including the Arab, Indian, and Chinese and their transactional relationships with one another. The classical interstate system was dealt a severe blow by the advent of the colonialists, who were responsible for the destruction and complete breakdown of the trade network in Asia. This subsequently had one of the most significant effects on the conquest of Malacca by the Portuguese (Morris, 2010).

The major colonizers of Southeast Asia over almost 400 years from the 1500s to the 1940s were Europeans, Japanese, and the US. The seven colonial powers in Southeast Asia were Portugal, Spain, the Netherlands, Great Britain, France, the United States, and Japan. Before the arrival of the Portuguese in the Indian Ocean in 1498, no single power had attempted to monopolize the sea-lanes that connected the ports of the Indian sub-continent with the Middle East and East Africa on the West and the ports of Southeast Asia and China to the East.

According to Kristof, Asia's grand failure was a result of the complacency of the East, its tendency to look inwards, its devotion to past ideals and methods, respect for those in authority, and being suspicious of new ideas. Asia lacked the excitement of Europe. Both China and India were self-satisfied, the former believing that they had nothing to learn from outsiders, whom they considered barbarians (Kristof and WuDunn, 2001, p. 42).

On the contrary, Europeans were explorers. It was the demand for silks from China and spices from SEA via India that spurred European traders and crusaders to travel to the Exotic East. The land route or the Silk Road that passed through erstwhile Persia, across the Himalayas to gain access to China was the more popular route. During the 13th century, under the reign of Genghis Khan, the Mongols established an empire which extended from Persia to China. Although the Mongols were known to be brutal, there were no restrictions on the flow of trade; hence, trade from Asia to Europe flourished. However, the European euphoria was short-lived, and with the fall of the Mongol Empire in the 14th century, a vast number of the land routes were nearly blocked. The Arabs, however, conducted trade through the sea routes and benefited tremendously.

2.2.1 *Southeast Asia's Appeal*

One of the most influential theses in Southeast Asian history in recent decades has been that put forward by Anthony Reid in his *Southeast Asia in the Age of Commerce*. In this work, Reid suggests that the age of commerce had its roots in changes that occurred during the 15th century. The commercial boom and the emergence of port cities as hubs of commerce including Pegu, Aceh, and others, spurred the political, social, and economic changes which marked the Age of Commerce in the region, extending from the 15th to the 17th century. He points to changes in the spice and aromatic wood trade, a trade boom beginning sometime around the year 1400, and new systems of cash cropping across the archipelago (Reid, 1993).

With the booming maritime trade came the emergence of the Southeast Asian "junks" or vessels as well as new navigational techniques. Increased commercialization and the growth of cosmopolitan urban centers, usually port cities, was accompanied by the demand for more money, which brought demand for more sophisticated financial systems and promoted the emergence of mercantile elites. Other social manifestations of the Age of Commerce as depicted by Reid included both a religious revolution, with the introduction of Islam and Christianity in the region, and a military revolution with new war technologies aiding in the strengthening of new regimes (Reid, 1993). China, India, and the Arab world introduced the people of Southeast Asia to ideas and technology that benefited their well-being significantly. The three major influential powers directly brought Southeast Asia to prominence on the national frontier, sped up their development, and allowed them to capitalize on their valuable assets. In hindsight, it is a sad and ironic rise to significance because this new-found glory made Southeast Asia an appealing target for the colonizing Europeans who were looking to bypass the middlemen (merchants) and gain direct control of the goods and people in Southeast Asia. The Chinese, Indian, and Islamic interactions with Southeast Asia positively changed the area's culture, religion, and economy, but it also led to the eventual deprivation of their independence at the hands of Europeans.

Beginning in 9th century, Angkor, associated with the Khmer Empire, began to gather power and territory in mainland Southeast Asia. It would grow to be one of the largest empires in Southeast Asian history, and at one stage reached beyond the current boundaries of Cambodia and into present-day Southern Vietnam, Laos, and Thailand, stretching into the Malay Peninsula. Moreover, at this time, there emerged in Southeast Asia, a trend toward a smaller number of supra-regional powers. This feature became dominant in the post-11th century history of SEA. In Southeast

Asia, after the decline of Angkor, most of continental SEA was under the influence of the Thai kingdom of Ayutthaya. From the middle of the 11th century to the end of the 13th century, the Western part of the continental SEA was under the kingdom of Pagan. In the 14th-century Java, it was Majapahit who held sway.[1]

It is also apparent from observing both the Chinese and Southeast Asian evidence that the period from the last decades of the 13th to the first few decades of the 14th century was likely a period of stagnation in Southeast Asian maritime trade. It was a possible offshoot of the warfare the Mongols waged against the Southern Song dynasty in China, during which the Yuan efforts to tightly manage maritime trade and the major Yuan military missions launched in the maritime realm increased. Coedes saw the 13th century as *une periode critique* or a critical period in Southeast Asia. This was because as the classical states declined, the Mongols expanded, Tai polities burgeoned, and Islam began to spread in the maritime realm. This was also a critical and hugely important period as it marked the end of the early Age of Commerce (Wade, 2009).

2.3 Europeans: The Masters of the Seas

At this stage, it is worth recalling that global exploration and empire-building were initiated by the Portuguese (early Age of Discovery), who were eventually joined by the Spanish (late Age of Discovery). Following the Age of Discovery, the Iberian nations (Iberian Peninsula is located in Southwestern Europe and includes mainly the three countries Andorra, Spain, and Portugal) were joined by Britain, France, and the Netherlands. The European nations had built ships to sail across the world's oceans during the Early Modern Age. Asian navies stood no match to the European marine vessels.

When the search for sea routes commenced, it stemmed from the belief that they had discovered two sets of islands. They began referring to Southeast Asian islands as the East Indies. By the end of the

---

[1]The empire of Majapahit was the last of the major Hindu Empires of the Malay archipelago and is considered one of the greatest states in Indonesian history.

15th century, Europe was looming large on the maritime space ready to take hold of the treasures of Asia. As Ian Morris said, "By 1914, Europeans and their colonialists ruled 84% of the land and 100% of the sea" (Rachman, 2016, p. 5).

It is well known that the empires of the greatest significance were those of India and China. The Mughals, who were Muslims of Turkic descent, brought Persian culture to India, which was dominated by a largely Hindu population. In India, the Mughal Empire held sway till the last Mughal king Bahadur Shah Zafar died in a British prison in 1862. British East India Company effectively ruled in India from 1757 to 1858, after which the British Crown assumed direct control of the Indian subcontinent.

Similarly, in China, it was the Manchus of the Qing dynasty who ruled over the Han people (who formed a majority). Both India and China were rich in terms of produce that could be exported and thriving manufacturing sectors — Indian cotton and indigo, and Chinese silk and porcelain. The taxes from the peasantry also filled the coffers of the empires, giving them little reason to look beyond their frontiers toward the trade and wealth that could potentially be theirs. They continued to be confined to the boundaries of land with gross neglect of the seas and maritime geography. Both countries had efficient methods of farming and even had trade surpluses with the rest of the world.

Although Zheng He's voyages from 1405 till 1433 are well documented, China is known to have focused only on the continental space till recently.[2] In 1405, the Chinese admiral Zheng He had a fleet of nearly 300 vessels and 27,000 sailors from Nanjing to Sri Lanka. It is also known that Zheng He visited the Southeast Asian ports multiple times in the early 1400s. He also visited Indian ports in Bengal and Kerala (Basu, 2017, p. 59). In other voyages, he reached the Malacca Straits, East Africa, and Java (Gideon, 2016).

---

[2]From 1405 until 1433, the Chinese imperial eunuch Zheng He led seven ocean expeditions for the Ming emperor that are unmatched in world history. These missions were astonishing as much for their distance as for their size: during the first ones, Zheng He traveled from China to Southeast Asia and then on to India, all the way to major trading sites on India's Southwest coast.

It is believed that a request for trade from King George of England was summarily dismissed by the then Chinese emperor Qianlong, stating that there was no use for China of British goods.[3]

Since both India and China, with poorly equipped navies, had no advantage or interest in sea-borne trade, it was the European traders who were able to dominate the trade in the Indian Ocean. They reaped huge profits by selling their merchandise to countries in South, Southeast Asia, and China. Europe had secured vast quantities of silver from having looted the Americas. This was used profitably during their trade with China, which comprised opium and other products. China, in turn, needed silver for pursuing a stable currency policy, and with silver in short supply, they were forced to trade for it. While silver was inexpensive in the Americas and Europe because of its abundant supply, this metal was scarce in China.

It is important to note here that in the 16th and 17th centuries, the naval capabilities between Europe and Asia differed vastly, with the former being the superior one.

2.4 Southeast Asia in Europeans' Colonial Capture: Maritime and Mainland

While the Europeans gained mastery over the seas, the Arabs had not left. They, in fact, secured Malacca as the core trading center for the Southeast Asian region. The Portuguese entered this region and gradually took control. Malacca was one of the three key points with Goa and Hormuz, which gave the Portuguese control over the Asiatic trade routes. This geographical sphere of Southeast Asia had been accustomed to trading with the Arabs, Indians, and Chinese. The Europeans here appeared as an aberration.

When the Portuguese arrived with their display and exercise of military might, the Southeast Asians were unprepared and unguarded. Like India, Southeast Asian states were a victim of the neglect of maritime

---

[3]Two edicts from the Qianlong Emperor, on the occasion of Lord Macartney's mission to China, September 1793. From http://afe.easia.columbia.edu/ps/china/qianlong_edicts.pdf; accessed on November 22, 2018.

power (Devare, 2005, p. 92). The commerce-fueled harmonious relations were destroyed by the Portuguese. When Malacca fell to the sophisticated weaponry systems of the Portuguese in 1511 and continued to be in their control till 1641, the Malays established a new Sultanate at the tip of the Malay Peninsula — Johar. As a result, the Arab trade shifted base from Malacca to Johor. The Portuguese onslaught throughout the Indian Ocean took place in a period of weak principalities and distracted empires, such as Ming China, Safavid Persia, and Ottoman Turkey (Kaplan, 2011). The Portuguese held command over this region for about a century. The Portuguese also acquired Macao from China in 1557, vastly contributing to their further domination of the Asian sea routes.[4]

It was the profitability of the textile trade that brought the Dutch first, followed by the English and the French. In 1656, Colombo fell to the Dutch, and in 1663, the Portuguese lost Cochin to the Dutch. Competition with the British East India Company had led to the loss of Hormuz earlier.

Thus, in a short period, the Dutch, and later, the English attempted to replace the monopoly of the Portuguese with their own. This led each of them to form their well-guarded settlements along the chief trading routes as alternatives to the former Portuguese trading strongholds. In the beginning, the Dutch appeared to be more successful than their British and French rivals and succeeded in establishing their pre-eminence in Indonesia, and once they had outmaneuvered the Portuguese, they came to control trade out of Gujarat and Sind. It was now the Dutch who began to impose their will on most Indian shippers, exacting the taxes that were earlier levied by the Portuguese. At the same time, each of Portugal's European rivals began setting up local factories and trade outlets of a size akin to Goa.

It is important to understand that by the 14th century (1350–1400), the Majapahit Empire based in Eastern Java conquered most of Sumatra and controlled a vast part of Peninsular Malaysia and the Malay Archipelago. Several states in Sumatra, Malay Peninsula, Borneo, Sulawesi, Nusa Tenggara islands, Maluku, New Guinea, and some parts of Philippines

---

[4]While the Portuguese could keep only their island colony of East Timor, the island of New Guinea was controlled by the Dutch, the British, and the Germans.

islands were under Majapahit realm of power — in essence, all of Malaya belonged to Indonesia.

The Majapahit Empire was an Indianized kingdom based in Eastern Java from 1293 to around 1500. Due to its strategic position on the spice trade route, the Majapahit Empire grew immensely wealthy by levying duties on goods shipped through its area of control. The golden age of the Majapahit Empire was during the reign of Hayam Wuruk, the fourth ruler of the empire, who ruled from 1350 to 1389. By 1365, the entire Malay Archipelago, except Srivijaya and two of its colonies, had been conquered by the Majapahit Empire. However, the empire was short-lived, as its power declined after Hayam Wuruk's death. At the beginning of the 15th century AD, a war of succession broke out and lasted for about 4 years.

2.4.1 *Maritime Southeast Asia and the Colonial Powers*

Meanwhile, Islam was spreading in the region, and many kingdoms converted to this faith. One among these was the continually rising Malaccan Sultanate of the last Raja of Singapura. As Hindu-Buddhists, the Majapahit Empire was unable to compete with its Muslim neighbors and continued to disintegrate, finally collapsing toward the end of the 15th century.[5] Islam was imbibed and accepted due to its principle of equality for all, while the focus on kings and devarajas resulted in the decline of Hinduism. With the Hindus losing their earlier predominance, it was the Muslims who were accorded higher status with best positions favoring them. Across a majority of the Southeast Asian islands, several traders converted to Islam. This included Malacca, Sumatra, Borneo, and some of the Northern Javanese ports. Bali and East Java, however, continued to be under the influence of Hinduism.[6] Since the kingdoms of Java were constantly at war with one another, it was easy for the Western powers to infiltrate and take control of both Malacca and Ceylon. Treaties were also

---

[5]The Majapahit Empire: The Short Life of an Empire that Once Defeated the Mongols, 19/08/15. From https://www.ancient-origins.net/ancient-places-asia/majapahit-empire-short-life-empire-once-defeated-mongols-003623; accessed on November 14, 2018.
[6]The people of Java refer to themselves as Hindus/Buddhists.

signed with East India, Japan, and Vietnam, enabling the Dutch to gain control over the major trading ports in the Indian Ocean and the trade in rice, sugar, coffee, and spices.

The Dutch party, however, was soon to be disrupted by the French. The *Vereenigde Oostindische Compagnie* (VOC) or *the Dutch East India Company* was forced to declare bankruptcy in 1799,[7] due to its mounting defense expenditure for defending their territories from Napoleon Bonaparte.[8] The Dutch, after Napoleon's conquest, had to forego the Straits of Malacca to the British in exchange for the Dutch East Indies. This loss of the Straits was a direct result of the Anglo-Dutch Treaty of 1824. The British, who were already in the Indian subcontinent since 1750, also seized the opportunity created by the departure of the Dutch and assumed control of the Malay Peninsula as well as Borneo, now known as Malaysia. The Europeans thus distributed maritime Southeast Asia into spheres of influence.

Meanwhile, Spain conquered most of the Philippine Islands from the local Muslims. The islands were named the Philippines in honor of King Philip II of Spain, with its capital being established in Manila. Over three centuries of Spanish rule till 1898, with the conversion of the inhabitants to Roman Catholicism, the Filipinos became almost completely Christianized and Westernized. The US colonized the Philippines in the aftermath of the Spanish-American War of 1898.

Toward the end of the 16th century, Portuguese pre-eminence in this region began to decline, particularly after 1580 when their royal line died out, and Portugal was united — forcibly — with Spain under Philip II. (Portugal regained her independence 60 years later, in 1640.)

In 1641, the Dutch drove the Portuguese from Malacca, and in 1658 from Ceylon. Portuguese possessions in the East began to shrink and were soon limited to Goa in India, Macao in China, and a part of Timor in the

---

[7]Founded in 1602, the Dutch East India Company (*Verenigde Oost-Indische Compagnie*, VOC) flourished and survived for two centuries. The company, a combination of commercial organizations in various cities of Holland and Zeeland, traded both in Asia and between Asia and Europe.

[8]Napoleon Bonaparte dominated European and global affairs for more than a decade while leading France against a series of coalitions in the Napoleonic Wars.

East Indies. The French had lost all their territories in this region; the Dutch continued to hold sway over Java. The Dutch East India Company managed to keep control over large parts of Indonesia.

2.4.2 *Mainland Southeast Asia and the Colonial Powers*

During the 17th and 18th centuries, when the Dutch were securing the East Indies, and Spain was consolidating her rule in the Philippines, countries on the mainland continued to be at war against one another. Since there was a decline in the demand for spices, the Dutch sought other avenues for profiteering. This resulted in conflict and power struggles with the local rulers of the islands. The resistance over the period 1825–1830 was firmly dealt with, and the Dutch imposed a system whereby a portion of the cultivable land of locals had to be designated for production of cash crops like coffee, tobacco, sugar, and cotton, with procurement prices fixed by the Dutch. Despite some relaxation in the colonial policy, the revolts continued in Java during the 19th century. It was only toward the end of the 19th century that the Dutch finally gained control of the island of Bali and conquered the Sultan of Aceh in Northern Sumatra.

In Vietnam, it was the Nguyen dynasty that became famous during the Nguyen Trinh War from 1627 to 1673. Southern Vietnam was under the control of Cambodia until about 1760, and for over 100 years, the rival Nguyen family ruled over a separate kingdom based in Hue in Central Vietnam. (The Northern kingdom during this period of division came to be known as Tonkin.) In 1802, Vietnam was unified under the Nguyen dynasty, with its capital at Hue. In 1803, the authority of the ruler was formally recognized by the Chinese Ch'ing dynasty. The Nguyen dynasty lasted until the resignation of Bao Dai at the end of World War II.[9]

Under the Nguyen dynasty, more than two centuries of struggle between Vietnam and Siam (Thailand) for control of Cambodia reached a critical stage, and in the process, the two competing powers earned the

---

[9] From https://www.globalsecurity.org/military/world/vietnam/vietnam-nguyen.htm; accessed on November 12, 2018.

intense enmity of the Cambodians. Whenever the opportunity presented itself, Vietnam proceeded to impose its own culture and institutions on the Cambodians, and after 1834, Cambodia was subjected to direct Vietnamese rule. Shortly after that, the Cambodians, encouraged by Siam, rebelled against the Vietnamese, and this ensuing inconclusive military conflict between Siam and Vietnam ended in 1845. A final resolution was settled upon only when the two powers agreed to set up joint control over Cambodia. This dual vassalage was terminated in 1863 with the establishment of a French protectorate over the area (*Ibid.*).

While Laos was comparatively peaceful during the 17th century, toward the end of the century, an internal struggle divided the country into three separate kingdoms. They were centered on Luang Prabang in the North, Vientiane in the center, and Champassak in the South. Cambodia, driven from the Mekong Delta in Southern Vietnam between 1700 and 1760, continued to be a prey to Siamese interference in the West.

Meanwhile, the British Empire, realizing the importance of ports, entered SEA in 1786, where their first colony was the Port of George Town on the island of Penang. This was one of the first seeds to be sown in terms of colonial establishments of the British, who took control of Ceylon at first, followed by Malacca, Singapore, and Sabah, by 1867. After that Java, which was also in British possession, was administered for 5 years (1811–1816) by Stamford Raffles, an East India Company officer. In 1819, as a result of Raffles' instigations (who had liberal ideas about governance), the Company acquired the lease of the island of Singapore from the Sultan of Johor. At the time when the British acquired Singapore, it was nothing but a swampy jungle, but with Raffles' foresight and guidance, it soon grew to become one of the most strategically advanced ports of SEA and soon overtook Malacca as the favorite stop for ships.

Once the British had won the Opium War against China in 1842, and the trade treaties included France, it became easier for the French to spread their influence. The French took Cochin China or South Vietnam (in 1862, 1867) as a colony and gained protectorates over

Cambodia (1863), Annam (1884), and Tonkin (1884). By 1885, France had established colonies in Central Vietnam (Annam) and the North (Tonkin) as well.[10] The King of Cambodia, who sought foreign aid in 1861, was forced to become a French protectorate. Earlier, the previous ruler, King Chan (1806–1834), had turned to the Vietnamese for protection from the Thais, which had infuriated the latter. They subsequently tried to take advantage of the volatility in Cambodia but were rebutted by the Vietnamese (Lambert, 2019).

Meanwhile, the French, taking advantage of the prevailing animosities, challenged Siamese intervention in Laos, and in 1893, Laos also became a French protectorate. The next task for the French was to initiate administrative reform and economic development in their new empire of Indo-China (Cochinchina, Annam, Tonkin, Laos, and Cambodia). In terms of the cultural influence of the French, it was most influential in Cochin China (Southern Vietnam). With the British taking over Malaya and Burma, and the French controlling Vietnam, Laos, and Cambodia, the only native kingdom to retain and defend its independence during the 19th century was that of Siam (Thailand).

2.4.3 *Britain and France in Southeast Asia*

During this second half of the 19th century, Siam found itself in a difficult situation due to the increasing pressure from French advances in the East, but her resistance to this pressure was helped by Britain's desire to keep Siam as a buffer between the British and French possessions. This was a case similar, if not identical (in terms of policy and polity), to that of Awadh's status as a buffer state in India, during the British Raj. By conceding French possessions of Cambodia and Laos, Siam succeeded in surviving within her traditional borders, and in 1896, both Britain and France guaranteed her an independent status.

---

[10] Indo-China (Indochine in French) consisted of the French colony of Cochin–China and the French protectorates of *Annam, Tonkin, Laos* and *Cambodia*. Cochin–China, *Tonkin*, and *Annam* were later combined to form a new country: *Vietnam*. The capital of Indo-China was Hanoi.

By 1885, the conquest of Upper Burma by the British, and involuntary abduction of the last Burmese king, Thibaw, had already taken place. They grew to control a majority of the Muslim states of the Malay Peninsula, in Southern Siam. It was the French who were considered a more significant threat by Siam because of their occupation of Southern Vietnam, around the Mekong Delta in 1863, and beyond to Cambodia. Assuming Vietnam's traditional interests, France obliged the Cambodian king, Norodom, to accept a French protectorate. Siam had to relinquish its right to Cambodia in 1867, in exchange for French recognition of Siam's sovereignty over the Cambodian provinces of Siem Reap and Battambang. France, who had ambitions of outdoing Britain, developed a trade route to Southwestern China through the Mekong Valley, assuming control over Vietnam in the 1880s. For realizing their ambitions, it was also imperative for the French to take control of the small Laotian kingdoms, which were under Siamese suzerainty. The French claimed these territories based on the mandate of being a supervisory power in areas that were ruled over by Vietnam. Siam, however, was unwilling to cede Laos and it was only after a bitter war was fought in Laos in 1893 that the Siamese agreed to the cession of Laos. Britain and France signed a treaty in 1896 which recognized a border between French territory in Laos and British territory in Upper Burma. The expansionist forces of the French were successful in securing the surrender of Battambang and Siem Reap to French-occupied Cambodia in 1907. King Chulalongkorn was also made to give up Siam's claims to the Northern Malay states of Kelantan, Terengganu, Kedah, and Perlis to the British in exchange for legal jurisdiction over British subjects on its soil and a large loan for railroad construction. Although Siam maintained its independence, it has already lost many of its territories even as it became a buffer state between the two European powers. In 1824, the British East India Company also acquired Malacca from the Dutch, exchanging it for a British trading post in Sumatra. The three British settlements — Penang, Singapore, and Malacca — were administered from 1826 as the "Straits Settlements"; hence, Britain became increasingly involved in the political affairs of the neighboring native Malay states.

In addition to taking control over the port cities, the British ventured further into the Malay Peninsula to exact the profits emanating from rubber cultivation. By the early 20th century, all of the Malay Peninsula was under some form of British control, which had systematically replaced Siamese influence in some of the Northern states. There was great economic development during the 19th century, not only in tin mining, with the help of the Chinese immigrants, but also in the arena of rubber (labor for which was provided mainly for by workers from Southern India). The intermingling of races created some problems owing to the overwhelming numbers of Chinese. However, it would suffice to state that the different communities — British, Malays, Chinese, and Indians — lived in peaceful separation from each other, and nuisance or volatility was at a minimum.

To understand the fall of Hong Kong to the British, it is important to trace the historical events in China. The Manchu dynasty toward the end of the 18th century commanded immense power, controlling China, with Annam, Siam, and Burma in a tributary relationship. However, not fully realizing the threat the Europeans posed to their empire, the Manchus imposed restrictions on European trade and refused to allow any foreign embassies in Peking. Consequently, the first Opium War was fought from 1839 to 1842 over British trade in China. Another Opium War was fought from 1856 to 1860; the wars unleashed a century of humiliation for the Chinese (Allingham, n.a.).

The consequence of the Opium wars on China was devastating. The Manchu armies were no match for the British forces who wielded absolute command of the seas. Hong Kong — a hilly and rocky island then, with few inhabitants and a haunt of pirates — was ceded to Britain and some Chinese ports were opened to British trade. Similar trade treaties with other Western nations followed. After subsequent agreements with China, Britain obtained the Kowloon Peninsula on the mainland opposite Hong Kong in 1860, and in 1898 the 99-year lease of the "New Territories" on the mainland, greatly increased the expanse of the colony. Hong Kong, with a magnificent harbor, became one of the main ports of the East.

With a rich appetite for trade, the British well understood the importance of Burma, located to the East of India in order to seize control of the trade between India and China. Thus, another important sphere of influence emerged for the British in Burma, which had settlers from Tibet, known as the Burmese. The British were well prepared to stop the advances of the Burmese into Arakan toward the end of the 18th century, and then into Manipur and Assam in 1822. This led to the first

Anglo-Burmese War in 1824–1826. The war concluded with the British annexation of Arakan and Tenasserim (the latter is the long strip of territory between Siam and the Western coast). Burmese interference with British trade caused a second war in 1852–1854. As a result of this, Britain annexed Lower Burma, including Rangoon and Pegu.

Subsequently, a revolution in Burma led to the deposition of the reigning monarch; and a new king, Mindon Min (1853–1878), who shared friendly terms with the British, ascended the throne. He built a new capital, Mandalay, near Ava. However, his successor, Thibaw, reverted to anti-British trade policies, causing a third Anglo-Burmese War in 1885.[11] This third war ended the Kingdom of Burma. Thibaw lost his crown in 1885 at the age of 27, and Britain assumed control — both administrative and trade — over the rest of the country. The Shan states in the East, however, close to Siam, could not be secured for several years. For the next 50 years, Burma was governed as a province of British-India.

2.5 Siam's Tryst with Colonizers and the Role of Mongkut's Diplomacy

Almost through the 18th century, Siam tried to stay away from Western influence. The Ayutthaya period, which began in 1350, came to an end in 1767, when Siam was conquered by the Burmese. Although Siam was defeated in that war, a small Thai army was able to find its way out of the ruins and despite more Burmese raids was able to regain control of the Chao Phraya River Delta. Hence, it was an army officer known as General Chakri, who established a new capital at Bangkok, in 1782. He came to be known as Rama I (the Chakri dynasty, in which all the kings take the name Rama, which continues at present) (Mason, 2000). Under the new dynasty, Siam expanded its borders, at the expense of Burma, Cambodia, Vientiane (Laos), and Northern Malaya. With the expansion, there came the burdensome tax system; in fact, the so-called tax farming system meant that people who collected tax could keep whatever they realized above

---

[11]By now, India itself was now directly under British government rule, East India Company rule having ceased in 1858. From http://aerocomlab.stanford.edu/jameson/world_history/A_Short_History_of_South_East_Asia1.doc.

their bid. Most of these tax collectors were Chinese immigrants. This tax system created a large slave class, and a feudal society was developed; a slavery system allowed the slaves to transfer themselves from one owner to another. Rama III, wishing to circumvent colonization, reluctantly agreed to enter a trade agreement with Britain in 1826. His successor, King Mongkut,[12] an established religious scholar, devoted himself to studying Western science and humanities, mastering several languages, including Latin and English, and learned about his people and culture through a kingdom-wide pilgrimage.[13]

It was King Mongkut (Rama IV, 1851–1868) who opened the economy to foreign trade and led the process of Thailand's modernization. He not only introduced Western education and medicine but also encouraged schools of new thought(s). Mongkut's reign coincided with a particularly complex era of international relations for South Asian countries. European political powers had begun circling Siam because it occupied an attractive position between Burma. At this time, Burma was annexed by England and French-occupied Indo-China. To retain independence and avoid capture by the British, Mongkut instituted a series of measures that assimilated his country into the modern world, sacrificing some traditional aspects of Thai culture. He corresponded regularly with European leaders and welcomed them as royal visitors and employed Western experts and advisors. He enacted several modernization reforms, from health and medicine standards to education and administration regulations. In 1854, Mongkut agreed to an important negotiation. John Bowring, an advisor to Queen Victoria, visited the King in the hopes of abolishing Siam's monopoly on international trade. Although it was asymmetrical in terms of

---

[12]Mongkut was born in the Old Palace in 1804 where he lived until his father, Isarasundhorn, was crowned King Rama II, and the family moved to the Grand Palace. At the age of 19, Mongkut followed Siamese tradition that men of his age become Buddhist monks. Although he was the crowned prince, Mongkut was not immediately sworn in as Siam's new monarch when his father died. From https://kingandiolney.wordpress.com/historical-context/king-mongkut/; accessed on January 3, 2019.

[13]*Ibid.* A short description of King Mongkut is taken from the famed "The King and I", a book written by Margaret Landon in 1944, is as follows, *"Eyes inquisitive and penetrating, he was the massive brain proper to an intellect deliberate and systematic"* — Anna Leonowens, from The English Governess at the Siamese Court.

favoring the English, the Bowring Treaty[14] opened Siam to Western economic relations and eased the British interest in Siamese colonialism. Mongkut continued to navigate difficult foreign relations by retaining a balance between self-protection and submission. Ultimately, this diplomacy saved Siam from further foreign intervention, making it the single country in continental Southeast Asia to avoid Western colonization.[15]

Mongkut died in 1868 after a reign of 17 years. Rama V, King Chulalongkorn, who reigned till 1910, continued his reforms and further modernized the financial system, the army, and communications, with the help of his European and American advisors. Siam, under Chulalongkorn, was forced to return all territory to the East of the Mekong River to the French. Britain and France agreed in 1904 to uphold an independent Siam as a buffer between their colonial empires. In 1909, Siam was also forced to surrender few territories, which, in the present day, are known as the four Northern provinces of Malaysia (Mason, 2000).

Siam was able to consolidate its independence thereafter, as the Europeans were involved in World War I (1914–1919). However, European advisors continued to remain in important positions for the next two decades, with the Siamese State Bank being led first by a German and then by an Englishman (Basu, 2017, p. 86).

2.5.1 *The Military in Thailand*

It is important to bring into discussion the role of the military in Thailand's historical development. From 1932 to 1958, the country went through 12 *coups d'etat*. Post 1958, there have been 8 more coups, several of them having been successful in changing the incumbent government. In fact, Thailand has depended on military rulers ever since its transition from an absolute monarchy to a constitutional monarchy in 1932. According to Roger Kershaw, in Thailand, the constitutional monarchy was not just the

---

[14]The Bowring Treaty is the name given to an agreement signed on April 18, 1855 between the United Kingdom and the Kingdom of Siam that liberalized foreign trade in Siam. The treaty was signed by five Siamese plenipotentiaries and by Sir John Bowring, Governor of Hong Kong and Britain's envoy.

[15]https://kingandiolney.wordpress.com/historical-context/king-mongkut/.

object of politics, but was the subject of politics, or in a way, it was an autonomous factor (Kershaw, 2000, p. 68). The relationship between the military and the monarchy, began in 1957, when the Thai military general Sarit Thanarat with the blessings of King Bhumibol aligned with the United States. Post the death of Sarit in 1963, Thailand's closeness to the United States continued; this provided the much-needed support to not only pursue anti-communist policies but also ensure the country's continued independence. Regimes which followed that of Sarit continued with policies of development. Prior to 2006, there was a coup in 1991, the latter placing a military general in power only for a year (Chibber and Shishodia, S.K, in Kumar, 2013, p. 132).

In 2001, Thaksin Shinawatra came to power and was re-elected in 2005, mainly as a result of his populist policies. However, in 2006, a military coup was staged against him, mainly due to allegations of corruption against his government. The present general Prayut Chan-o-Cha who overthrew the Yingluck Shinawatra Government has been in power since the 2014 coup, making sure that with the 2019 elections, there was no threat to his position.

2.6 Conclusion

Lieberman (2003, pp. 4–5) has drawn parallels between political consolidation in Europe and Southeast Asia. This connection includes an explanation of how between 1340 and 1820, almost 23 independent Southeast Asian kingdoms collapsed to three. The situation was similar to the one in Europe, where ~500 political units in 1450 were reduced to 30 by the late 19th century. Cultural and commercial relations became more and denser, and political integration became a reality, making it more inclusive and specialized. This was so in varying degrees in Burma, Siam, and Vietnam on the mainland; in Europe, it was in France and Russia that centrally defined cultural norms became a symbol of political inclusion (Lieberman, 2003).

Thus, it would not be incorrect to state that the present nations of South and Southeast Asia follow the boundaries defined by the calculations, political maneuvering, and at the convenience of the colonizing powers. Their superiority in fighting and winning wars was unmatched. This was because it was in war-torn Europe that firearms developed most rapidly, and hence, when the European and Asian armies clashed in the 18th and 19th centuries, the Asians were invariably outgunned (Gideon, 2016, p. 23).

Traditional trade networks were disrupted by the colonizers. For example, the Spanish relied on the trans-Pacific link to Mexico for retaining control over their possessions. The cultural and political traditions were dealt a severe blow and had one of the most damaging impacts on interstate relations in Southeast Asia. Inevitably, there was a breakdown of a regional configuration of states. This, along with the construction of artificial boundaries under colonialism, disintegrated the landscape of Southeast Asia.

Each of the countries in Southeast Asia is a colonial creation carved by the needs of the metropole. Even Siam, which retained independence, was formed in response to European colonialism and, like other colonial creations, expanded to absorb a hinterland populated by different people than those at the core. Each of these states in the region is, in fact, multi-ethnic, with peripheral areas that extended well beyond easy colonial control.

Moreover, the traditional rulers of these nations, even when faced with threats from the European colonial powers in the 20th century, met the challenges individually and not collectively. Siam, through its diplomatic endeavors, was successful in maintaining its independence, even though it lost some of its territories. According to Hopkins, Siam in the early 1950s, was the haven for the gunrunners of most of Asia as well as a clearinghouse for insurgents. It had problems in the North, East, and South (Hopkins, 1952, p. 96).

Hence, it would be appropriate to state that before the advent of European colonialism, the Asian world-order was made up of transacting boundaries of several ancient civilizations. The existing order was permeated by European colonialism, resulting in the concept of sovereignty and the state — a European conception which emphasized sovereign exclusivity. The 19th-century notion of the sovereign state eventually found fertile ground in an Asia, which was not only interested in overthrowing colonial oppression but also finally able to do so.

Post-independence, each of the Southeast Asian nation-builders was faced with the challenge of establishing and reinforcing central control.

This challenge was easier in some places than others, and many of the security issues in the region today can be traced to efforts to consolidate artificial entities along colonial boundaries. The border regions — Mindanao, Aceh, the Burma–Thailand, Cambodia–Thailand, Malaysia–Thailand borders — have been the source of internal separatism from the outset. As a result, state concerns about security were, primarily, internal rather than external (Davis, 2005).

Moreover, the traditional rulers of these nations, even when faced with threats from the European colonial powers in the 20th century, met the challenges individually and not collectively. Siam, through its diplomatic endeavors, was successful in maintaining its independence, even though it had to partake of several of its territories. Hence, the boundaries of Southeast Asian countries were fluid due to the intervention- and influence-seeking behavior of Western colonial powers. Evidently, then nation-building became an exercise of great challenge.

Thailand's tryst with democracy and the realization of people's aspirations for freedom of speech seem illusory. It is also interesting to note how young men have entered into military careers, simply to be able to secure power and position through the military hierarchy. With so many people with ambition, it is difficult to understand how aspirations of these people would be accommodated. (Butwell, 1964, p. 54). About the 2019 elections, as stated in the *Diplomat*, "the junta set out from day one to figure out how it could hold on to power indefinitely, while still going through the process of holding elections. In short, the military sought to put in place a system in which they would not have to stage a coup again, but would control everything from within" (Abuza, 2019).

Here, Wang Gungwu's assertion is recalled; although Thais have sought control by a democratic party rather than the military, they have not done better in nation-building in the Southernmost and Northeastern parts of the country (Gungwu, 2010, p. 53).

Aspects of Siam's histories during the 20th and 21st centuries are provided in Chapter 3 which focuses on Thailand and its historical-religious and cultural relations with India.

Chapter 3

Thailand–India: Through the Lens of Southeast Asian History and Culture

Those who love Ramakien (Ramayana) love to study about India.

Srisurang Poolthupya[1]

3.1 Introduction

The influence of Indian culture on Southeast Asian religion and culture has been discussed in Chapter 1. Chapter 2 focused on the colonial struggles of Southeast Asia and Siam's relative insulation from colonization.

It is well known that Thailand and India have been in contact economically, socially, and culturally since the early formation of the Thai kingdom of Sukhothai in the 13th century AD (Poolthupya, 2008, p. 669). Hence, Thailand's relationship with India has a long history that resulted in the adaptation of Indian culture to suit the contemporary Thai environment. There are Tai communities settled in Assam, in India since the 13th century. It is through the movement of people that cultures get enriched. Hence, the two-way cultural and religious connections are discussed in this chapter. A section on Tai communities is also included.

The map of Thailand, in Figure 3.1, shows some of the important places referred to in the report.

---

[1] Srisurang Poolthupya in an interview to the author on May 31, 2018, Bangkok, Thailand.

Figure 3.1:   Map of Thailand

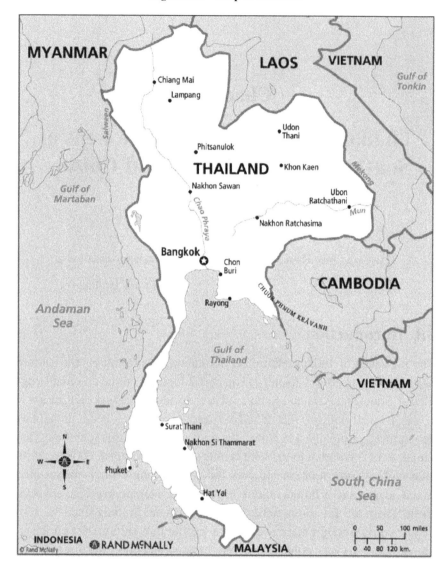

According to Coedes (1996), the introduction of Indian culture was a gradual process, and the local people readily accepted the superior cultural endowments of the immigrants, and "assured the newcomers of a welcome". Brahmanism attracted the monarchy, and Buddhism attracted the masses. Although ever since the *Dvaravati* era (i.e., the period from the 7th to the 11th centuries), before the arrival of the Khmers,[2] the monarchy and a majority of the commoners had predominantly converted to Buddhism, and Brahmanical (Hindu) faith acquired an important place of its own. At present, Hinduism is one of five official religions of Thailand. The other religions are Buddhism, Sikhism, Christianity, and Islam.

This chapter explores the religious and cultural links between India and Thailand through politico-religious history, including Buddhism and Brahmanism. It also provides an insight into the cultural practices as well as aspects of art and architecture, whose origins can be traced back to India. A section on Tai communities, who came to India in the 13th century and settled in Assam has been included as well.

3.2 Advent of Buddhism and Brahmanism

According to Wales (1931), the very early settlers of present-day Thailand were the Lava who lived in the Northern hills, and the Mon-Khmer, who had settled over the entire area from present-day Cambodia to as far as Pedu, in Malaysia. It is believed that it was traders from India who made the initial contact with these people. Soon after, two missionaries were sent by King Asoka, viz. Sona and Uttara, in the 3rd century BC, to Suvarnabhumi. It was Hinayana Buddhism that was brought from Sri Lanka, and spread further to Cambodia — this is evident from the ancient wheels that have been discovered at Nakhom Pathom. The Mahayana sect also reached the kingdom of Srivijaya in Sumatra, Central and Southern Siam, as well as Cambodia. From India, King Kanishka, the

---

[2]From http://www.Thailandsworld.com/en/Thai-art/mon-dvaravati-art-Thailand/index. cfm. Dvaravati also refers to the Mon communities that ruled what is now Thailand. Nakhon Pathom, Khu Bua, and U Thong in Central Thailand are important sites for Dvaravati art and architecture. The art objects are of Hinayana Buddhist, Mahayana Buddhist, and Hindu religious subjects. Objects are stone sculpture, stucco, terracotta, and bronze. The style is influenced by India, Amaravati (South India), and Gupta and post-Gupta prototypes (4th–8th centuries in India) but have local elements to reflect Southeast Asian facial features. Found throughout the Dvaravati Kingdom, these symbols of the Buddha's first sermon were erected on high pillars and placed in temple compounds. Today, good examples can be seen at the Bangkok National Museum.

Mauryan ruler, sent missionaries to China, Tibet, and Southern India, thus helping Buddhism spread further (Wales, 1931, p. 3).

Baker discusses how Buddhism originally came to the Chao Phraya Basin by the 5th century, at a time when awareness about Indic gods was neither well defined nor separated into different sects (Baker and Pasuk, 2005, p. 7).

It is well known that in the 5th century, the East Borneo inscriptions, called Yupas, which are dated 400 AD notes on Sanskrit verses, that Mulavarman,[3] the lord of kings, in Borneo was known to have been generous to the Brahmanas and gave them valuable presents. These priests were gifted cattle and land. A Sanskrit rock inscription from circa 450 AD speaks of an occasion in which Brahmanas were presented with a thousand cows. A 5th-century Chinese text says that in the kingdom of Dun-sun, "there are more than a thousand Brahmanas of India" (Embree, 1997).

According to Prof. N.A.K. Sastri, as cited by Mukhopadhyay, it was the resident Indian merchants, who married the locals and became the basic transmitters of Indian culture. The adventurous Kshatriyas who married into the families of local rulers subsequently brought with them Brahman priests to authenticate and assert their political authority (Mukhopadhyay, 2017). The introduction of the Brahmanical culture was a continuing process. Such contacts, beginning at a relatively remote period, were first substantiated archaeologically during the 2nd and 3rd centuries AD.

3.2.1 *A Contiguous Civilization*

Wales (1931) further states that through the remains of the Dvaravati kingdom of the Mons (which is in present-day Thailand), from the 3rd to the 7th century AD, it can be inferred that the Sarnath school of India had a profound influence on the people. It was after this period that Brahmanism gained traction in India, but the Indians, who settled among the Mons, as well as the local people, embraced Buddhism and continued

---

[3]The names of Khmer kings like those of certain Hinduized monarchs in Java, all end with suffix *varman*, which means protector.

to practice the faith. Although the Indian settlers in Suvarnabhumi contin-ued to maintain contact with their country, one cannot accurately ascer-tain when the Brahmanas commenced their real influence. It is well documented that the Brahmanic Indians established a powerful empire in Cambodia, which extended further West into Suvarnabhumi. However, it is sometimes debated whether there was a movement of Brahmanas over-seas. The question is significant as to go "overseas" was considered impure, and a return to caste demanded prayaschit (redemption) in many forms. However, scholars have then agreed to the fact that Brahmins did not see the East as "abroad" for the civilization they found was contigu-ous to their own, fused by an intrinsic harmony. The West comparatively was "abroad".

3.2.2 *Hindu Gods: Repository of God's Divinity during 8th–11th Centuries*

After the Thai people moved Southwards from Southern China after establishing a strong independent state in the 7th century (Nanchao), they entered Siam; here they witnessed the absorption of Mahayana Buddhism and Brahmanism by the local people. While Buddhism was the religion of popular choice, Brahmanas were also treated with deference. In the 9th-century Angkor, it is believed that Indravarman I had a Brahman, Sivasoma, in his court who was said to have studied under Sankara (Manguin *et al.*, 2011). Further, it was during the time of Jayavarman II, who came to the throne in 802 AD, that the king came to be identified as the Hindu gods — Shiva and Vishnu. He was known as the *Jagat ka Raja* (king of the world) or the *Devaraja* (Royal God). The belief was that the "Royal God" was not the king of gods (i.e., Indra) but a god of the king, either Shiva or Vishnu. The *Devaraja* cult was a royal cult designed to legitimate and maximize the king's power by endowing divinity or quasi-divinity, onto kingship. The Indian ritual was the most sophisticated, and hence, the most powerful ideological device available at the time to which kings were readily attracted. Kings present at the cult were distinguished from Brahmins in that the cult was to bring down to this world legitimacy and authority of rulers over the ruled (Wales, 1931, p. 9). Sublimity and godliness emanated by gigantic shrines, and conspicuously placed *lingas*[4] could effectively produce a religious basis for the legitimation of the kingship. Hence, power was centered upon the king "[who] was the divine source of all authority" and the divinity of kingship was achieved by the king's proper ritual-service to god (Yeonsik, 2011).

In the words of Wales (1931):

> No doubt the Khmer cult of the Deva-raja and the deification of kings was only a highly specialized form of an earlier Indian conception of divine kingship, exemplified by the following passage from Manusmriti, (an important early Hindu text): "Even an infant king must not be despised (from an idea) that he is a mere mortal, for he is a great deity in human form".

Thus, a Hindu king was considered a repository of the divinity of god, but he was not a god himself. In Buddhism, the king is a *Bodhisattva* or a *Chakravartin* — a stature that was greater in the eyes of the Buddhists to any Hindu god (Wales, 1931, pp. 29–32).

It is important to note that there were early contacts between Kalinga (present-day Odisha, India) and Siam. It was during the 8th and 9th centuries CE that a wave of migration from the seaports of Kalinga to Siam helped in the 'Indianization' of Siam. The recent archaeological excavations in Central Thailand have unearthed tangible indicators of contacts with ancient Odisha in the form of bronze bowls and carnelian beads, especially, etched carnelian beads (Patra, 2017).

3.3 Buddhism — Influences from Burma and Sri Lanka during the 11th–13th Centuries

While Kusalasaya (2013) believes that Burmese-Buddhism had also made inroads into Siam, via Pagan (the Burmese capital under the powerful King Anuruddha (Anawratha) during the 11th century), Wales (1931) believes otherwise. While Kusalasaya recognizes the expanse of the kingdom from across Northern and Central Thailand, with authority provided

---

[4]In Hinduism, a *linga* is a stylized phallus worshiped as a symbol of the god Shiva.

by the Buddhist relics found there, Wales (1931) observes that the impact of Pagan Buddhism is insignificant because of the political enmity between Siam and Burma and the hostility in all exchanges between them (Kusalasaya, 2013). On this premise, the Thais, according to Wales (1931), would never have adopted any strand of Burmese culture. According to him: "Cultural resemblances are entirely due to a common origin, both the Burmese and Siamese owed much to the earlier Indian civilization of the Mons".

Between Thailand and Sri Lanka, the influence went both ways. It was about the 12th century when Sinhalese-Hinayanistic influences first appeared in Thailand. The mass conversion of the Thai from Mahayana Buddhism appears to have occurred during the 13th century.[5] While the Mahayana theory of divine incarnation requires that a temple occupy the center of the capital, the Hinayana sect, recognizing the king merely as a representative of the divine, requires that the palace occupy the center.[6]

In about 1257 AD (BE 1800)[7], Thailand sent her *Bhikkhus* to Ceylon, thereby obtaining the *upasampada vidhi* (ordination rite) from Ceylon, which later became known in Thailand as *Lankavamsa*. Apparently, the early batches of *Bhikkhus*, who returned after studies, often accompanied by Ceylonese monks, established themselves first in Nakon Sri Thammarath (South Thailand); many of the Buddhist relics bearing definitely Ceylonese influence, such as stupas and Buddha images, have been found there. Some of these relics still exist today. News of the meritorious activities of these monks soon spread to Sukhothai, the then capital of Thailand, and King Ramakhamhaeng who was ruling at the time, invited the monks to his capital, giving them his royal patronage and support for the propagation of the Doctrine. This fact is recorded in one of the King's rock inscriptions, dated about 1277 AD. The study of Pali, the language of

---

[5] Hinayana encompasses 18 schools. The most important for our purposes are Sarvastivada and Theravada. Theravada is the one extant today in Sri Lanka and Southeast Asia.

[6] From http://www.siameseheritage.org/jsspdf/1961/JSS_053_1i_Sternstein_KrungKao-OldCapitalOfAyutthaya.pdf; p. 88.

[7] The official calendar in Thailand is based on the Buddhist Era (BE), which is 543 years ahead of the Gregorian or Western calendar; hence, the year 2017 is equivalent to the Buddhist Era (BE) 2560 in Thailand.

Theravada or Southern Buddhism, also made great progress, and in all matters dealing with the *Dhamma,* the impact of Ceylon was perceptibly felt (Patra, 2017).

This is further reiterated by Baker and Pasuk (2005). They state that it was in the 13th century that monks brought with them the tradition of Theravada Buddhism from Sri Lanka, which was accepted with great enthusiasm. Theravada Buddhism, being the state religion of Thailand, constitutes an integral part of Thai identity and culture. Monks were venerated by the kings, and the kings built Buddhist temples. Despite the diverse strands of belief systems that the Thai society was exposed to, there was no antagonism between the different forms of Buddhism already in existence in Thailand as well as the *Lankavamsa,* which had been introduced from Ceylon.

Contrary to what was expected, religious consolidation occurred peacefully. This is evident in all religious rites and ceremonies of Thailand. Indeed, somewhat characteristic of the Buddhists, there had been a spirit of forbearance in all matters. This was/is the Thai way, and the Thai culture of tolerance and acceptance of ideas is considered suitable for societal harmony (Baker and Pasuk, 2005, p. 7).

3.4 Religion in Thai History

The history of Thailand can be broken into three very general periods — pre-Khmer, Khmer, and post-Khmer. The period called pre-Khmer is also called the *Dvaravati* period. *Dvaravati* itself is a Sanskrit word used to refer to the city of Shiva from the Indian epic poem *Mahabharata.* It translates to "a place with gates". It lasted from about the 6th century until about the 11th or 12th century, when it was overwhelmed by the Khmer civilization of Angkor. It consisted of many small city-states of uncertain ethnicity. It is interesting to note that the Khmer people ultimately became the masters of much of what is now mainland Southeast Asia. Their influence extended East to the China Sea, Westward through what is now Thailand, to the Burmese border, and as far South as the Isthmus of Kra (Mason, 2000, p. 38). Rather than being Thai speakers, it is believed that these people spoke a language of the Mon-Khmer family. They left behind magnificent art — including temples, Buddha images, giant terracotta heads, sculptures, and terracotta relief on walls and caves. It appeared to be a thriving culture as the Indian merchants referred it to as the 'Land of Gold'.

The *Dvaravati* period markedly ended in the 12th and 13th centuries with the expansion of the Khmer of Angkor into Thailand. Although the Khmer culture gradually moved into Thailand over a few hundred years, its influence was not enduring as they were always considered to be invaders.

3.4.1 *Thailand in the Post-Khmer Era: 1238 to the Present*

Thailand's post-Khmer era can be broken down into three parts: the Sukhothai and Lan Na Period (1238–early 1400s), the Ayutthaya period (1350–1767), and the Chakri dynasty (1782 to present). The Thais consider the Sukhothai Period to be the 'Golden Age' of Thailand. It is widely believed that the time was more egalitarian — everyone was taken care of and attended[8] (Lehman Jr., 2015).

3.4.1.1 *Sukhothai — The Golden Period (1238–1438)*

In 1237, the Sukhothai (or Dawn of Happiness) kingdom became free, resulting in the ascendancy of King Ramkhamhaeng the Great. Ramkhamhaeng was popular and was revered as a father; it is believed that he would listen to the petition of any subject who approached the palace.

King Ramkhamhaeng reinvented the Thai alphabet (which replaced the Khmer script) and went on to become the precedence of the people of the Thai nationality. He developed the *Lai Sue Thai* or the Thai alphabet by adapting them from the ancient Khmer, Mon, and Burmese alphabets for making reading easier.[9]

---

[8]Ayutthaya was a prosperous trading coastal city, close to the Gulf of Thailand on the Chao Phraya River, the main river of Thailand. Its kings became incredibly prosperous trading with Europeans and Asians alike.

[9]The Great Kings of Siam by Thai Laws. From http://Thailaws.com/download/Thailand/thegreatkingsofsiam.pdf; accessed on December 1, 2018.

After he died in 1317 AD, his successor King Dharmaraja I came to the throne in 1353. Unlike his predecessor, he was not only well versed in the *Tripitaka*, in Hindu rituals, and skilled in astrology but also an educationist. He set up a school for Buddhist and Brahman priests and sent a mission to Ceylon to bring certain relics. He also became a monk in the later part of his life.

3.4.1.2 *Ayutthaya Period (1350–1767)*

During this period, the Khmer influence resulted in the disappearance of the paternal aspect of kingship, and the monarchs withdrew behind a wall of taboos and rituals. There are different versions about the founding of Ayutthaya, but according to popular legend, it is believed that a Prince U-Thong migrated South due to a plague in his city-state and was in search of a suitable location to settle down. The prince came to an area called *Nong Sano* or *Sano Swamp*, where he encountered a hermit (*rusi*). The hermit claimed how he had been there since the time of Buddha and that the latter had prophesied that one day a great city would be built there. Prince U-Thong then decided to construct a new city on the spot and established Ayutthaya on March 4, 1351, and went on to rule over it with the title of King Ramathibodhi I (Vandenberg, 2009). This was the beginning of the present kingdom of Siam, and by 1400, the remnants of the old kingdom of Sukhothai passed in terms of rule and territory under Ayutthaya.

After the founding of Ayutthaya, despite the continuing connections between Siam and China, there was no cultural influence of the latter. On the contrary, Siam influenced China through its own rich culture.

During this period, i.e., from 1351 to 1767, the idea of kingship changed. Due to the ancient Khmer traditions in the region, the Hindu concept of kingship was applied and the king was believed to be the reincarnation of Hindu gods. Brahmanas took charge of the royal coronation. Ayutthaya's historical documents show the official titles of the kings in great variation: Indra, Shiva, and Vishnu, or Rama. Without a doubt, Rama was the most popular, as *Ramathibodhi*. However, Buddhist influence was also evident because many a time the king's title and "unofficial" name related to *Bodhisattva, Dhamma Raja*, or King of Dharma.

Baker and Pasuk (2005, p. 14) confirm this in their work(s). Ayutthaya's ancient links to the Angkorian Cambodia were reiterated by King Prasat Thong in the 1630s.[10] Hence, more Brahmanas were brought in and the number of rituals increased. The palace was built several times, to keep the inner portion of the palace well guarded and secure with successive outer courtyards and higher walls. The royal persons were well hidden from people's gaze and they emerged only on select occasions in a year. It is not surprising that a French writer remarked that Siam "[is] more monarchical" than any other state in the Indies. While the Brahmanic art of the later Ayutthaya period was divided between two general tendencies, one was Khmerizing and was more or less a continuation of the Lopburi school,[11] the other was inspired by the iconography of South India; the Bangkok school created an original and unique Brahmanic art (Boisselier, 1975, p. 88).

Here, the importance of Burma is not to be missed because Ayutthaya was first captured in 1569 for 15 years by the Burmese, and its second and final destruction was in 1767.

3.4.1.3 *Bangkok Period (Post-1767): Advent of the Chakri Dynasty*

This period witnessed the present Chakri dynasty from 1782. After a period of instability, the first king of the present Chakri dynasty established the capital in Bangkok. The first three kings of the Chakri dynasty made efforts to restore the Ayutthaya glory of the past in their new capital. Under the Bangkok period, the position of the Brahmanas had considerably weakened. Their role as astrologers, however, continued to be significant in deciding the king's expeditions and making other critical decisions related to the State. In present times, while auspicious dates and good

---

[10]Prasat Thong reigned over the period 1629–1656. He was the first king of the Prasat Thong dynasty, the 4th dynasty of the Siamese Ayutthaya kingdom.

[11]Lopburi was also known as Lavo and had its own culture. At present, it has a Museum with Dvaravati artifacts. King Narai fortified Lopburi in the mid-17th century to serve as a second capital when the kingdom of Ayutthaya was threatened by a Dutch naval blockade.

omens for the accession of the king are important due to their popularity with the masses, it is very rare for Brahmanas to be consulted. Instead, this function is assigned to a non-Brahman official who holds the office of the royal astrologer (one only) and is known as *Brahyd fiord* (Wales, 1931). Despite this, royal ceremonies continued to be largely Hindu based, given the fact that the Thai kings wished to retain the splendor of the former Khmer kings.

The Mahayanist gods were not recognized in Hinayanism and Hindu gods were reduced to the rank of attendants of the Buddha. According to Wales (1931), no Buddhist king would be pleased on being reduced to nothing more than an incarnation of a Hindu deity. The king's image was that of a *Bodhisattva* (or incipient Buddha) or that of a *Chakravartin* (Universal Emperor), borrowed from the Sinhalese kings and further strengthened in Thai society, by the evidence of the popular Indian *Jataka* stories. This brings us to the concept of accumulation of merit and merit-making, whereby a king is rewarded for the merit he had accumulated in his past births. It is a natural corollary to believe then that the king still being impacted by the Wheel of the Law would probably rule more justly in comparison to a Hindu monarch. However, history is replete with reigns of despotic rulers, who remained unrestrained despite the prevalence of Hinayana Buddhism. As a result, ironically, Buddhism led to the ideology of the Divine Kingship associated with absolute tyranny (Wales, 1931).

In all of the above accounts, the chief occupation(s) of a king may be classified under three headings: (1) duties to religion, especially in connection with the state ceremonies; (2) duties to the secular government, especially in the matter of conferring among his ministers and granting audiences; (3) recreation, especially in the harem.

3.5 Thai Kings and India

It is well documented that Thai kings of various eras have always tried to follow the Buddhist ideal of the "Ten Virtues (or Dharmas) of Kingship" (*Dasabidh Raja Dham*). The traditional names of many ruling Thai kings at least since the period of the Ayutthaya Kingdom (1351–1767) was either "Ramesuan" or "Ramathibodi" (Rama the Ruler), and of course, the old capital city of Ayutthaya itself was named after Rama's city Ayodhya.

Thailand's kings are considered to be the incarnation of the Hindu Lord Vishnu, as well as the Buddhist Bodhisattwa.[12]

In the Rattanakosin or Bangkok era (starting from 1782), the first King who founded the City of Bangkok and established the Royal House of Chakri — Thailand's current reigning dynasty — was King Phra Buddha Yotfa Chulalok, or Rama I. He took the traditional name "Ramathibodi" and decided to name his dynasty *Chakri*, as the *Chakra* of Vishnu. The emblem of the Chakri dynasty is Vishnu's discus intersecting with Shiva's *Trisula* or trident. Apart from being a Buddhist, a warrior, and an administrator, King Rama I was also interested in the arts and literature. With help from Brahmins, scholars and poets, he translated and composed a completed Thai version of *Ramayana* (called *Ramakien* — or "the honor of Rama", in Thai) and built the Temple of the Emerald Buddha in his own Grand Palace. The 2-km long walls of the temple's compound are decorated in murals telling the story of *Ramakien* in its entirety.

Ramakien is a favorite epic of Thai kings. There are a few surviving remnants of the Thai *Ramayana* from the time of the Ayutthaya kingdom. Just prior to the Bangkok period, in the Thonburi period, King Taksin the Great in fact, composed four short plays and it is believed that the most popular versions of *Ramakien* in Thailand are the ones authored by King Rama I. His son Rama II — King Phra Buddha Loetla — was creative too and wrote the script for the *Khon* mask dance play.

King Mongkut or Rama IV, one of Rama II's sons, who was educated in the West (popular as depicted in the "The King and I" films and musical plays), was ordained as a Buddhist monk for 27 years before ascending the throne. He was fluent in the Pali language (one of the Prakrit languages of India) as well as with Buddhism. Among the *Ramakien* plays he wrote was the episode of Rama's *Canvas* journey. His successor, King Chulalongkorn the Great or Rama V, added his work on the Thai *Ramakien* in the form of Thai sonnets along the compound walls of the Temple of the Emerald Buddha. These sonnets served as a kind of caption or description to each mural painting, relating the story of *Ramayana* in that particular part of the walls. Altogether, there are 178 murals with thousands of accompanying

---

[12] From http://newdelhi.thaiembassy.org/en/2018/07/kings-india-royal-thai-family-context-siam-bharat-relations/.

sonnets composed by the Siamese princes, ministers, nobles, and poets of the time. The King himself contributed 224 sonnets.

The Royalty has had close ties with India. King Chulalongkorn visited several Indian cities during the British rule in 1872 (see Figure 3.2). His experiences in India had greatly impressed him and inspired him later in his reign for his endeavor to modernize Siam.

King Vajiravudh, Rama VI, was a profound scholar well versed in Sanskrit and Hindu literature, including the *Ramayana* and the *Mahabharata* epics. He also translated many stories from these epics, wrote Thai plays inspired by Indian literature, such as the Thai versions of Kalidasa's *Shakuntala* and King Harsha's *Priyadarshika*, the tale of King Nala and Princess Damayanti, and a short play on how the God Ganesha lost one of his tusks. Based on his research, the King also wrote a book on the origins of the Thai *Ramakien*, tracing back to the Sanskrit and Bengali sources in India. It was he who first standardized the title and style of the

Figure 3.2:   King Chulalongkorn in India, 1872 (Rama V was King of Thailand from 1868 to 1910)

Chakri Kings in English, to be henceforth known as "Rama" (from the Thai word Ramathibodi).

King Vajiravudh's younger brother succeeded him and became King Prajadhipok, Rama VII. Another great-uncle of the present King, he received India's renowned poet, "Gurudev" Rabindranath Tagore, in Bangkok in 1927, on which occasion the Gurudev composed two poems (in Bengali and English) dedicated to Siam. One is entitled "To Siam", which was read out in the presence of Their Majesties the King and Queen of Siam, before the gathering of princes and ministers of the Siamese Court. The other is called "Farewell to Siam".

In the 1950s, King Bhumibol was the patron of the first Thai Buddhist Temple in India, i.e., the Royal Thai Monastery at Bodh Gaya (Wat Thai Bodh Gaya), Bihar, which was built by the Thai Government on an invitation of Indian Prime Minister Nehru for the international Buddhist community to build their temples in the land of the Buddha. The invitation was issued on the occasion of the grand celebration of the 2,500 years of Buddhism, the Buddha Jayanti, which was held in India in 1956. The chief Buddha statue in the main Congregational Hall of Wat Thai Bodh Gaya was cast in Thailand in a ceremony presided over by King Bhumibol himself. He also gave the name "Phra Buddha Dharmishra Jambudipaniwat Sukhodaya" (meaning "Buddha, Lord of Dharma, who returns to the Continent of Jambudvipa for the happiness to occur") to the statue. King Bhumibol (and Queen Sirikit) hosted President V.V. Giri, the fifth President of India, during a State Visit to Thailand in 1972 (Sugondhabhirom, 2018).

In October 2016, His Majesty King Bhumibol Adulyadej, Rama IX, passed away, after having served his people for 70 years, as Thailand's longest ruling monarch. In November 2016, Prime Minister Modi, on his way to Tokyo, paid his respects to the late King, in Bangkok.

King Rama X, Thailand's present King, Maha Vajiralongkorn, was crowned king of Thailand, at the start of 3 days of ceremonies on April 5, 2019. The king received the five Royal Regalia — the symbols of kingship — which include the Great Crown of Victory, the Royal Slippers, the Royal Fan and Fly Whisk, the Royal Sword of Victory, and the Royal Scepter. The celebrations lasted till April 8 and represent the king's transformation from human into a divine figure.[13]

---

[13] From http://www.asianews.it/news-en/King-Maha-Vajiralongkorn-crowned-as-Rama-X-of-Thailand-46924.html.

As Crown Prince, he visited India three times (in 1992, 1998, and 2010). He himself piloted his aircraft to Gaya Airport and paid his respect to the Mahabodhi Temple as well as the Royal Thai Monastery in Bodh Gaya. The late King Bhumibol's daughters, Princess Maha Chakri Sirindhorn and Princess Chulabhorn, are also frequent visitors to India. Princess Sirindhorn is a Sanskrit and Indologist expert. She is the recipient of the World Sanskrit Award and the Padma Bhushan Award from the Government of India. She was conferred the Honorary Degree of Doctor of Literature (Sanskrit) from Delhi University and the Indira Gandhi Peace Prize. Since her first visit in 1987, she has visited the country 18 times. Princess Chulabhorn, a biochemist with keen interest in public health, visits New Delhi to participate in official meetings of the World Health Organization (see Figure 3.3).

The affection for India runs deep in the Royal Thai Family, generation after generation. King Bhumibol's mother, Her Royal Highness

Figure 3.3:   HRH Princess Maha Chakri Sirindhorn Received the Padma Bhushan Award in March 2017

Princess Sri Nagarindra, was not only fascinated by Indian cultures but also a keen student in Pali and Sanskrit and Buddhist philosophy later in her life. The cordial ties between India and the Royal Family of Thailand are one of the most important factors contributing to the everlasting friendship between Thailand and India.

3.6 Cultural Manifestations of Bilateral Ties

Thailand is replete with temples comprising the statues and murals of Indian gods and goddesses. While Lord Indra, Brahma, and Vishnu are popular, a favorite is Lord Ganesha. Even the Buddhist stupas and temples are guarded by Hindu gods. As stated in an earlier chapter, the influence of India on the art and architecture as well as the beliefs is widespread. Here, the focus is on such influences in Thailand.

3.6.1 *Art, Architecture, Temples, and Beliefs*

The distribution pattern of the archaeological materials including knobbed wares, stamped wares, glass beads, and semi-precious stones, among others, shows that Thailand had established a well-organized maritime trade network across the Bay of Bengal, via Bengal. Furthermore, one learns about a completely new inventory of trading commodities. The peak period of trade was possibly between 100 BCE and 100 CE (Jahan, 2012).

The earliest works of art produced in present-day Thailand date from the Kingdom of Dvaravati (6th–11th centuries), whose main centers lay within a 100-mile radius of Bangkok and a capital in all probability in Nakhon Pathom. Other Mon kingdoms stretched Westwards as far as Thaton in Burma.[14] The distinctive Dvaravati sculpture is that of the Wheel of Law. Indian culture, primarily through Buddhism, having crossed over the high seas left permanent imprints in arts, folklore,

---

[14] From the 8th century onward, the Khmers pushed forward into the Menam plains until, at the beginning of the 11th century, they annexed the whole Kingdom of Dvaravati. From https://www.Thailandtourist.net/dvaravati-period/.

language, literature, religion, and thought of Thailand. The excavations at Pong Tuk and Phra Pathom have brought to light the remains of a temple sanctuary, buildings, and a small statue of standing Buddha, which highlights the Indian influence on Siamese culture, art, and architecture (Patra, 2017).

In the Khmer period, i.e., post the 11th century, it was Shiva who was worshipped more than any other Indian gods. Given the fact that mountains were a sacred entity for the Khmers, and in India, Shiva was believed to control the cosmological universe from his abode on the Kailash Mountain, drawing parallels and adopting influences was a natural process (Gosling, 2004, p. 37). The sculpture of the reclining Vishnu is another unique example of Khmer art. Sandstone and bronze both were used to produce statues and images in Khmer culture. Among the most important images is that of a headless female divinity — probably Shiva's consort Uma, found in Aranya Prathet, in Prachinburi Province. Examples can be found from the subsequent periods of Khmer and Khmer-influenced art in Siam until the 13th century (Boisselier, 1975, p. 171).

The murals of Wat Phra Kaew (Emerald Buddha temple) across 178 panels narrate the story of Phra Rama, the hero of *Ramakien*, vividly. *Ramakien*, or the "Glory of Rama", has the same basic narrative as Valmiki's version but is devoid of the religious significance it has in India. It was treated more like an epic, instead of a mythological-religious text, centered on Thai characters. Indian influence on the Thai art and architecture include the Phra Prathom Chedi in Nakhon Pathom, which closely resembles the Sanchi stupa (Srichampa, 2015). Traced back to the 18th century, an influence from South India was also perceived in the art of Ayutthaya (this may have been, however, transmitted by way of the peninsula together with Cambodia). Among sculptures, the most outstanding is a huge Shiva of 2.8 m in height, now preserved in the Bangkok National Museum.

It is important to understand that the possession of important Buddha statues played an important role for the Ayutthayan king's political legitimization. The possession of certain Buddha statues was interpreted as conferring legitimacy and power to kings and rulers, sacred objects believed to have the power to preserve the land. These Buddha images, till the present day, continue to be attributed to great virtues and powers. At least six images with their legends are called *Sihing* (interpreted as Sinhala or Lion) Buddhas. Five images *Phra Sihing* (at Hor Phrabhut Sihing), Nakhon Si Thammarat; *Phra Sing* (at Wat Phra Sing), Chiang Mai; *Phra Sihing* (at Wat Phra Chao Mengrai), Chiang Mai (dated 1470); *Phra Sihing* (at Wat Khok Kham), Samut Sakhon (dated 1689); and *Phra Sihing* at Trang (stolen).[15]

In the *Rattanakosin* or Bangkok period (1767–1932), the sculptors carved Brahmanical images. King Rama V undertook the creation of several bronze Brahmanical deities. The iconography was inspired by the *Tamradevarupa* — a Brahmanical iconological treatise written during the reign of King Rama III as a guide for artists. Although there are several hundred well-carved sculptures, the most outstanding are the 152 marble bas-reliefs of scenes from the *Ramakien* created during the reign of Rama III to decorate the base of Wat Chatpun. Murals of the *Ramakien* can also be seen in Wat Phra Keo, Chapel Royal of Emerald Buddha in Bangkok. Images of Brahma and Vishnu can be seen in Wat Bovoranibies Vihara. The resplendent images further emphasize the peaceful correlation of Brahmanism and Buddhism.

It was the migration of Tamilians to Siam that paved the way for the rapid spread of ancient Dravidian culture and civilization in Siam. The influence of Hindu culture, customs, and tradition gradually became immersed in Thai society. It is said that the ancient and the holiest Brahmanic Vedic book of Siam was written in the ancient Tamil script and is still available in the Siamese Brahmin temple in Bangkok. In 1872, King Chulalongkorn visited India, and on his return gifted a set of glass lamps to the temple as a token of friendship between India and Siam. The shrine of Goddess Mariamman in Bangkok became a place of worship for all, including the Siamese. In 1911, the temple was renovated. Gradually,

---

[15] Stanley Tambiah wrote that the word "Sihing" "had been interpreted in one case, as referring to Sinhala, because of its alleged Sinhala or Sri Lankan origin; and in another case as meaning "lion" because of the statue's metaphorical resemblance to the lion. The Sinhalese do call themselves the "lion race" and trace their origins to Prince Vijaya (543–505 BC) whose paternal ancestor was a lion, so both meanings converge.

the idols of Hindu gods and goddesses were brought from India and installed with due solemnity and reverence in the temple. Images included those of Lord Ganesha, Lord Subramaniam, and Lord Krishna. In 1953, a massive image of Lord Buddha was consecrated in the temple premises with a view of making it a place of worship for Hindus and Buddhists alike. At present, there are four Hindu temples in Bangkok. Sri Maha Mariamman Temple is the oldest among the Hindu temples in Bangkok. Hindu Dharma Sabha Mandir is commonly called 'Vishnu Temple' (Gupta, 1999, pp. 98–99). During a visit to the temple on April 26, 2019, the author spoke to one of the priests. He spoke about the strong belief in the Hindu deity, and what was surprising is that young Thais also flock to the temple frequently.[16]

In Bangkok, Hindus have their temples or *mandirs* — Sri Mariamman Temple or Wat Khaek, on Silom Road which is of South Indian style; Vishnu Temple or Hindu Dharma Sabha at Thung Wat Don, Yannawa, which was constructed by Hindus from Uttar Pradesh; and Dev Mandir or Thep Monthien on Siripong Road, Sao Chingcha, and so on. In other provinces where Hindu communities are found — such as Chiang Mai, Chiang Rai, and Lam Pang in the North, Phuket in the South, and Saraburi in Central Thailand — *mandirs* serve the religious interests of the people. In the Northern provinces, Hindus and Sikhs have particularly close relations and help each other (Srichampa, 2014).

In Thailand, the most sacred Brahma shrine is located next to the Erawan hotel on Ratchaprasong Road, in the heart of Bangkok. Brahma has been known to Thai society since long ago.[17] He is referred to as *Phra Phrom* and is considered to occupy a higher plane than other gods and deities. *Phrom*, from a Theravada Buddhist perspective, is a living creature. He was believed to be the highborn being from heaven, reborn as *Phrom* in the *Phrom*-world, as a result of his power to participate in and with supra-consciousness, when he was a human being (Srichampa, 2015).

---

[16]Visit by author to the temple on April 26, 2019.

[17]Trimurti or Hindu Triad are referenced in the Puranas (the Puranas are the pasts of the universe and have several stories which happened on earth or even on other planets) as Lord Brahma, the Creator; Lord Vishnu, the Preserver; and Lord Siva, the Destroyer.

During the establishment of the shrine, the eternal spirit of Brahma was invited to live within the statue and remove the sufferings of worshippers. It is believed that Brahma enters the statue daily in the evening, except on the Buddhist Holy Days — that is when he departs to meet Lord Buddha. Moreover, a worship ceremony is held on the 9th of November annually, since 1956 (Jangpanichkul, 1993, p. 100). The Brahma god, or *Than Thaao Maha Phrom*, is believed to relieve suffering, remove obstacles, and provide luck and success. The posture of the Brahma shows him radiating supreme serenity. *Brahma Erawan* not only is respected by Thais, often referred to as the "Brahma of Asia", but also has devotees from numerous neighboring countries such as Malaysia, Singapore, Brunei, Indonesia, Vietnam, China, Hong Kong, Taiwan, Korea, Japan, India, and some Western countries as well (Jangpanichkul, 1993).

3.6.2 *Indian Influence on Thai Language*

Buddhism was adopted as the national religion during the Sukhothai period, and it was in 1345, that a Thai scholar wrote a thesis titled *Traibhumikatha*, implying the story of the three planes of existence in Buddhist cosmology, in which the newly invented Thai script was used. The thesis is now regarded as one of the earliest literary works of Thai literature.

Many alphabets used in Southeast Asia have been borrowed or adopted from South Indian alphabets. Thai alphabets were developed from Cambodian and Mon alphabets, both of which inherited the written form from the South Indian alphabets called *Pallava*. Even *Grantha*, which was used in South India to write Sanskrit, was developed in the 18th century. Pali and Sanskrit were ancient languages and influenced Thai language since ancient times. Despite the growing popularity of the English language, Thais continue to use Pali and Sanskrit more frequently. An important point to be noted is that the Brahmanas in Thailand also used *Grantha* to write the scriptures that were used in crucial royal ceremonies until the days of Rattanakosin era. As a result, *Thai Grantha* or *Grantha* used in Pali, Sanskrit, and Tamil scriptures of the Brahman in Thai royal court was created with a unique identity, different from the one used in South India (Mesangrutdharakul, 2015).

Although Tamil too is an ancient language, it is not as important as Pali and Sanskrit as an influencing element in the Thai language. Tamil is not commonly used or well known in Thailand because it is the exclusive language of the Tamil Brahmans in the Thai royal court, and its use is forbidden to outsiders. Tamil, considered to be a holy language, is used on special occasions when the Thai Brahmanas pray during ceremonies held in the royal court. As stated in the first enacted Thai law, the punishment for the Brahman who misreads the mantra is — *To be hung with a big rosary* (Royal Institute in Mesangrutdharakul; Waradet, 2015).[18]

The *Rajasabdas* or vocabulary, used in the royal house is Sanskrit-based. The Royal Institute of Thailand is engaged in coining new words related to areas of usages in different subjects such as royal vocabulary, official language, trade and commerce, management, philosophy, and others. All these make substantial use of Sanskrit terms. The reasons why the study of Sanskrit is important are — first, it is a useful tool to understand written Thai literature; second it provides more choices for coining new words, naming people and places; third, the Sanskrit language helps compose poetry in Thai. Sanskrit has also motivated Thai scholars to coin words with the help of derived words from Sanskrit. The most frequently used words *Kara* (action) and *Bhava* (state or being) have helped to build Thai vocabulary. Thai people believe that when a Sanskrit word is adapted into the Thai language, it becomes phonetically sweeter. Undoubtedly, the Thai language has been influenced by Sanskrit and has helped in enriching the volume of Thai vocabulary.

Another aspect of Indian influence is manifested in the usage of words with Sanskrit origins in the royal court. The more polite words have their origin in the Khmer language. The language was a medium through which a marked distance was maintained between the king and the subjects, affirming the superiority of the former. According to Manu, the king was appointed by the Almighty to protect the people. However, it was another matter that the benefit would accrue mainly to the Brahmanas, who would enjoy both status and wealth. The duties of the king included inspecting the armies and their equipment, the beasts of burden, as well as

---

[18]There is a 543 years difference between the Buddhist calendar and the Gregorian calendar. Hence 2550, is 2007.

being aware of the happenings in the State. Recreation was an integral part of their daily routine. According to Wales (1931), there were conspicuous similarities between ancient Indian maharajas and kings of Siam at least up to the middle of the 19th century.

3.6.3 *Thai Ramayana or Ramakirti/Ramakien*

The city-state of Sukhothai, which was known as Lawo Ayodhya, believed in powerful Hindu gods especially in Shiva, Brahma, and Vishnu — together known as Trimurti. These Gods, according to Hindu mythology, work together to continue the cycle in birth and rebirth of living things. The interest of the Thais was in the curative power of Lord Vishnu, the protector, whose main role was to cure living beings of their illnesses. The center of this interest was focused on *Ramavtar* or the seventh *avatar* (form/manifestation) of Lord Vishnu on earth, as explained in the *Dashavtar*. Thai people believe in the sovereign power of the ruling monarch, who is till date considered an incarnation of God and who lives on earth in the name of King Rama, or an incarnation of Lord Shiva. As explained earlier, Thai culture and its evolution have been influenced by both the Buddhist Tipitaka and the *Ramayana*.[19]

The book of *Ramayana* was preserved in the name of *Ramakirti*. It is said that when Ayutthaya had fallen into ruins after a foreign invasion, the Thai culture had to be again restored from scratch. King Rama I commanded that the new capital city of Bangkok replace Ayutthaya and ordered that three works of literature be revived, viz. the Law of the Three Seals, Tipitaka, and *Ramakirti*. In the book *Ramakirti*, Rama I added a statement that the book had been restored for entertainment alone and not for the governance of the nation.

When the new capital city of Bangkok was founded, King Rama I ordered the restoration of the Grand Palace on the likes of the palace in ruins of Ayutthaya. After the completion of what is now known as the temple of the Emerald Buddha within the Grand Palace, the king also initiated the painting of a mural explaining the story of *Ramakirti* in

---

[19] Author's interview with Thai scholars including Chirapat Prapandvidya and Nonglucksana; Bangkok, May 31, 2018.

panels all around its walls. The series of murals are considered to be the longest mural painting in existence. Along with the entrance doors, sculptural figures of demons, which were to serve as *Dwarapalas* (guards), were also made and these characters can be recognized from the *Ramakirti*.

During the rule of King Rama II (1767–1824), the great stupa at Wat Arun Raja Vanaram, also known as the temple of Dawn, was built. This stupa was meant to represent the Buddhist cosmography as explained in the *Traibhumikatha*. From the time of reign by Rama V (1868–1910), the interest of Thai people turned toward European culture. Despite this, the interest in the *Ramakien* continued, especially in performing arts and stylistic presentations. At present, the masked dance drama also known as *Khon* is considered a classical art form, wherein episodes from *Ramakirti* are performed. Thailand has been instrumental in bringing together the presentation of the *Ramayana* traditions of all the ASEAN nations.

How King Rama I's Ramakien reflects the Thai historical situation' during that time by Poolthupya (2015) can be referred to here to substantiate the above. The *Ramakien* story reflects frequent wars during the reign of King Rama I also known as Chula Lok the Great. After King Thaksin (*Maharaj*) managed to drive away the Burmese and gained independence for the Thai people, peace remained elusive. Even after Bangkok was established as the new capital in 1782, there were frequent wars between Thailand and its neighbors. It was King Rama I who realized that the country needed people of courage and intelligence to ward off the invading powers. He decided to gather the Thai poets for them to compose the *Ramakien* so that it could reflect Thai beliefs and cultural traditions, knowing very well that the *Ramayana* was known to the Thai people since the 13th century. Hence, it is known as *Rama I's Ramakien*. It is possible that the king himself contributed some verses.

Given that the country required consolidation, Rama I became cognizant of the fact that many of the wars were unavoidable. Hence, additional aspects of bravery, loyalty, and discipline were included in the *Ramakien*. According to Srisurang, Rama's bravery extended beyond the killing of Ravana and his brothers. Thus, *Ramakien* includes verses which have been added by the Thai poets to suit the needs and interests of the country.[20] The imbibing of India's traditions and customs also resulted in their impact on festivals and ceremonies.

3.6.4 *India's Influence on Festivals and Ceremonies*

Several Thai ceremonies have been adopted from the Indian tradition, especially those regarding ordination, marriage, and cremation. Brahma and other Hindu deities are widely worshipped by the Thais (who also worship Lord Buddha) due to the popularity of the Hindu ceremonial rites, used particularly for royal ceremonies.

3.6.4.1 *Thai Royal Ceremonies and Festivals*

(1) The Triyambavay Trigavdy Ceremony or the Giant Swing Ceremony

The important ceremony of Triyambavay Trigavdy, popularly known as *Lo Jin Ja* (pulling the swing) is one of the most interesting as well as one of the most difficult to understand of all Siamese State Ceremonies (Wales, 1931, p. 238). The Swinging Festival was formerly performed in the first lunar month, but was later changed to the second month. It was not only an important State Ceremony in Bangkok and in the former capitals Ayutthaya and Sukhodaya but practiced in other cities as well. At Nagara Sri Dharmaraja, the Swing still stands, but there is no longer a State Ceremony there. According to the common Siamese belief, the purpose of the Triyambavay Tripavdy is as follows: Once a year, god Shiva comes down to visit this world and stays here for 10 days. He used to arrive on the seventh day of the waxing moon in the first month and depart on the first day of the waning moon. But it was not difficult to postpone the date of his arrival until the second month, because, according to King Rama V, it is the Brahmanas who keep the keys of Heaven and, Shiva could not come down till they had opened the door for him. For the Thais, Shiva is a jovial god who likes to be amused, and the swinging and

---

[20]Srisurang Poolthupya, the first Director of the India Studies Centre at Thammasat University, interview in Bangkok on May 29, 2018. Sanskrit importance for Indianization.

the acrobatic feats which accompany the procession, are devised for his entertainment. Vishnu, who arrives on the day Shiva leaves and stays only 5 days is considered by the Thai people to be of a quiet and retiring disposition. He is accordingly honored only by the rites performed by the Brahmanas, in the temple dedicated to him.[21] It is strange that the Siamese conception of the characters of the two high gods is the reverse of that held in India. Shiva is received with great devotion; Divine beings like the Sun, the Moon, the Earth, and the Ganges assemble and wait upon him. The lesser gods are represented by the carved panels which the Brahmanas fix in front of the pavilions, from which Shiva is expected to watch the swinging (Wales, 1931, pp. 239–256).

It is believed that this was originally a Sun ceremony for the following reasons: (1) it occurs during the winter solstice, (2) the swinging is performed from East to West, in the direction of the apparent movement of the sun, and (3) the circular dances which follow the swinging probably symbolize the revolution of the earth and the sun's rebirth on the occasion of its return to the Northern hemisphere. In India too, it is in the middle of March when Hindus observe a swinging festival in honor of the god Krishna, whose image is placed in the seat (or cradle) of a swing and then, just when the dawn is breaking, is rocked. This ritual symbolizes the three steps of Vishnu — as a manifestation of solar energy, through the seven regions of the universe, and where the sun rises, culminates, and sets. This further confirms that the Siamese swinging ceremony was originally a ceremony dedicated to the Sun. This ceremony was performed to pay homage to Lord Shiva by inviting him to Earth, once a year. This ceremony was held in Kalinga, India, and a swing was used to symbolize the center of the Universe. This ceremony was abolished during the period of King Rama VII. However, Brahman priests continued to make an offering to God Shiva.

(2) The Royal Ploughing Ceremony

This ceremony is held annually in May. It is usually overseen by the king at Sanam Luang. Originally a Brahmanic rite, it was adopted to mark the

---

[21] Chirapat Prapandvidya in Interview to author, April 24, 2019.

beginning of the farming season and to bless the farmers with year-long prosperity. The Ceremony of the First Ploughing, known as *Bidhi Carat Brah Ndngdla*, or popularly as *Eek Nd*, is entirely Brahmanical and takes place outside the city in the Crown padi (or paddy) field called *Dun Jam Poy* in the sixth month (Vaisakha). The date is chosen with great caution. On the afternoon of the same day, Buddhist monks carry out the special image of the Buddha in procession in connection with the minor degree of the *Barna Sutra*; the Brahmans also carry in procession the images of the Hindu gods to the Crown padi fields. Here they are placed on an altar in a ceremonial pavilion for the performance of rites. For this ceremony, the King usually appoints a substitute for himself. On the morning of the day fixed for the Ploughing Ceremony, the "temporary king" is carried on a palanquin in procession to the Crown padi field. This procession consists only of ceremonial drummers, umbrella bearers, a bodyguard, and others carrying the insignia of the Minister. On arrival at the field, protected by fences erected at each corner, the presiding official goes to the pavilion of the Brahmanas and lights incense sticks before the images of the deities. After performing the relevant rituals, he takes the gilded handle of the plough, which has been wrapped in a red cloth by the Brahman Raja Guru and whips up the pair of magnificent oxen, while the Brahmanas blow the conches (*Ibid.*). He then ploughs three concentric furrows after which he is handed two silver and two gold rice baskets containing seed-rice, by ladies of the nobility. When the Brahmanas blow the conches and mantras are recited by the Buddhist monks, the "temporary king" scatters the seeds as he ploughs three more concentric furrows, while an official scatters holy water simultaneously. After this, the oxen are unyoked and seven vessels are placed before them containing padi, Indian corn, beans, sesame, rice spirit, water, and grass, and whichever commodity the animals choose to partake of will be plentiful during the coming year, respectively. This marks the end of the ceremony, and the "temporary king" then departs. It is then that the people who have gathered to witness the proceedings, collect the blessed rice grains, which they believe, when mixed with their own seed-rice, will be very efficient fertilizers. The king himself does not preside over this ceremony. The *Baladeva* (the one chosen by the king) and others go around ploughing from left to right. Earlier, during the Sukhodaya period, the king himself would be present during the ceremony.

(3) Loy Krathong

This Festival of Lights is celebrated with the floating of lanterns on rivers and streams at the end of the rainy season. The Hindu Gods who are worshipped in this festival are *Isuan* or Shiva, *Phrom* or Brahma, and *Narai* or Vishnu. This festival is celebrated to worship the Goddess of Waters or *Chao Mae Kangka*. The Thai people thank the Goddess for providing water and also ask for forgiveness if they have harmed the river. Thai people refer to it as the festival of "Mother Water". Some historians believe that this festival follows from the Indian tradition in which Hindus go to the banks of the rivers on the first night of the new lunar year carrying bamboo poles, with hanging lighted lanterns. This is very similar to the ritual of floating of boats in Odisha on the day of *Kartika Purnima*, or full moon day in winter months.

(4) Songkran Festival

The Sankranti, or astrological (solar) New Year, falls on either the 12th or 13th of April — the date of the assumed entrance of the sun into Aries, according to the traditional Hindu calculation. The day is termed Maha-*Sankranti* and with it commences a three-day-long festival. The third day is regarded as New Year's Day. This is one of the 17 occasions in the year on which, according to the KM (Kata Mandirapdla or the Book of Palace Law) the King must take a ceremonial bath of purification. For the Thai people, this season is one of rejoicing and merrymaking. They undertake several activities such as washing images in the temples, building hillocks of sand to cover the monastery courtyards, and making offerings of candles and incense before the images of Buddha. This festival marks the Thai New Year Day. *Songkran* signifies the sun's movement into the first house of the zodiac. On the eve of Songkran Day, images of Buddha are assembled in the *Dusidabhirom* pavilion where monks chant special passages to bestow blessings upon the royalty. The festival is usually attended by the King, who graciously presents food and other offerings to monks and sprinkles fragrant water on the Buddha images. The Thai people also celebrate their New Year by going to the temples and seeking blessings from the monks. They also pay respect to the elderly members of their family and those in the superior position and, in turn, receive their blessings. This tradition is believed to have been introduced by the Indian Brahmanas (*Ibid.*).

(5) Indrabhisheka

It is believed that the Siamese *Rajabhiseka* (King's coronation) contains many ideas derived from the Vedic *Rajasuya* or consecration of emperors. There was also in Vedic India another ceremony for the consecration of emperors, known as the *Indrabhisheka*. Although the Siamese have preserved the ancient name, the ceremony has little in common with the one of the Vedic times (Wales, 1931, pp. 121–122). The only recorded instance of it ever having been performed in Siam seems to be the occasion on which King Ramadhipati II was consecrated in 1510 AD.

(6) Visakha Puja Day

This is an important day for the Buddhists as it is this day which marks the birth, enlightenment, and attainment of Nirvana by Lord Buddha. On the eve of *Visakha* Puja Day, food is offered to monks, who chant their blessings in the Grand Palace and temples throughout the country. Buddhists take the opportunity to pay homage to Lord Buddha and express their gratitude for his sacrifices and renew their devotion to Buddhist ideals. In Bangkok, *Visakha* Puja is the year's biggest religious holiday, which is celebrated during the seeding and ploughing season. The author was witness to the *Visakha* Puja at the Thai Bharat Cultural Lodge, where both Indians and Thais joined together to express gratitude to the Buddhist monks.[22]

(7) The Royal Ceremony for Preparing Celestial Rice or *Khao Thip*

This ceremony is held to worship God Indra. A portion of the special rice is offered to monks and what remains is given to members of the royal family, courtiers, and others.

Other popular holy days include *Magha Puja* in February and *Asalha Puja* in July, which commemorates the day on which Lord Buddha delivered the First Sermon to his five disciples, namely, Konthanya, Vassapa,

---

[22] Author at Thai Bharat Cultural Lodge on *Vishakha* Puja on May 30, 2018.

Bhattiya, Mahanama, and Assashi, at Esipatanamaruekathayawan forest, and explained his theory of the Four Noble Truths (*Ariyasai*).

It is important to delineate the historical connect between peoples of our two countries. This helps to further understand the affinity for Thailand, among communities settled in the Northeast of India.

3.7 Tai Communities in India and People-to-People Connections: The Cultural Continuum

Many communities in India trace their origin South of the Yarlung Zangbo, source of the Brahmaputra River, including the Tai-Ahoms or Ahoms, an offspring of the Tai people who are called Shan in Myanmar, Thai in Thailand, Lao in Laos, Dai and Zhuang in China, and Tay-Thai in Vietnam (Laishram, 2011).

This section focuses on the connections through the history of the Tai communities, and hence, it highlights the significance of people-to-people connections.

As history confirms, it was a group of Tai, led by a prince named Chaolung Sukapha of Mong Mao, who in his search for a fortune, traveled toward the South from Yunnan with his queens, retinue, and a large army. After 13 years, he finally arrived in the plains of the Brahmaputra valley and called it the Golden Kingdom or *Mung-Dun-Chun-Kham*. He established the Ahom dynasty in 1228 CE, which ruled in the Brahmaputra valley for 600 years (Morey, 2008). Historian Edward Gait stated that the progenitors of the Ahoms were an offshoot of the great Tai or Shan Race. He further stated that Sukapha crossed the Nongnyang Lake at Sagaing, where he met with fierce resistance from the Nagas. Later he came to Assam (Gait, 1906).

According to Stephen Morey, more than a million people in the Northeast of India claim Tai ethnicity. There are Tai Ahom (the earliest migrants, in 1228 AD), Tai Khamti, Tai Phake, Tai Khamiyang, Tai Aiton, and Tai Turung. Other than Tai Ahoms, the other groups are not more than 10,000 in population. Tai language is spoken, to varying extents, in all of these communities (Morey, 2008).

It was this group of Tai people who had been able to carve the second largest Tai Kingdom in the world, next to Ayutthaya. The kingdom, having enjoyed independence for six centuries (even though they were attacked by the Mughals 17 times), was able to build a repository of a highly developed culture in the form of manuscripts, buildings, rituals, and customs. Their chronicles are supposed to be rich sources of knowledge of ancient Tai society and culture (Gogoi, 2018).

It is documented that for about 70 years after 1826, the Ahoms as a community were subjected to extreme hardship in their political, economic, and social life, by the British who virtually turned the Ahoms into political "untouchables". "They were not only marginalized within society but also impoverished due to systematic discrimination, which deprived them of other benefits of the new economic order" (Phukan, 1990).

A distinguishing feature of this culture is that these people inhabiting the Eastern region of the world who were predominantly Mongolian in origin had remained comparatively isolated for a very long period from the remaining communities of the world. This happened because of their geographical isolation, a result of the natural barriers (including the Himalayas, the Tibetan Plateau, as well as the vast deserts and steppes of Central Asia (Gogoi, 2018).

Sathip Nartsupha of the Chulalongkorn University of Bangkok, who had undertaken a major project of social and cultural history of Tai people in Burma, Southern China, and India, says "these findings suggest that the ancient Tai society was an Asiatic type and that the ancient Tai culture revolved around worship of nature and ancestors" and this is very much true to Ahom and "The Ahom worship of nature and ancestors is a belief system different from Aryan Hinduism" (Nartsupha and Wichasin, 1998). In 1901, L.A. Waddel wrote "still the majority of the Ahom even now, although professing Hinduism, eat beef and pork and bury their dead unlike the Hindus, who burn their dead" (Waddel, 2000).

The drinking of rice wine called *nam lao* was universal and is still favorite among many Ahoms in the villages in Upper Assam. In many families, no ritual is complete without rice wine; offering of rice wine to the ancestors is customary and obligatory for those Ahom who still perform traditional rites. Moreover, their festival *Bihu* of the Tai Ahoms has a close association with the *Poy Sangken* of the Thais of Thailand. This folk festival is mainly associated with cultivation and offerings for mother earth and nature. There is feasting and merrymaking and families visit their parents, elders, relatives, and friends. Bihu, besides being a primary identity of Assam, is also a harvest festival. It is celebrated thrice during important junctures of the agrarian calendar. The Bihu songs and dances mark the spring season.

In terms of language, the Ahoms had brought to India a new speech — the Sino-Tibetan Tai speech — with a new script, a unique culture, a religion, and a civilization with tremendous historicity. However, once they settled in Assam, they discarded their speech, script, and religion as well as their relationship with their ancestral homes in the Shan State. Toward the beginning of the 19th century, Ahom people spoke Assamese as their mother tongue. Ahom language continues to be used in religious ceremonies, such as the Ahom Soklong wedding which includes the chanting of prayers. The language is being revived and it is important to mention here that two Ahom dictionaries by G.C. Barua in 1920 as well as B.K. Baruah and Phukan in 1964 have been produced. These are mostly based on a late 18th-century manuscript word list, known as the *Bar Amra*. This manuscript, written entirely in Ahom script, gives definitions for several thousand Ahom words in Assamese (Morey and Post, 2010).

However, given the fact that Tai communities in India and the Thai in Thailand have been conditioned according to their special societal norms and religious affinities over the last few decades, there are differences as well. According to Edward Gait, it was toward the end of the Ahom rule when the King and nobility adopted Hinduism, and the love for the land and commitment to royal duty was gradually replaced by an obeisance before the gods in the name of religion. The Ahoms intermarried and incorporated many of the conquered tribes into their fold. Several of these tribes were already Hinduized then. Their offspring, however, were of mixed origin given the fact that the Ahoms married or re-married as they settled in the Brahmaputra valley (Gait, 1906).

They worshipped several gods and goddesses with sacrifices and offerings. The Ahoms had ceremonies for good crops and the prosperity of the State. They also had elaborate ceremonies connected with marriage and burial of the dead.

The Tai Ahom tradition and culture are fairly similar to the Thai culture. A Tai Ahom and a Thai usually address each other as *Pinong*.

The Tai Ahoms can also relate to both objects and customs on visits to Thailand; examples being objects of cultivation (the paddy fields, the plough, the bell on the neck of the buffalo), the weaving loom, the fishing equipment, the delicately crafted woodwork, the canals or moats surrounding the palaces, the worship of the ancestors performed in the village with chicken and rice wine, sticky rice, one village producing one product, as the one tambon one product (OTOP) of Thailand, and the smiling faces of people (Gogoi *et al.*, 2018). Hence, it was in 1926, when Sir Edward Gait observed, "They (the Ahom) are genuine Shans, both in their physical type in their tribal languages and written character" (Gait, 1906).

3.8 Conclusion

It can be concluded that the prime influence of India on Siamese culture, albeit indirectly, was through the Indianized kingdoms of Dvaravati, Srivijaya, and Cambodia. To trace this influence, one can trace four such strands including the Mahayanistic influence (which originated in the Punjab, travelled to South India, then spread to Siam and Cambodia), the Vaisnava Brahmanism (which influenced Cambodia in the early centuries of the Christian era), and Saiva Brahmanism (which reached Suvarnabhumi possibly between the 8th and 12th centuries AD) and the influence of Sinhalese Hinayana. For the Thais, Buddhism continues to be the prime reason for their gratitude to India.

Up to the present times, Brahmanic rites thrive side by side with Buddhistic ceremonies in Thailand and Cambodia, especially in the royal courts. Thailand is known as a Theravada Buddhist country, in which the king is essentially the patron and protector of the religion and people. In fact, the Brahman and Buddhist systems concur in their fundamental characteristics, i.e., their circular form, constituted by concentric zones around Mount Meru. In Thailand and Cambodia, the circumambulation of the city has formed one of the essential elements of the coronation ritual, implying that the king takes control not only of the city but also of the entire empire (Kershaw, 2000, p. 175).

According to 2000 census, 94.6% of Thailand's population belongs to the Theravada sect of Buddhism. The conception of a king is that of a superior being — to be obeyed implicitly. The king has no wish for a share in the government and neither does he engage himself with day-to-day politics. It is certain, therefore, that any conception of the kingship that strengthens peoples' belief in the ruling power is of the highest sociological value. There are a few Mahayana monks and monasteries, but they are mostly confined to foreign communities, primarily the Chinese. All, however, live in peace and cooperate (Kusalasaya, 2013). Chirapat Prapandvidya, Professor and Head of Sanskrit Studies, Silpakorn University, in an interview with the author, explained the role of Sanskrit language in understanding the similarities in Hinduism and Buddhism.[23]

The science of astrology continues to have a tremendous impact on several important stages of Thai life. Both Buddhist monks and Brahman astrologers are sought by the Thai people, who seek advice regarding the auspicious or inauspicious days for important personal events. In the 21st century also, we notice Hindu temples predominating in Buddhist Thailand. In the present day, one also finds modern sculptures of *Phra Phrom* (Lord Brahma), *Phra Narai* (Lord Vishnu), and *Phra Pikanesvara* (Lord Ganesha).

The influence of India extends not only in terms of Buddhism and Brahmanism but also in cultural ceremonies as well. It is also visible in the Thai form of greeting — *Namaste* in India is similar to the Thai *Sawadee Kha*. *Nam-mon* (holy water) has originated from the Sanskrit word *Namamah*. It is customary, both in India and Thailand, that sacred water be sprinkled over the devotees as a blessing, after the *Arti Puja* (or the ceremonial worship) (Patra, 2017).

The influence of Thai culture is also very visible among the Tai communities in India, who trace their settlement in the Brahmaputra valley way back in the 13th century. These communities are closely linked to the Thai people, especially in Thailand's Northern provinces.

It was Thailand that initiated a search for kin groups spread over the neighboring countries, in India, Laos, Vietnam, and Southern China in the 1970s when a new school of thought called "Community Culture" emerged in Bangkok. The group aimed to help the Thai villages withstand the intrusion of the state and Western norms of economic development and

---

[23]Chirapat Prapandvidya in an Interview to the author in Bangkok, May 31, 2018.

empower them to generate a "native" economy. For this, they needed an archaic Tai village system to serve as a model. Chatthip Nartsupha, the leader of the Community Culture School in Bangkok, saw in the buranjis of Assam the possibility of an imaginative space for return to pastoral village life. Ahom, the unspoken subject of Assam and Indian history, was adopted to fulfill the aim of the Thais. Hence, Thai history and pan-Thaiism transcended the boundaries of Southeast Asia and moved beyond to include areas in South Asia. Since 1981, exchanges between Ahom and Thai activists have generated exchanges among the communities to make Assam a meeting place for historical, cultural, and commercial exchanges between South and Southeast Asia.

Ever since the exchanges have continued, the author met several members of the Tai community as they were participants in the 13th International Conference on Tai Studies, held in Chiang Mai University in July 2017.

Moreover, Indians settled in Thailand have generally avoided conflict. It was different for the Chinese, who not only engaged in mostly commercial transactions but also, from earliest times, took advantage of the fact that in a non-Muslim country as Thailand, it was easy to marry a Thai and even adopt local family names (Pauker *et al.*, 1977, p. 147).

The fact that the Royalty of Thailand has always paid special attention to their relations with India reiterates the fact that not only in the past but also through the kings of the Chakri dynasty, India continues to influence the monarchy as well as everyday life in Thailand. Princess Sirindhorn regularly visits not only the Buddhist sites in India but also the Tai communities in Assam, continuing the age-old links. The Thai people understand and are grateful to India for giving them a cultural fusion of Hinduism and Buddhism, which not only provides them with a religious anchor through the manifestations of cultural embodiments but also provides guidelines for their everyday living and relationships in society.

Chapter 4

ASEAN Centrality: A Contemporary Strategic Perspective

4.1 Introduction: ASEAN Centrality Decoded

This chapter focuses on ASEAN, its genesis, macro-economic indicators, and its centricity in the Asian geostrategic landscape. It also assesses ASEAN's internal and ASEAN-led external mechanisms for strategic cooperation. The last section assesses India's possible role in the region, bringing into discussion the Indo-Pacific and the Regional Comprehensive Economic Partnership (RCEP). The China factor continues to be discussed throughout the strategic dimensions and in impacting ASEAN's unity.

While delineating ASEAN's centrality, the term centrality has three components; viz. a. geographical centrality, institutional centrality implying that it is at the core of trade agreements and at the center of maritime power security including the freedom of navigation; and third, ASEAN provides a forum where leaders and people meet. At present, ASEAN is at the center of the largest trade agreement — the Regional Comprehensive Economic Partnership being negotiated among ASEAN plus six countries as well as the evolving Indo-Pacific construct at the strategic level (INSSL, March 29, 2019).

While understanding ASEAN centrality, it is important to underline that ASEAN's unity is the hallmark of its central position in the evolving multilateral trading and security — strategic architecture. With the transformations in the regional and global space, dominated by China's rise, there is a visible change in the way countries in Southeast Asia are being bilaterally engaged by China (*Ibid.*).

The imperative for discussing ASEAN's centrality is because as a collective body, it has assumed a distinctive position in the ambit of Asian affairs. Its shared vision and strength have been lauded as a model for other regional groupings such as the South Asian Association for Regional Cooperation (SAARC). However, ASEAN's unity has been impacted, as was visible in the 2012 Summit where the contentious issue of the South China Sea was shelved. The normative order constructed by ASEAN is also being challenged, even as many ASEAN countries, as well as India, assert the importance of a rules-based order.

4.2 ASEAN Conception and Evolution

On August 8, 1967 the "Bangkok Declaration" gave birth to ASEAN, the Association of Southeast Asian Nations, an organization that initially united five countries in a joint effort to promote economic cooperation and the welfare of their peoples.

However, its genesis was not easy. According to Thanat Khoman, "In effect, this historical event represented the culmination of the decolonization process that had started after World War II. Following their victory in the war, the colonial powers tried their best to maintain the status quo". He further explains that it was the Japanese invasion and the defeat of the colonizers that undermined their rule. This led to the initiation of freedom from the colonial masters, and several independent and sovereign nations took birth (Khoman, 1992).

Thailand, as the only nation which had been spared from colonization, due to its far-sighted kings, felt it a duty to deal with the new contingencies. It was Thanon, the first Thai diplomat in the newly independent India, and Pridi Panomyong, a former Prime Minister, who made efforts to promote new relationships and cooperation within the region. Given the fact that the world was then divided by the Cold War into two rival camps vying for domination over the other, initially, it was a small organization of three countries viz. ASA or the Association of Southeast Asia, comprising Malaysia, the Philippines, and Thailand that was set up in 1961 (Beng *et al.*, 2015).

With the colonialists having discouraged any form of intra-regional engagement, for a grouping to emerge and sustain itself, there were obvious factors. First, an imperative for neighbors to will to work together. Second, especially with the Southeast Asia Treaty Organization (SEATO), cooperation among members located in distant lands could be ineffective. There was thus a need for those people who lived close to one another and shared common interest, to engage through a formal alliance. Third, the need to join together was important for the Southeast Asian countries to be heard and to be effective to deal with big power rivalry. Lastly, it was inevitable that only cooperation and integration could serve the interests of all.

However, it was not long after the ASA was established that problems arose for the fledgling organization when a territorial dispute (British colonial issue of Sabah) emerged between Philippines and Indonesia on the one hand and Malaysia on the other hand. While ASA was paralyzed by the dispute on Sabah, efforts continued to be made in Bangkok for the creation of another organization. (Thailand remained neutral in the Sabah dispute). It was in 1966, when a larger grouping, with East Asian nations like Japan and South Korea as well as Malaysia, the Philippines, Australia, Taiwan, New Zealand, South Vietnam, and Thailand, was established and known as ASPAC or the Asian and Pacific Council.[1] However, soon again, ASPAC was adversely impacted by the ramifications of polities. The admission of the People's Republic of China and the eviction of the Republic of China or Taiwan made it impossible for some of the Council's members to sit at the same conference table.

With the initiative of Thailand, once again, an effort was made to bring the members of ASA together. It was the Thai foreign office which prepared a draft of the new institution. Singapore was invited to join the meeting. The first formal meeting of representatives from the five countries — Indonesia, Malaysia, the Philippines, Singapore, and Thailand — was held in the Thai Ministry of Foreign Affairs.[2] The group

---

[1] ASA was in existence only till 1975.

[2] The five Foreign Ministers who signed it — Adam Malik of Indonesia, Narciso R. Ramos of the Philippines, Tun Abdul Razak of Malaysia, S. Rajaratnam of Singapore, and Thanat Khoman of Thailand — are considered as the Founding Fathers. The document that they signed is known as the ASEAN Declaration.

moved to the Thai seaside resort of Bangsaen, where the ASEAN charter was worked out. The participants returned to Bangkok for final approval of the draft, and on August 8, 1967, the Bangkok Declaration gave birth to ASEAN — the Association of Southeast Asian Nations.[3] For Thailand, the formation of ASEAN, was driven by its disappointing experience with SEATO, through which it learned well that "it was useless and even dangerous to tie its destiny to distant powers who may cut loose at any moment their obligations with lesser and distant allies" (Khoman, 1992).

Moreover, the focus of ASEAN, which was in a way inspired by the model of the European community, was to be principally economic, or non-military. However, the ambit of ASEAN's mandate soon had to be widened due to several events including the defeat and withdrawal of the United States from Vietnam in 1973 and growing ambitions of the Vietnamese to the extent of fixing its gaze on taking over the rest of French Indo-China in addition to the Northeastern provinces of Thailand.

The perceived threat from a heavily militarized Vietnam made the anti-communist countries in Southeast Asia pull more closely together. The Bangkok Declaration stated that ASEAN aimed at ensuring member countries' "stability and security from external interference in any form or manifestation to preserve their national identities in accordance with the ideals and aspirations of their peoples" (ASEAN, 1967). However, in reality, this had meant working closely with the United States against what the leaders of these countries saw as Soviet and Chinese threats (Westad, 2017).

It is interesting to note here that Thailand's position during the Cold War was ambiguous. Although the country's political leadership was keen to maintain the country's independence on the world stage, yet concurrently, it wished to project itself and establish credentials as staunchly anti-communist. As Mathew Philip argues, Thailand, though never formally a client state of the United States, was very firmly embedded in the Western camp through the commitment of Thailand's cosmopolitan urban communities to developing a modern, consumerist lifestyle (Phillips, 2017).

---

[3]ASEAN owes its name to Adam Malik, the erstwhile Foreign Minister of Indonesia.

Historians have argued that there were several obstacles to regionalism, especially due to the colonial legacy of political and economic isolation of State from State (Pauker *et al.*, 1977, p. 110). Thus, when the Association of Southeast Asian Nations (ASEAN) was launched on August 8, 1967, it was essentially a political initiative meant to end disharmony within the anti-Communist bloc in the region and strengthen the anti-Communist bloc in facing the then Communist threat seen in the Vietnam War. Brunei Darussalam then joined on January 7, 1984, Vietnam on July 28, 1995, Lao PDR and Myanmar on July 23, 1997, and Cambodia on April 30, 1999, comprising the present 10 member states of ASEAN. Over time and especially after the Asian financial crisis of 1997, the very nature of the ASEAN changed with the entry of new members and the focus began to shift away from a purely strategic one toward closer economic integration.[4]

ASEAN has made progress in the 50 years and more of its existence. Its importance as a regional organization too has grown, especially as the 10 countries believe that it is their unity, which lends them strength as well as greater bargaining power with the big powers. Its regional identity should, however, be seen as an evolving phenomenon (Acharya, 2013, p. 28). Managing relations with countries such as USA, Japan, China, India, and others would not have been easy through bilateral engagement. It is the multilateralism and regionalism that make ASEAN portray itself as a unified grouping. Although the ASEAN framework is underpinned on three pillars — The Economic, the socio-cultural, and politico-security, tremendous progress has been made in the first one, having moved toward establishing the ASEAN Economic Community in 2015.

4.3 ASEAN's Economic Emergence and Centrality

ASEAN's importance as a regional grouping can be traced back to the 1990s, when the following trends emerged: first, the Southeast Asian economies became strong performers relative to other emerging economies until the late 1990s when simultaneously two things happened — the Asian financial crisis which devastated their economies and the

---

[4]From https://asean.org/asean/about-asean/overview/.

accelerated rise of China. The ASEAN economies grew rapidly in the period 1980–1997, registering real growth rates of 6% between 1990 and 1997. After 1997, they slowed down not only in absolute terms but also in comparison with other major developing economies. The slowdown spurred them toward integration, possibly as a path to enhancing their ability to match China's improved competitiveness.

The second trend that emerged was that the ASEAN countries delivered rates of return to foreign investors that were higher even than China and India. However, after 1997, i.e., after the Asian financial crisis, ASEAN lost out to China, mainly because of the perception of risks which deterred the inflow of foreign direct investment (FDI) (Government of Singapore 2002). Since then, ASEAN has been collectively engaged in consolidating its power as a regional grouping (Kaplan, 2014, p. 174).

Third, ASEAN is at the core of multilateral arrangements, which began with the US-led Asia-Pacific Economic Cooperation (APEC) forum in the early 1990s. This was followed by the 10-member Association of Southeast Asian Nations (ASEAN) in 1999, the Regional Forum (ARF) with its present structure in 2000, the first exclusive East Asian institution, and the ASEAN Plus Three (APT), institutionalized in 1999, which brought together China, Japan, South Korea, and 10 ASEAN countries to cooperate on regional financial management. In 2005, the East Asian Summit (EAS) was established among 16 countries — the APT member countries plus Australia, New Zealand, and India — and later joined by the US and Russia. In terms of issue-specific regional institutions, the APT countries set up in 2010 a multilateral reserve pooling arrangement totaling US$120 billion, named the Chiang Mai Initiative Multilateralization (CMIM), to help with managing regional financial crises. In the meantime, 16 Asian countries in 2004 concluded the Regional Cooperation Agreement on Combating Piracy and Armed Robbery against Ships in Asia (ReCAAP) that institutionalized multilateral information-sharing and other forms of technical cooperation to address the growing maritime piracy problems in the region. Meanwhile, ASEAN and its member states are also playing an important role in the future of shaping the regional architecture in the Indo-Pacific region (The Maritime Executive, 2014).

Within its economic centrality, aspects of trading agreements as well as economic indicators of member countries are discussed.

4.3.1 *ASEAN: The Hub of FTAs in Asia*

With the establishment of the ASEAN Free Trade Area (AFTA) in 1992, ASEAN developed as the core of free trade agreement networks in East Asia, thus taking the "driver's seat" in the economic integration of the region. The main goals of the AFTA were reflective of the ASEAN's character as an FDI-dependent and export-oriented region. It was the endeavor of AFTA to enhance the region's collective competitiveness and emerge as the production base for the world economy as well as attract more FDI into the region.

At present, there are several bilateral FTAs and multilateral FTAs centering around ASEAN members (the APT, the ASEAN plus 6, etc.). This region has seen a surge of FTAs, from 4 in 1990 to 123 in 2011, and adding up to 245 if we include those which are proposed and under negotiation. The creation of these bilateral and multilateral structures has resulted in the so-called Asian "noodle bowl" or "spaghetti bowl" effect, which is widely discussed in the literature (Masahiro Kawai and Ganeshan Wignaraja, 2009). Once China became a member of the World Trade Organization (WTO) in 2001 (and it was brought into the organization by the dominant powers), the multilateral trading environment witnessed a change in relationships and balance of power moving from West to East. This was because China prepared itself to become competitive in almost all products and soon became the "factory of the world". In addition to its membership in the WTO, it negotiated and signed the FTA with ASEAN in 2005. It is important to add here that the ASEAN–China Free Trade Area (ACFTA), constitutes the world's largest FTA with about 2 billion consumers and the third FTA in terms of total trade volume. China and the six more advanced ASEAN nations had progressively removed 90% of tariffs by 2010, while Cambodia, Laos, Myanmar, and Vietnam (CLMV) did so in the following 5 years.

Also, there have already been more than 25 rounds of negotiations for the region-wide free trade agreement — the Regional Comprehensive Economic Partnership (RCEP) composed of ASEAN plus China, South Korea, Japan, Australia, New Zealand, and India. The expectation is that the RCEP will be signed by the end of 2019. Given the withdrawal of the

United States from the Trans-Pacific Partnership (TPP), the drive to launch this agreement has become more vigorous. RCEP is discussed later in this chapter.

4.3.2 *ASEAN Contemporary Economics: An Overview*

ASEAN is a group of 10 member countries comprising a population of more than 650 million, with trade, investment, and security cooperation links with all the major countries of the world. The ASEAN is a major global hub of manufacturing and trade, as well as one of the fastest grow-ing consumer markets in the world. The latest data from ASEAN Statistics revealed that ASEAN economies remained resilient in 2014 amid uncertainty in the global economic environment. The real Gross Domestic Product (GDP) grew by 4.6% to reach US$2.76 trillion in 2017. The sustained growth in GDP led to an increase in the GDP per capita from US$3,908 in 2013 to US$4,305 in 2017.

Services is an increasingly important sector throughout the world, and ASEAN is no exception. By 2016, the services sector had accounted for 53.1% of ASEAN's Gross Domestic Product (GDP). In terms of trade, ASEAN's export reached US$326.8 billion in 2016 or almost 2.5 times in a decade. ASEAN's import, over the same period, reached US$316.5 billion in 2016, which was almost double of the earlier figure. This development indicates that ASEAN, as a region, has transformed from a net importer to a net exporter of services. The services sector is also a major recipient of Foreign Direct Investment (FDI) flows into the region. FDI in the services sector reached US$72.1 billion in 2016 or 74.6% of total FDI, up from US$41.2 billion or 66.4% a decade ago (ASEAN, 2017). Intra-ASEAN trade constitutes about 25% of its total trade with the world.

However, the 10 countries in the Association vary greatly in terms of geographic area and economic indicators. Table 4.1 shows the vast diver-gence in the size of the ASEAN economies in terms of GDP and GDP per capita and in trade volumes. GDP per capita ranges from less than US$1,500 for Myanmar and Cambodia to more than US$50,000 in the case of Singapore. Such disparities breed divergent interests, and integra-tion itself becomes a difficult proposition. In terms of population,

Indonesia is the largest country, with the Philippines in the second place. Singapore has the highest per capita income of US$57,000 (approx.), whereas the CLMV countries had per capita incomes of less than US$3,000 in 2017. Singapore and Thailand together account for almost half of the total trade of ASEAN countries.

Thailand, with the third highest per capita income among ASEAN, has the highest trade in value, after Singapore. Thailand's trade with India is discussed in a subsequent chapter.

Given the extraordinary economic divergence of the countries as reflected in Table 4.1, there are apprehensions about further deepening intra-ASEAN engagement. For India, a more integrated and united ASEAN holds greater promise.

4.4 ASEAN's Geopolitical and Geostrategic Centrality

ASEAN's geographical location and the fact that it is one of the most successful regional groupings in Asia makes it a fulcrum for several multilateral security arrangements; the latest being the Indo-Pacific construct.

This was articulated by Ambassador-at-Large at the Singaporean Ministry of Foreign Affairs, Bilahari Kausikan, during the ASEAN Roundtable 2017 organized by the Singaporean think tank, ISEAS — Yusof Ishak Institute as follows, "ASEAN centrality is not a magic incantation whose mere invocation makes all our dreams come true. Nor is it an objective reality that exists irrespective of perceptions — ASEAN centrality is more akin to the sound of Berkeley's falling tree than Johnson's immovable rock". He further added, "It is a political construct. If you do not recognize it, it does not exist" (Gnanasagaran, 2017). He implied that national interests of ASEAN member states must be secured while also serving the interests of big powers like the USA, China, India, and other countries (*Ibid.*).

It is evident that SEA centrality is not only about its geography, which makes it sit astride both the continental and the maritime space. In geostrategic terms, it is also central to the interests of major powers and hence here is where various major powers intersect. All the big powers need to be mindful of the intricacies of major power contestation and cooperation

Table 4.1:   ASEAN: Incomes, Population, Trade, and Economic Size, 2017

Country	Total Population (millions)[a]	Gross Domestic Product (current prices USD) 2017	Gross Domestic Per Capita Income (current prices USD[b]) 2017	International Trade 2015[c] (As of Nov. 2016)		
				Exports (USD million)	Imports (USD million)	Total Trade (USD million)
Brunei Darussalam	423.0	12,212	28,465.6	6,354	3,238	9,592
Cambodia	15,158.2	22,340	1,421.3	8,839	10,838	19,676
Indonesia	2,58,705.0	1,013,926	3,866.7	150,366	142,695	293,061
Lao PDR	6,621.1	17,090	2,530.8	3,714	3,049	6,763
Malaysia	31,633.5	317,042	9,892.2	199,158	176,011	375,169
Myanmar	52,917.0	65,607	1,228.6	12,197	16,907	29,104
Philippines	1,03,242.9	313,875	2,991.5	58,648	70,295	128,944
Singapore	5,607.3	323,954	57,722.2	366,344	296,765	663,109
Thailand	67,454.7	455,704	6,735.9	214,396	202,751	417,147
Vietnam	92,695.1	223,927	2,390.3	162,014	165,730	327,744
ASEAN (Average)		2,765,679	4,305.0	1,182,031	1,088,279	2,270.310

Notes: [a]Refers to/based on mid-year total population based on country projections; ref: ASEAN-Statistical-Leaflet-2017_Final.pdf. [b]Based on AMS' data submission to ASEAN statistics and the Official National Statistical Offices website. [c]ASEANStats.org.

Sources: ASEAN Finance and Macro-economic Surveillance Unit Database, ASEAN Merchandise Trade Statistics Database, ASEAN Foreign Direct Investment Statistics Database (compiled/computed from data submission, publications, and websites of ASEAN member states' national statistics offices, central banks, and relevant government agencies and international sources).

when approaching the region (Chong, 2013). The region is not only important for India along with USA, Japan, and Australia in its Quad grouping but also of great significance for countries such as South Korea and Taiwan.

The Quad is viewed by the ASEAN as a strategy by USA, Japan, Australia, and India, the world's major democracies, to contain China while the Indo-Pacific construct warrants and merits an ASEAN response. It was at the 33rd ASEAN summit in Singapore in November 2018, when the leaders discussed the Indo-Pacific concept broached by the Quad countries and decided to formulate a regional architecture of their own, in which ASEAN centrality would not be compromised. While the majority believed that the EAS was the appropriate grouping to discuss this concept, given that over the past 13 years, it had grown into a body confident of discussing strategic matters, there were outliers. The most reluctant among the 10 were the Philippines and Cambodia, while Laos, Brunei, and Myanmar chose to be silent. It was Vietnam, Thailand, Singapore, and Malaysia who were keen that this construct be discussed within the ASEAN framework (Chongkittwarn, 2018).

In Chiang Mai on January 18–19, 2019, ASEAN foreign ministers discussed their formulation in detail, but the Chairman's statement after the close of the retreat merely stated that they had noted progress of the discussions of a collective modality. It stated, "Indo-Pacific Outlook is one that reinforces ASEAN centrality, and that is based on key principles of openness, transparency, inclusiveness, rules-based approach, mutual trust, mutual respect, and mutual benefit. We believe that such an approach would generate concrete benefits for the peoples of the region and complement existing regional and sub-regional frameworks of cooperation. In this regard, we looked forward to further development of this Outlook, with a view to finalizing it for adoption by ASEAN".

4.5 Mechanisms for Cooperation and Dispute Resolution

ASEAN in Asia is often cited as a model of regional cooperation and has been lauded for its efforts in integration through several joint endeavors such as the formation of ASEAN Community, which comprises the ASEAN Economic Community (AEC), ASEAN Political-Security Community (APSC), and ASEAN Social-Cultural Community (Anand, 2017).

The mechanisms discussed here are primarily two — the ASEAN Way and external mechanisms for cooperation and dispute resolution.

4.5.1 *Internal Mechanisms: The ASEAN Way*

ASEAN's key principles for its internal functioning are unanimity in decision-making and non-interference in the internal affairs of a member country. Hence, a unanimous vote of its members is required for any action to be taken, and the principle of non-interference emerged from the painful experience of colonialism in Southeast Asia (Hoontrakul *et al.*, 2014, p. 180).

4.5.1.1 *China in Southeast Asia*

While the ASEAN Way described earlier, combining the informal processes of decision-making with the principle of non-interference in the affairs of another country, does have its advantages, there are several limitations too. According to Woltersdorf, there are many different perspectives on ASEAN's success. It was only in the 1980s that Deng Xiaoping managed to turn generations of distrust between China and conservative Southeast Asian leaders around. As the economic interaction between China and SEA grew, the diplomatic relationship grew. China has always preferred to engage with each country bilaterally. He points out that China continues to succeed in dividing ASEAN members over the territorial conflict in the South China Sea.

An example of this is when Cambodia in 2012 — for the first time in ASEAN history — avoided mentioning the South China Sea conflict in a closing statement. The Philippines position also clearly changed substantially under President Duterte, i.e., from taking the dispute over the reefs and islands in the SCS to the International Tribunal to negotiating a Joint Development Agreement (JDA) with China in overlapping claimed areas. According to Richard Javad Heydarian, "Even if the two sides never actualize the broached JDA, the mere discussion of such arrangements will allow China to divide further and rule its smaller resistant neighbors while providing new diplomatic veneer on its ever-expanding military footprint across the wider South China Sea" (Kausikan, 2018).

Differing threat perceptions (especially over China) result in ASEAN members having their own anxieties. However, at the same time, given China's economic weight, are wary about anything that smacks of "containment", particularly at a time when China appears more cooperative about negotiating a code of conduct (CoC) for the South China Sea. In fact, a first reading of the CoC has been done in July 2019, to set the tone for the finalization of the document. The principle of consensus on security issues constrains ASEAN's ability to address urgent matters, especially the South China Sea disputes.

During interviews with Thai experts, including Panitan Wattanayakorn, Wisarn Pupphasvesa, and Chulacheeb Chinwanno,[5] on the issue it was shared with the author that institutional innovations should be developed to allow for a certain level of flexibility. This would enable member countries to effectively address important regional security issues in general and the South China Sea disputes in particular. It is being advocated that ASEAN should maintain the consensus-based decision-making mechanism where possible and adopt a majority-vote system where the consensus seems impossible. These innovations may be in the form of an ASEAN Commission for the Management of the South China Sea Disputes, an intra-ASEAN caucus on the issue, or a caucus of regional states inside as well as outside ASEAN, which share concerns about the disputes (Hie, 2016). This is further reiterated by Salleh Buang as he writes, "ASEAN leaders must revisit this provision if it wishes the expanding organization to be effective in maintaining and enhancing 'peace, security and stability' in the region (as stated in Clause 1 of Article 1, Purposes of the Charter)" (Buang, 2017).

As Bertil Lintner shared with the author, "ASEAN is a golf club". The ASEAN leaders can take decisions while playing golf as their agenda is often quite informal, and there is not much clarity on the process to be adopted. It is well known that ASEAN functions on two key principles: consensus and non-interference in member states' internal affairs.

---

[5]Interviews to the author in April 2019.

According to Bertil Lintner, in effect, ASEAN finds it impossible to take any unified stand in regional conflicts — or address bilateral issues between its various members. He predicted that this weakness would result in the benefits accruing to China as the small countries in ASEAN would be wary and overly cautious of antagonizing China.[6]

According to Amitav Acharya, the ASEAN Way is not so much about the substance or structure of multilateral interactions, but a claim about the process through which such interactions are carried out. This approach involves a high degree of discreetness, informality, pragmatism, expediency, consensus-building, and non-confrontational bargaining styles, which are often contrasted with the adversarial posturing and legalistic decision-making procedures in Western multilateral negotiations (Acharya, 1997).

The ASEAN Way is best described by John Ciorciari, Associate Professor and Director of the International Policy Center at the University of Michigan. While speaking to *The Politic*, he said, "The idea of the ASEAN Way is to bring everyone along in a style of diplomacy that takes a lot of time, that requires a lot of rounds of consultations, and tries to build consensus, so the organization does not contribute to divisions among its members" (Jany, 2017).

4.5.1.2 *Questioning Consensus: Limits to ASEAN Unity*

The ASEAN dispute resolution mechanism has jurisdictional flexibility. Before bringing a dispute to the ASEAN dispute resolution mechanism, member states can use other dispute resolution forums (ASEAN Secretariat). There have been several issues within and among the ASEAN member countries which have not brought any resolution mechanism from within ASEAN. In recent times, whether it was the silencing of opposition by the Cambodian government or the war on drug peddlers by the Duterte government in the Philippines, ASEAN countries chose to remain silent. China, which uses its statecraft in government-to-government negotiations, has scant interest in encouraging models of sustainable development of its smaller neighbors and their peoples'

---

[6]Bertil Lintner in an interview to the author in Chiang Mai on May 21, 2018.

well-being. This was shared by several speakers from Thailand with the author at the ICTS 13, in Chiang Mai in July 2017.[7]

In terms of land acquisition for banana plantations, Chinese expanding footprint has moved from Laos to Thailand, Myanmar, and Cambodia, wreaking health and environment havoc along its path. Yet, there is little that is being done collectively to prevent this from happening, as was articulated by Yos Santasombat, from Chiang Mai University.[8]

Testimony to the fact that environmental issues have been completely ignored is the continuing dam-building activity of the Chinese on the Mekong River. According to Brahma Chellaney, China has erected eight mega-dams on the Mekong and is building or planning another 20. This nutrient-rich sediment is essential to the livelihoods of 60 million people in Southeast Asia. With its clout, Beijing has rejected the treaty-linked Mekong River Commission and instead co-opted the vulnerable downstream nations in its own Lancang-Mekong Cooperation initiative, which lacks binding rules (Chellaney, 2018).

The 700,000 Rohingyas who fled from the Rakhine State of Myanmar to Bangladesh since the middle of 2017, is considered as one of the greatest of refugee crisis in the world. The ASEAN response has clearly received one of the sharpest criticism from the ASEAN Parliamentarians for Human Rights, when a member articulated, "If ASEAN leaders want to stop making excuses and actually help, they should do more to pressure the Myanmar government and military to halt the attacks, end policies that promote and institutionalize discrimination, and enable conditions for the safe return of Rohingya refugees to their homes in Myanmar" (APHD, 2017).

However, there are voices such as that by Rahimah Abdulrahim, Executive Director of the Habibie Center, a think tank based in Jakarta, who argues that ASEAN gives its members a shared identity. The Indonesian government sent 34 tonnes of aid, including tents, rice, sugar, and sanitation supplies to Rohingya refugee camps in Bangladesh.

---

[7]13th International Conference on Thai Studies on the theme "Globalized Thailand?" *Connectivity, Conflict, and Conundrums of Thai Studies* July 15–18, 2017.
[8]Yos Santasombat, Professor in Chiang Mai University, in an interview to the author on May 23, 2018, in Chiang Mai, Thailand.

Abdulrahim emphasized the importance of proximity and joint involvement in ASEAN as a motivation for this aid. "We feel such a large responsibility towards Myanmar because the conflict is a part of our community. It is in our backyard", she added.

Thailand's response to the refugee crisis has also been mixed. Thai law does not give refugees and asylum-seekers legal status, nor does it establish any formal measures to protect those fleeing persecution and human rights violations in another country. Therefore, refugees, like all other irregular migrants are considered "illegal" and are subject to arrest, detention, and deportation (Gaughran, 2017).

However, despite the law, it is well known that there are refugee camps along Thailand's Western border, near Mae Sot, and these have sheltered villagers fleeing Myanmar's brutal counter-insurgency operations against ethnic armed groups. It is believed there are at least 100,000 refugees on the Thai border with Myanmar. However, in 2015, the Thai navy did push back the boats with Rohingya refugees to Malaysia and Indonesia (*Ibid.*). This was reiterated by Prof. R. Naruemon Thabchumpon, of the Institute of Asian Studies, Chulalongkorn University, in an interview to the author when she confirmed that the Rohingya refugees would have to be taken care of by Bangladesh, Malaysia, and Indonesia, these being countries with large Muslim populations. She also confirmed that Cambodia would not take Rohingyas; Thailand will not get involved in Myanmar's or Cambodia's internal conflicts. She further added, "Cambodia and Laos hate Thailand because in the past Thailand invaded the countries of Cambodia and Laos". The historical baggage of Burmese aggression in Thailand also holds back Thailand from getting involved in the issue.[9]

However, at present, ASEAN's only acknowledgment of the crisis is a statement at the United Nations' General Assembly expressing "concern" and "deepest condolences".

Wen Zha elucidates the ethnicity issue as infusing uncertainties in bilateral cooperation, especially between Thailand and Malaysia, due to issues emanating out of the ties between the Thai-Malays and the Malaysian Malays. ASEAN's ignoring of this bilateral conflict in its

---

[9]Interview to the author on May 30, 2018, at Chulalongkorn University, Bangkok.

statement also deprives the ASEAN Security Community of necessary substance (Zha, 2017, pp. 320–321).

Inevitably, despite ASEAN's motto of "One vision, one identity, one community", there are still limits to ASEAN-inspired unity. In the present time, the political situation in ASEAN is quite fragile, with weak democracies in the Philippines and Indonesia. There is an absolute monarchy in Brunei. In Thailand, there is a military dictatorship with a 36-member Cabinet having been sworn in July 2019 and single-party communist rule in countries like Laos and Vietnam.[10]

Cambodia has been ruled for more than 30 years by the authoritarian leader Hun Sen. With disparities in culture, religion, and development, it is to the credit of ASEAN leaders that the organization has been able to realize the ASEAN Economic Community, with credit going to the ASEAN Way.

4.5.2 *ASEAN External Mechanisms for Strategic Cooperation*

While ASEAN centrality has been discussed in the preceding section of this chapter, it is also essential to further discuss and evaluate the mechanisms for strategic cooperation in which ASEAN countries are engaged.

(a) ASEAN Regional Forum (ARF) established in 1994 is an important forum for security dialogue in Asia. It brings together 27 members which have a bearing on the security of the Asia Pacific region including the 10 ASEAN members, the 10 ASEAN dialogue partners (Australia, Canada, China, the European Union, India, Japan, New Zealand, the Republic of Korea, Russia, and the United States), one ASEAN observer (Papua New Guinea), as well as the Democratic People's Republic of Korea, Mongolia, Pakistan, Timor-Leste, Bangladesh, and Sri Lanka.[11]

---

[10]From https://www.dw.com/en/the-asean-way-where-is-it-leading/a-39998187, accessed on January 12, 2019.

[11]Department of Foreign Affairs and Trade, Government of Australia, ASEAN Regional Forum (ARF), Department of Foreign Affairs. From https://dfat.gov.au/international-relations/regional-architecture/Pages/asean-regional-forum-arf.aspx; accessed on December 7, 2018.

The ARF is a forum for security dialogue in Asia, complementing the various bilateral alliances and conversations. This forum enables members to discuss current regional security issues and develop cooperative measures to enhance peace and security in the region. Consensus decision-making and frank dialogue are its key pillars. In its first phase, the ARF focused on confidence-building measures and made some progress in building a strategic community. At the 16th ARF Ministerial Meeting in July 2009, ministers endorsed an ARF vision statement. The vision included an undertaking to move toward the ARF's second phase — the development of a preventive diplomacy capacity. This was followed by the adoption, in July 2010, of the Hanoi Plan of Action to implement the Vision Statement (*Ibid.*).

The ARF also has a 1.5-track body called the ARF Experts and Eminent Person group (the EEPs) that meets annually to provide advice and recommendations to ARF officials (known as Track One). Second-track (i.e., non-official) institutions, such as the Council for Security Cooperation in the Asia Pacific (CSCAP) and the ASEAN Institutes of Strategic and International Studies (ASEAN ISIS), also generate ideas and inputs for the ARF's consideration (*Ibid.*).

The Vision Statement for ARF for 2020 was adopted at the 16th ARF Ministerial Meeting held in Phuket, Thailand. It continues to underline that ARF is a central pillar in the emerging regional security architecture. Members also emphasized the need for strengthening ARF's role in raising awareness of security challenges and intensifying confidence-building and cooperation. However, the ARF as an extension and instrument of ASEAN has stalled at the confidence-building and preventative diplomacy stage (Whelan, 2012). As the main forum for ASEAN security dialogue is the ASEAN Regional Forum (ARF), India has been attending annual meetings of this forum since 1996 and has actively participated in its various activities (Government of India, n.a.).

(b) The East Asia Summit (EAS), an 18-member grouping, is also a key forum for strategic dialogue. This is the only leader-led forum in which all key partners engage in discussing all the possible political, security, and economic challenges facing the Indo-Pacific and has an important role to play in advancing closer regional cooperation.

The EAS has 18 members — the 10 ASEAN countries (Brunei, Cambodia, Indonesia, Laos, Malaysia, Myanmar, the Philippines, Singapore, Thailand, and Vietnam) along with Australia, China, India, Japan, New Zealand, the Republic of Korea, the United States, and Russia. Discussions take place at the annual leaders' summit, usually held alongside annual ASEAN leaders' meetings. EAS ministers and senior officials also meet throughout the year to take forward leaders' initiatives.

At the most recent, i.e., the 12th EAS held on November 14, 2018 in Manila, (Philippines), India, was hailed as a balancer in the region. The *raison d'etre* for balancing emanates from China's Belt and Road Initiative overwhelming the region with its influence. Officials of the "Quad" countries (India, USA, Japan, and Australia) also met on the sidelines of the Summit and post 2007, when Australia had moved out of this configuration, were no longer hesitant to take forward their format of multilateral engagement (Government of Australia, n.a.). Hence, from a somewhat "outlying" position, India has come to the center stage of geopolitics and geoeconomics in the region represented by the East Asia Summit countries (Borah, 2017).

(c) The ASEAN Defense Ministers' Meeting (ADMM), since its inception in 2006, is the highest defense consultative and cooperative mechanism in ASEAN. The ADMM aims to promote mutual trust and confidence through a greater understanding of defense and security challenges as well as enhancement of transparency and openness. Cooperation in the ASEAN defense sector has grown steadily since its inception in 2006. Work in humanitarian assistance and disaster relief (HADR), in particular, has been progressing at a significant pace. The ASEAN Defense Ministers have adopted many concept papers to enhance cooperation in HADR. Follow-up workshops on the ASEAN Defense Establishments and Civil Society Organizations (CSOs) Cooperation in Non-Traditional Security and on the Use of ASEAN Military Assets and Capacities in HADR were also conducted.

Similarly, cooperation in the area of peacekeeping operations and defense industry moved in tandem with the adoption of the Concept

Papers on the Establishment of ASEAN Peacekeeping Centers Network and on ASEAN Defense Industry Collaboration by the 5th ADMM in 2011. Initiatives on establishing ASEAN Defense Interaction Programme and an ADMM Logistics Support Framework were also adopted by the 7th ADMM in 2013. Implementation of these initiatives is currently underway. Another important new ADMM initiative is the establishment of a Direct Communications Link, which was adopted by the 8th ADMM in 2014. This Link, when established, will be a security-building measure that will promote fast response cooperation in an emergency, in particular relating to maritime security. Work is also currently in progress to establish the Direct Communications Link.[12]

The ADMM-Plus is a platform for ASEAN and its eight dialogue partners to strengthen security and defense cooperation for peace, stability, and development in the region. The Inaugural ADMM-Plus was convened in Ha Noi, Vietnam, on October 12, 2010. The Defense Ministers decided on five areas of practical cooperation to pursue, namely, maritime security, counter-terrorism, humanitarian assistance and disaster relief, peacekeeping operations, and military medicine. To facilitate cooperation on these areas, Experts' Working Groups (EWGs) are established.

In 2013, a new priority area of humanitarian mine action was agreed, and the EWGs on Humanitarian Mine Action (HMA) was established following the endorsement of the 7th ADMM in Brunei Darussalam on May 7, 2013. Practical cooperation has been moving apace on the six priority areas. Since 2016, the priority areas have been expanded to include cybersecurity and the EWG on Cyber Security has been established following the endorsement of the 10th ADMM in Vientiane, Lao PDR, on May 25, 2016. The 3rd ADMM-Plus was convened in Kuala Lumpur, Malaysia, on November 4, 2015. The 4th ADMM-Plus was convened in Clark, Pampanga. The Philippines, on October 24, 2017. The 12th ASEAN Defense Ministers Meeting (ADMM) and 5th ADMM-Plus were held on October 19 and 20, 2018 in Singapore. It was here that the ASEAN Defense Ministers' Meeting (ADMM) saw the adoption of the guidelines for air military encounters. The Guidelines for Air Military

---

[12]ADMM, ASEAN Defense Minister's Meeting. From https://admm.asean.org/index.php/about-admm/about-admm.html.

Encounters (GAME), are a voluntary, non-binding set of measures. These are a practical confidence-building measure for militaries to improve operational safety in the air. They are meant to help manage unintentional encounters in flight between military aircraft over the high seas to avoid potential safety hazards. With the adoption of GAME now finally occurring, the focus will move to the expansion of its support as well as efforts to see its gradual implementation. Therein will be its true test — as with other confidence-building measures, the effectiveness of GAME will lie in the willingness of states to actually adopt and then use the guidelines in practice over time (Parameswaran, 2018).

ADMM added the guidelines would also help reinforce the spirit of ASEAN Political-Security Community Blueprint 2025, which calls on all ASEAN member states to promote shared norms as well as principles of international law, in building a rules-based community.

Shangrila Dialogue is another multilateral dialogue on issues of peace and security that has been organized in Singapore since 2002. India has looked upon this mechanism (organized by the International Institute for Strategic Studies of UK) as an important forum for raising issues of security concerns (Devare, 2005, p. 81). The 2019 Dialogue focused on issues of maritime security, cybersecurity, and confidence-building measures, amid the China–USA tensions. India asserted that common prosperity and security require the evolution of a common rules-based order for the region (MEA speeches, June 01, 2018).

4.6 Evaluating the Mechanisms for Strategic Cooperation

The ASEAN Defense Ministers have, in the October 2018 Joint Declaration, admitted that there are challenges facing the grouping. They highlighted that there is growing uncertainty in the global landscape, including the increasing complexity of non-traditional and transnational security encounters challenging the region. While underscoring the importance of the ADMM and the ADMM-Plus as part of the region's key security architecture, they reaffirmed the imperative for upholding a rules-based regional order with respect for international norms and laws

(Philstar, 2018). Contending visions of the East Asian multilateral order by China and the United States have put a strain on the present regional architecture. While Sino-US competition in the region is the most visible in the economic sphere and South China Sea disputes, defense multilateralism — in the form of the ADMM and the ADMM-Plus — is also a key part of the regional order and would surely be affected by growing major power rivalry. The ADMM and the ADMM-Plus have typically focused on confidence- and capacity-building — avoiding the more politically sensitive issues.

There are several strengths of these mechanisms. First, these are the only meetings where the defense ministers of ASEAN and the other eight countries can exchange views on security issues of mutual concern. Second, these mechanisms of ADMM and ADMM-Plus envisage cooperation through joint tabletop and field exercises and thus contribute to capacity-building for ASEAN states to respond to regional security challenges. Third, humanitarian assistance and disaster relief (HADR) are also important for cooperation in shoring up capacities of member countries. The earthquake and tsunami in the islands of Indonesia in late 2017 and 2018 point to the growing need for joint relief operations. Fourth, in the ADMM-Plus, there is a central role for ASEAN, given its perceived independence and neutrality amid major power rivalry (Teo, 2017).

However, as pointed out earlier, there are several limits to the ability of these mechanisms. Despite the existence of dispute settlement mechanisms, the fears of the past colonial and post-colonial experiences in the region prevent the peaceful settlement of intra-ASEAN conflicts. The Thailand–Cambodia border conflict for the temple of Preah Vihear is a case in point.[13] The International Court of Justice, which in its decision on November 11, 2013, declared unanimously on the basis of a 1962 judgment that Cambodia had sovereignty over the whole territory of the

---

[13] In a June 1962 judgment, the ICJ found that the temple is situated in territory under the sovereignty of Cambodia and that Thailand is under an obligation to withdraw any military or police forces, or other guards or keepers, stationed at the Temple or in its vicinity on Cambodian territory. In April 2011, Cambodia requested the ICJ to interpret the 1962 judgment, arguing that while Thailand recognizes Cambodia's sovereignty over the temple itself, it does not appear to acknowledge the sovereignty of Cambodia over the vicinity of the temple.

promontory of Preah Vihear and that Thailand is obligated to withdraw its forces from that territory (UN News, 2013). Cyclone Nargis in Myanmar in 2008 could barely evoke humanitarian assistance missions. Military modernization and an arms race are not without reason. Operational activities have been undertaken primarily on a bilateral or trilateral basis, such as the anti-piracy patrols in the Malacca Straits, or multilaterally in areas such as disaster management simulations. The South China Sea dispute continues to divide members' perceptions with countries such as Cambodia and even Laos, completely overwhelmed by China's deep pockets. There is scant progress in dealing with terrorism, smuggling of drugs and narcotics, and human trafficking. Moreover, ASEAN countries themselves have a weak capacity for peacekeeping and peacebuilding activities, as it was the United States which has been for decades the security provider in the region.

Several challenges continue to pre-occupy ASEAN countries, the most striking being the Sino-US rivalry which has accentuated in the Trump era. Taking sides is not an option for most Southeast Asian countries, as was articulated in an interview to the author by several experts in Thailand. However, it is with China that each of the ASEAN countries has the largest trade, given that this large neighbor has been more engaged with them in every sphere than USA in the past two decades. ASEAN countries' trade with China is more than eight times that with India.

China has continued to convert the reefs and shoals in the vicinity of ASEAN countries, assert its claims in the nine-dashed line, and also enhance its military and naval footprint in the South China Sea. The ARF meanwhile is yet to move beyond confidence-building to preventive diplomacy and conflict resolution. It faces difficulty and delays in negotiating a binding Code of Conduct. All that ASEAN security and defense cooperation has been able to achieve are continuing confidence-building through dialogue.

It is evident then that the rivalry of the big powers including not only China and the USA but also India, Japan, and Australia will continue to impact ASEAN centrality and unity.

According to Amitav Acharya, in Southeast Asia, realist perspectives link the fortunes of Southeast Asian regionalism to international dynamics of power (Acharya, 2013, p. 43).

"ASEAN's weaknesses may mean that it's vulnerable to [becoming] irrelevant", said Ciorciari. "For example, in the South China Sea issue, there is a tendency of the Chinese government to adopt a strategy of bilateralism, where they negotiate one-on-one with individual countries and hamstring the ability of ASEAN itself from negotiating their issues" (Jany, 2017). The underlying premise is that ASEAN will stay united, even as China continues to engage each country bilaterally (Gnanasagaran, 2017).

In the past, ASEAN has struggled to adopt a joint stand on the South China Sea, with Myanmar, Cambodia, and Laos — opposed to interfering in the issue. China and the United States are not members of ASEAN, but both nations routinely participate in its conferences. "The risk is that these big elephants, like China and the United States could push the nations apart", noted Terry. The organization's prime challenge, says Abdulrahim, is to utilize its resources and take concrete action. "ASEAN needs to remember that it has a seat at the table and has a role in maintaining international order", he said (Jany, 2017).

4.7 India's Evolving Role in the Regional Architecture

India's Look East Policy of 1992 was embarked soon after the country's liberalization reforms with a narrow focus limited to trade, investment, and science and technology in its engagement with ASEAN countries. By December 1995, India became a dialogue partner covering much broader areas of mutual interest. In 2002, India became a Summit partner, and by 2012, India had become a strategic partner of ASEAN. During this period, India also became a member of the regional security dialogue platform — the ARF and also participated in the ADMM-Plus meetings. The India ASEAN FTA in Goods was signed in 2009, following which it was enlarged to include services, technology, and investments in 2015. Through BIMSTEC (which was launched in 1997 in Bangkok), Mekong Ganga Cooperation (which was launched by the Vajpayee Government in 2000), and the East Asia Summit (EAS), India has been shaping the regional economic and strategic architecture (Ram, 2018).

As explained in the preceding sections, the end of the Cold War, the hub-and-spoke US alliance system, and the dominant presence of the United States had enabled ASEAN to be placed at the center of the Regional Security Architecture in East Asia. ASEAN-led institutions including the ARF, PMC+1, ASEAN+1, ASEAN+3, EAS, and the ADMM-Plus were intended to mediate relations between regional powers on their periphery, while the United States guaranteed and underpinned the regional order.

The Global Financial Crisis of 2007–2008 altered this scenario. First, there was an acceleration in the relative decline of US power in Asia as the US was preoccupied with the conflicts in Iraq and Afghanistan. Second, Obama's "rhetorical" pivot to Asia was a case of "too little and too late". China made its territorial grab through land reclamation and militarization of features in the South China Sea. Third, under relentless Chinese pressure, ASEAN unity on the South China Sea has remained broken since 2012. ASEAN was no longer able to provide an effective platform to mediate issues and address hard security issues between ASEAN states and major regional powers on its periphery. In the changing regional environment, marked by China's not-so-peaceful rise and assertions in the periphery of both South and Southeast Asia, it is doubtless that ASEAN unity is at stake. The United States and regional powers — India, Japan, and Australia — are turning to mini-laterals, including trilaterals and the Quad, to help restore the balance of power in the Indo-Pacific region.

The imperative of bringing in India, to balance the overwhelming weight of China, in regional affairs, has been a significant strand of strategic thinking among some ASEAN countries. It was no surprise, therefore, that way back in 2005, on the eve of India's participation in the inaugural East Asia Summit, Singapore Senior Minister Goh Chok Tong had spoken of India and China as two wings of a "mega jumbo jet" whose fuselage was the ASEAN (Brookings India, 2017). In his words, "I like to think of new Asia as a mega jumbo jet that is being constructed. Northeast Asia, comprising China, Japan, and South Korea, forms one wing with a powerful engine. India, the second wing, will also have a powerful engine. The Southeast Asian countries form the fuselage. Even if we lack a powerful engine for growth among the ten countries, we will be lifted by the two wings". This was further reiterated by Prabir De in an interview to the author at the ASEAN India Center (AIC), in New Delhi.[14] Tong, as Prime Minister of Singapore, had also spoken of his desire for India to take on a greater role in Southeast Asia, particularly due to the closure of US bases in the Philippines and China's assertiveness in the South China Sea (Mun, 2015, p. 25).

Thailand as one of the economically largest member countries of the ASEAN (second in terms of size of the economy) has signaled that India's linkages with the Association could be more robust. During the fourth East Asia Summit in 2009 in Hua Hin, Thailand, India joined the debate on Asian integration, with the then Prime Minister Manmohan Singh calling for an Asian Regional Trade agreement as a pivotal step toward the integration of the region into a broader "Asian Economic Community" (AEC) (Varadarajan, 2018). At the ASEAN–India Dialogue III in New Delhi in March 2011, Thailand's Foreign Minister Kasit Piromya stated that India's peaceful rise would benefit the region and the world and highlighted that the ASEAN was desirous of India "jointly shaping a more balanced and dynamic regional architecture" (Vu, 2011). Indonesia and Vietnam also seek deeper cooperation with India, as is evident from the former having joined the Asia Africa Growth Corridor[15] and the latter continuing to underline the role of India in Asian affairs. In fact, during the visit of India's President to Vietnam in November 2018, India and Vietnam agreed to expand defense cooperation and oil exploration to further boost their bilateral ties, even as they reaffirmed the importance of freedom of navigation, overflight, as well as unimpeded economic activities in the South China Sea, amid China flexing its muscles in the Indo-Pacific region. Malaysia and Singapore are also partners of significance for India, in terms of both economic and strategic cooperation. The

---

[14]Prabir De in an interview to the author, April 12, 2019.
[15]AAGC is currently being carried out among a group of think tanks in India, Japan, and Indonesia which have been state-designated as partners. The operational module, financing opportunities, and administrative mechanisms to formally operationalize the AAGC still need to be finalized. From https://www.risingpowersinitiative.org/publication/the-aagc-indias-indo-pacific-fulcrum/; accessed on January 21, 2019.

fact that Prime Minister Modi visited these two countries along with Indonesia on his 5-day 3-nation tour in June 2018 confirms the above.

4.7.1 *Contemporary Issues: RCEP and the Indo-Pacific*

The presence of the 10 ASEAN Heads of State/Government as Chief Guests at the Republic Day celebrations in January 2018 was also, therefore, reflective both of the importance India attached to its dialogue partnership with the ASEAN and the importance ASEAN nations have begun to attach to relations with India in their search for balancing China's aggressive behavioral and territorial assertions in the South China Sea. ASEAN and India had a special Summit on January 25, 2018 to commemorate the 25th Anniversary of ASEAN–India Dialogue Relations under the theme of "Shared Values, Common Destiny". Prime Minister Modi also delivered a Keynote Address at the Shangri-La Dialogue in Singapore in July 2018, through which he shared India's vision for the Indo-Pacific region. The vision articulated upholding respect for the common civilizational ethos of pluralism, coexistence, openness, and dialogue (De, 2018).

It is tempting to ask the question whether in light of these developments there is a renewed interest among ASEAN countries in India and a desire to have India playing a major security role in the Indo-Pacific region? ASEAN leaders have in the past been skeptical of India's capacity to deliver on its promises and India was perceived as a reluctant trade liberalizer. Chinese assertiveness and its expanding footprint through the BRI have also placed India in a difficult situation, even as it is challenged in its backyard, viz. South Asia. The renewed vigor of India's "Act East" policy under Prime Minister Modi and the strategic shift of India's ties closer to the United States may have changed that presumption. Moreover, India also seeks a central role for ASEAN in the Indo-Pacific construct, even though most countries in the region do not wish to be identified as "anti-China".

This has been evident in the June 23, 2019 ASEAN Outlook on the Indo-Pacific, which was presented by the Thai PM Prayuth Chan-o-Cha at Bangkok during the 34th ASEAN Summit. While ASEAN centrality was underlined, the importance of rules-based engagement was also emphasized. This concurs with India's stand on the Indo-Pacific regional architecture. Point No. 10 of the statement is as follows:

> ASEAN Outlook on the Indo-Pacific is based on the principles of strengthening ASEAN Centrality, openness, transparency, inclusivity, a rules-based framework, good governance, respect for sovereignty, non-intervention, complementarity with existing cooperation frameworks, equality, mutual respect, mutual trust, mutual benefit and respect for international law, such as UN Charter, the 1982 UN Convention on the Law of the Sea, and other relevant UN treaties and conventions, the ASEAN Charter and various ASEAN treaties and agreements and the EAS Principles for Mutually Beneficial Relations.[16]

The ASEAN Outlook clearly does not see the grouping taking sides, either with China or with USA.

China's rise has been factored on its economic surpluses boosted through trade. The Belt and Road Initiative (BRI), which has already expanded to more than 60 countries, is all about building infrastructure and expanding China's economic outreach coupled with a trillion dollars of investment. In contrast, India's initiatives marked by the three Cs of connectivity, commerce, and culture are quite pale and less visible. To link the strategic connections with the economic, it is important to outline here the challenges India faces in our Economic Partnership with the ASEAN as we move ahead?

First, a complicating factor is the pushback against globalization and the potential for the rise of protectionism. As India and the ASEAN work to further trade liberalization under the RCEP and through the implementation of the bilateral FTA for services, we must contend with the fact other nations including the United States are becoming increasingly protectionist. These attitudes are spawning hostility toward further trade liberalization.

Second, there is also a view in the United States that China has not played by the rules; unfairly denied market access and violated IPR protections. Many other countries, which have been the victims of China's mercantilist and predatory behavior — like India — would agree that a

---

[16]From https://asean.org/storage/2019/06/ASEAN-Outlook-on-the-Indo-Pacific_FINAL_22062019.pdf; accessed on June 26, 2019.

major stumbling block on the path to further liberalization is China's protectionist attitude toward trade, investment, and connectivity. This becomes a stumbling block for India in regional trade negotiations like the RCEP, and this explains India's reluctance to give China enhanced market access with reduced tariffs under the RCEP.

Third, while ASEAN centrality and the considerable achievements of the grouping are well recognized, it is an undeniable fact that ASEAN unity on the South China Sea issue has crumbled since 2012. The failure of ASEAN to present a united front in the face of challenges to the territorial integrity of some of its members challenges the idea that ASEAN is central to the Regional Security Architecture in East Asia. As individual ASEAN countries take sides in the great emerging game in East Asia, this also puts efforts at regional integration at risk in the future.

Thus, in the economic domain, it is the RCEP negotiations which have become the dominant discourse between ASEAN and six countries, including India. As India's former Commerce Secretary articulated, "India is a market of 600 million middle-class consumers, and it is for this reason that India is central to the signing of RCEP". Moreover, "India's persisting demand for services being included in RCEP is being met with stiff resistance from ASEAN".[17] Indian industry has expressed fears over competition from China and due to the latter's well-integrated production chain can enter the Indian market even through ASEAN. Thus far, India has an FTA or is in the process of negotiating one with all countries of RCEP, except China. However, for how long can India continue to deny itself the opportunities that RCEP presents, given the fact that the success of "Make in India" and the manufacturing sector does hinge on improving manufacturing competitiveness.

4.7.2 India: Meeting ASEANs Expectations

How should India pursue the economic pillar of its Strategic Partnership with the ASEAN? The answer should be that if India seeks a leadership role in the Indo-Pacific region, it must, as it has done in the past, approach

---

[17] India's former Commerce Secretary addressed the Young Diplomats Conclave at RIS, New Delhi, on January 17, 2019.

the RCEP negotiations from a strategic perspective. India cannot project its influence as a regional power in the ASEAN unless it assumes a dominant economic presence in the region.

What can India do to meet the expectations of the ASEAN in the realm of security? India as a rising power will be faced with expectations set by established powers, for example, when it comes to participating in global public goods provision. At the same time, a rising power will have to understand that immediate regional neighbors would have their expectations, and the latter could request them to commit to the solution of regional problems and the provision of regional public goods, while denying them any role in their internal affairs.

If India is to meet the expectations of its neighbors in ASEAN, it must first focus on developing comprehensive national power. A rapidly growing Indian economy, with an expanding manufacturing base marked by increasing competitiveness, could narrow the gap between itself and Asia's largest economy, China. India's economic prowess must be ensured to instill hope among ASEAN countries.

Second, there is an imperative to strengthen bilateral security ties with ASEAN countries, particularly in the maritime domain. We must move beyond token patrols and exercises to activities that promote interoperability and simulate potential threats to maritime security at sea. India's successful pursuit of military modernization and particularly naval modernization would go a long way in encouraging our partners in the ASEAN. We also need to focus on maritime domain awareness and conclude White Shipping Agreements with major ASEAN countries.

However, latest data from SIPRI for the year 2018 show that India's defense budget was less than a third of China's. The increase in defense expenditure in 2018 as compared to 2017 was 5% for China and 3% for India (SIPRI, 2019). In the budget presented to the Indian Parliament in 2019, it was evident that India struggles to increase its budgeted expenditure for defense modernization.

Third, we must strengthen security coordination with the ASEAN in platforms like the ARF, EAS, and the ADMM-Plus. Here, we need to move beyond Non-Traditional Security issues like HADR to hard security issues like combating terrorism, piracy, crime, and smuggling.

Fourth we must engage the larger ASEAN countries like Indonesia and Vietnam in mini-laterals or trilaterals to promote coordination and joint activities, including joint exercises and training. Mini-laterals have the potential of aggregating the hard power of participating countries and of working toward the restoration of the balance of power in the region. This has been discussed in Chapter 5.

4.8 Conclusion

ASEAN was established in 1967 as a bulwark against authoritarianism in the form of communism. The organization never proved a bastion of democracy, although it briefly exemplified popular demand for it. The Association of Southeast Asian Nations sees itself as a model of diversity, with coexisting cultures, religions, and systems of government. It certainly offers abundant economic opportunity. But the space is narrowing for those who seek political pluralism in Southeast Asia.[18]

At present, the 10-member organization seems the face of what the American political scientist Larry Diamond has called a "democratic recession" sweeping the world. Seven ASEAN countries are ruled by dictators, military juntas, monarchs, communist regimes, or single dominant parties that for decades have manipulated democratic processes (*Ibid.*). Both Thailand and Indonesia have witnessed elections in 2019.

It is evident that the ASEAN Way will prevail as far as the process of seeking internal solutions to issues is concerned. At the World Economic Forum meeting on ASEAN in Hanoi in September 2018, it was none other than the Cambodian leader Hun Sen who invoked ASEAN's founding principle of non-interference in the internal affairs of member countries, defending the communist and military regimes of Cambodia, Myanmar, Laos, Thailand, and Vietnam. "The countries that do not know our countries", he said, "please leave us to solve our problems for ourselves". In the present times, performance seems to prove legitimacy. And ASEAN is performing legitimately well, with economic growth expected to average

---

[18] From https://asia.nikkei.com/Opinion/Southeast-Asians-will-regret-giving-up-political-rights-for-affluence; accessed on March 12, 2019.

5.2% a year from 2018 to 2022, according to a 2018 report on Southeast Asia, China, and India published by the Organization for Economic Cooperation and Development (OECD) (*Ibid.*).

ASEAN's progress in terms of maintaining its centrality and significance is commendable. It has successfully brought together countries from Asia and the rest of the world together on a common platform through various formal as well as other networking arrangements. This is best articulated by Woltersdorf, former director of the Friedrich Ebert Foundation's regional cooperation office in Singapore, when he said, "Other than ASEAN, there is no other organization in Asia that can bring so many countries, including Japan, China and South Korea, to one table", adding that multilateral conferences and networking are an important accomplishment of ASEAN.

As discussed in the preceding sections, there are questions being raised about the future of ASEAN's centrality in the Asian regional architecture. Given the rising aspirations of China and its capacity to keep USA out of Asia, can there be another grouping or construct which can balance China? It's a given that China's ascent on the global landscape can no longer be contained. Moreover, the US defense department in a report of May 2019 suspects that China could build more military bases around the world to protect its investments in its BRI global infrastructure program. There is a fear that a military base could be built on the port of Gwadar in Pakistan and elsewhere.

Whether it is the countries in Quad or the Indo-Pacific region, each country has its bilateral connection with China and hence will avoid any provocation. The ASEAN countries are engaged in constructing their own all-inclusive Indo-Pacific vision with focus on a rules-based engagement. For India to assume a pivotal role in the Indo-Pacific region, it must primarily rely on Singapore. For, as Tommy Koh has written, "Singapore is India's best friend in ASEAN" (Koh, 2016, p. 72).

The most monumental challenge for the regional grouping hence is staying strong on the inside as Kausikan puts it, "the greatest challenges are internal, not external". International politics and diplomacy is a delicate game of chess where the pieces are your interests that are being pitted against the interests of your opponents. At times, countries reduce the risk of competition by aligning mutual interests. However, in changing times,

ASEAN must be wary of changes on the domestic front that can alter pre-existing mutual interests of member states. When those interests misalign, it can have severe repercussions to the behavior of the association as a regional grouping (Gnanasagaran, 2017).

While China is seeking its grandiose ambitions of replacing the United States and re-writing the rules and norms of the international order, it has no qualms about disintegrating ASEAN unity. However, India's interests can best be served by a united and strong ASEAN. India and ASEAN are aligned in terms of seeking a rules-based and inclusive international order, with freedom of navigation in the seas. This was articulated by Dr. Suriya Chindawongse, Director General, Department of ASEAN Affairs, Ministry of Foreign Affairs of Thailand, on April 10, 2019. He also highlighted the importance of connectivity for building an Indo-Pacific that encourages cooperation rather than competition.[19]

---

[19] India and ASEAN are aligned in terms of seeking a rules-based and inclusive international order, with freedom of navigation in the seas. This was articulated by Dr. Suriya Chindawongse, Director General, Department of ASEAN Affairs, Ministry of Foreign Affairs of Thailand, on April 10, 2019.

Chapter 5

ASEAN–India Relations: Multilateral and Bilateral Dimensions

5.1 Introduction

India shares extensive cultural and civilizational ties with Southeast Asia (SEA). These have already been detailed in a previous chapter.

To briefly recapitulate, it was in the 1st century AD that Indian traders sailed to the region, thereby facilitating the spread of Hinduism and Buddhism in pre-colonial kingdoms like Srivijaya in Sumatra, Majapahit in Java, Bali, and the Philippine archipelago. At the time of European colonization, the Indian subcontinent was used by the colonizers, especially the British, to gain control over large parts of SEA. The previous chapter delineates the growing significance of SEA, especially in the post-ASEAN phase.

To refer to International Relation theorists at this stage is relevant. Caporaso's assertion is of significance. According to him, "Given that interdependence is on the increase, it is a surprise that little attention has been given to multilateralism as an organizing principle of international political economy". He defines multilateralism, as grounded in and appeals to the less formal, less codified habits, practices, ideas, and norms of international society (Caporaso and Levine, 1992, p. 602). The ASEAN Way, in a way, conforms to this definition. At the bilateral level, the balance of relationships theory is cited to highlight why and how states manage their relationships. Shih underlines the fact that nation states have an interest in balancing relationships and may not always pursue "apparent national interests". He also highlights that countries may draw on cultural memory to forge relations (Shih, 2019, pp. 2–7).

This chapter discusses India's relations with ASEAN to contextualize its relations with Thailand in the succeeding chapters.

5.2 India–ASEAN Ties — From Looking West to Acting East

In the initial years of the 1960s, India's relations were SEA were fairly stable as India supported the anti-colonial struggle. However, the situation changed in the 1970s with India becoming closer to the Soviet Union. There was a certain discomfort among the ASEAN states regarding India's neglect of the region. Initially, in fact, India had been considered as a possible balancer to Communist China (Sridharan, 2001, p. 72).

Once the Cold War ended, India's "Look East" policy, for which India's former Prime Minister P.V. Narasimha Rao is credited, was pivoted around improving relations with the Asia Pacific region.

During his Prime Ministership, P.V. Narasimha Rao (1991–1996) visited several ASEAN countries including Thailand, Indonesia, Singapore, Vietnam, and Malaysia. India became an active participant in various ASEAN organizations, becoming a Sectoral Dialogue Partner of ASEAN in 1992, a full ASEAN Dialogue Partner in 1996, and also a member of the ASEAN Regional Forum (ARF) in 1996. This coincided with India's reform and liberalization policy, leading to a transformation in India's annual growth rates, further aiding its vision to engage outside the limited sphere of South Asia. Hence, the momentum continued with succeeding governments of Prime Ministers Atal Bihari Vajpayee and Manmohan Singh during the 1990s and early 2000s. India and ASEAN became summit partners in 2002 and strategic partners in 2012. In December 2005, India became a partner with ASEAN, through the ASEAN plus six formulation, i.e., the East Asia Summit. Other five members of EAS include China, Japan, South Korea, Australia, and New Zealand.

With the India-led South Asian Association for Regional Cooperation (SAARC) having become a victim of the India–Pakistan relations, there was an imperative for India to engage Eastwards. Prime Minister Narendra Modi as well as India's External Affairs Minister Sushma Swaraj made several visits to these countries since the AEP was launched in 2014. This is discussed in the next sections.

What is the rationale for India to Act East since 2014? This necessitates understanding ASEAN's importance for India — culturally, economically, and strategically.

5.3 ASEAN's Importance for India

In the preceding chapter, titled ASEAN centrality, the grouping's importance to the economic and security architecture has been discussed in detail. Areas specific to India are delineated here:

(a) First, the location of the ASEAN countries, both on the continental shelf and the maritime space, providing access through the Malacca Straits makes this region of strategic importance. Both Myanmar and Thailand open the gates for India to the East. The geopolitics of this region has also been impacted by the opening up of Myanmar in 2011 as well as the resolution of territorial conflicts within the ASEAN member countries.

(b) Second, ASEAN–India dialogue relations have grown rapidly from a sectoral dialogue partnership in 1992 to a full dialogue partnership in December 1995. India, therefore, participates in several dialogue mechanisms including the annual summits, ARF, PMC+1, East Asia Summit, ADMM+, SOMs, and meetings of experts. As a precondition of participating in the East Asia Summit as a founding member in 2005, India signed the Treaty on Amity and Cooperation in 2003 at the second India–ASEAN Summit. During that summit, India and ASEAN countries also concluded a "Joint Declaration on Combating International Terrorism". India and the ASEAN countries signed the "Partnership for Peace Progress and Shared Prosperity" in 2004 at the third India–ASEAN Summit. This was significant as it laid down the agreed pathway for the Partnership and was also detailed in the "Plans of Action". The ASEAN–India Centre within the Research and

Information System for Developing Countries (RIS) in New Delhi was established in November 2012 after the summit. ASEAN and India launched the center to promote, among other things, trade, investment, tourism, and cultural exchanges. India has also committed US$50 million to the ASEAN–India Cooperation Fund.[1]

To commemorate the anniversary of 25 years of the India–ASEAN Dialogue Partnership, 15 years of summit-level interaction, and 5 years of strategic partnership, Prime Minister Narendra Modi hosted 10 ASEAN country leaders for the Republic Day celebrations on January 26, 2018. On the occasion of the 2018 ASEAN–India Summit in New Delhi, PM Modi underlined India's commitment to Act East through the following: (1) ASEAN–India cooperation on ICT, digital, and rural connectivity in CLMV countries. Hence, India offered a $1 billion Line of Credit to promote digital and physical connectivity, as well as Rs. 500 crore to create manufacturing hubs in Cambodia, Laos, Myanmar, and Vietnam; (2) training programs in telecom, networking, regulation, and technology development; (3) a dialogue on financial inclusion, investment promotion, and infrastructure; (4) declaring 2019 as the ASEAN–India year of tourism; and (5) 1000 Youth Fellowships to ASEAN students (Nanda, 2018). In February 2019, India also organized the Fourth India–ASEAN Expo and Summit bringing together business delegations from all the SE Asian countries.

(c) Third, India seeks deeper engagement with a more globally integrated ASEAN Economic Community (AEC). Despite economic disparities within ASEAN, its members were committed to building the ASEAN Economic Community (AEC), which was formally launched in Kuala Lumpur, Malaysia, on November 22, 2015 (Albert, 2017). The key components of the AEC blueprint are defined as: a single market and production base, a competitive economic region, equitable economic development, and integration into the global economy (Plummer and Siow, 2009). Intra-regional trade in goods — along with other types

---

[1]From https://asean.org/vision-statement-asean-india-commemorative-summit/; accessed on January 28, 2019.

of cross-border flows — is likely to increase with the implementation of the AEC integration plan, which aims to allow freer movement of goods, services, skilled labor, and capital. A more globally integrated AEC has the potential for enhanced cooperation with India. Moreover, with rising per capita incomes in countries such as Singapore, Vietnam, Laos, Philippines, and Thailand, India will have greater trade and investment opportunities in the East (Tonby *et al.*, 2014).

(d) Fourth, the China factor also motivated India to not only modernize its economy but also engage more deeply with Southeast Asian countries (Singh, 2001, p. 193). Balancing China was in fact a strategic goal since the inception of India's LEP, according to Frederic Grare (Grare, 2017: 11). Although China commenced its liberalization program before India, India also considered itself as an attractive destination for foreign direct investment (FDI) since 1991. Moreover, Southeast Asian countries such as Thailand and Singapore were also keen to expand investments into India so as to diversify their risks. In terms of the post-Cold War geopolitical sphere and its own strategic positioning, there was an imperative for India to be viewed as a balance to China, in its neighborhood.

(e) Fifth, post 2014, there is growing involvement of India in its East Asian neighborhood especially in the field of maritime affairs. This has resulted in India acknowledging its security responsibilities. That India is a net security provider in the region has manifestations including its recent advances in maritime domain awareness, enhancing joint patrols, and humanitarian assistance as well as disaster relief (HADR) cooperation. India has also contributed to the maritime security of its neighbors through weapon transfers. Securing the seas and ensuring safe passage for its ships is another concern for India.

(f) Sixth, Maritime cooperation in the Indian Ocean is another reason for India's Act East Policy. China has also modernized and constructed a number of facilities along the Myanmar coast on the Bay of Bengal and the Andaman Sea. China's outreach of port-building activities in the Indian Ocean countries as well as the fact that its naval capabilities are far superior to that of India make India wary (Grare, 2017:35).

(g) Seventh, India seeks the cooperation of ASEAN countries on strategic issues — in developing the concept of the Indo-Pacific, while seeking a pivotal role for itself along with the United States, Japan, and Australia. However, it is important that they develop a common understanding on how it will develop. India has also launched the Asia Africa Growth Corridor, for which Indonesia is an important partner.

(h) Eighth, Issues of non-traditional threats, ecological sensitivity, as well as cooperation in transnational crime, drug trafficking, narcotics, etc., remain key areas of cooperation with ASEAN countries.

(i) Ninth, India's cultural bonding with Southeast Asia has further provided it a lever for enhancing cultural diplomacy and soft power initiatives. Sanskrit, yoga, art, religion, language, and literature have all been elements of the Modi government's impetus to building bridges of understanding and harness India's historical linkages.

5.4 India's Importance for ASEAN

Without a doubt, India has been a latecomer in forging ties with Southeast Asia, despite the Look East policy of the Narasimha Rao government of the early 1990s. This has been well articulated in the book by Kishore Mahbubani and Jeffery Sng titled *The ASEAN Miracle: A Catalyst for Peace*. "Even though it (India) became politically decolonized in 1947, it remained colonized for several decades and continued to look towards Europe and America for inspiration", the authors lament.[2] They spell out the importance of India's strong civilizational and cultural links with almost all countries of Southeast Asia.

What are then the specific possibilities for India to be considered an important partner for Southeast Asian nations?

First, while underlining the importance of initiatives to Act East by Prime Minister Modi since 2014, Mahbubani and Sng opine, "As ASEAN comes under renewed stress from the growing geopolitical rivalry between the US and China, India could provide a strategic balance". They further add, "India has an opportunity to develop a 20-year plan to enhance its relationship with ASEAN". The Council on Foreign Relations, a US-based think tank also underlined this, "Specific Southeast Asian states are now

---

[2]From https://www.thestatesman.com/books-education/india-important-ASEAN-150254 4277.html; accessed on March 9, 2019.

seeking to diversify their strategic partnerships, beyond a binary choice between Beijing and Washington. A key element of those diversification efforts is working with India as a counterweight to China and hedge against a declining United States" (Chandran, 2018).

Second, this geopolitical rivalry is manifest not only in terms of the race for influence but also in terms of impacting the manufacturing and growth rates of some countries in SEA. As China slows down, as is evident from Figure 5.1, the impact has been visible in terms of its industrial profits falling and consequent growth slowing down for the first time in 3 years, in 2019. China's slowing down can be attributed to, in addition to other factors, a low birth rate, which persists despite its revert to the one-child policy, as well as an aging population. Thailand became the latest Asian economy to slow down due to the trade war, as the economy grew merely by 3.3% in the third quarter of 2018 on an annual basis, below forecast of 4–4.2% expansion. In the second quarter of 2019, China's growth rate has slumped to its lowest in 27 years.

Figure 5.1 and Table 5.1 predicted a slower rate of growth in China in 2019, in comparison to 2018. India is expected to rise faster in 2019 than

Figure 5.1: World Economic Outlook Projections (GDP)

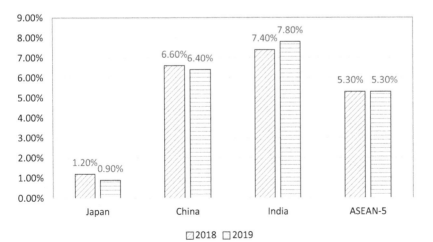

Source: World Economic Outlook, 2019.

Table 5.1:   Economic Growth Forecasts for ASEAN-5, India, China

	2016	2017		2018		2019	
ASEAN-5	4.4	5	(4.8)	4.9	(4.8)	4.9	(4.8)
Indonesia	5	5.1	(5.2)	5.4	(5.5)	5.5	(5.5)
Malaysia	4.2	5.8	(5.4)	5.3	(4.9)	5	(4.6)
Philippines	6.9	6.7	(6.5)	6.7	(6.7)	6.8	(6.9)
Singapore	2	3.4	(2.7)	2.7	(2.3)	2.5	(2.3)
Thailand	3.2	3.9	(3.6)	3.9	(3.5)	3.9	(3.4)
India	7.1	6.7	(7.0)	7.4	(7.6)	7.7	(7.8)
China	6.7	—	(6.8)	—	(6.4)	—	(6.2)

Note: Forecasts for 2017 onward, figures in parentheses represent average forecasts as of previous survey in September, annual figures for India are those of fiscal year (April to March).
Sources: JCER/Nikkei Consensus Survey, Nikkei/NON Survey, Haver Analytics.

the previous year. ASEAN's growth projection for 2019 remains constant as in 2018.

India's GDP in 2018 was US$2.7 trillion. With India projected to be the third largest economy by 2030 after USA and China, it will continue to influence both geopolitics and geoeconomics in Asia and beyond. The estimate by the United States Department for Agriculture Economic Research Service (USDA), based on data collated by World Bank and IMF, assumes the Indian economy will expand annually at an average 7.4% to $6.84 trillion by 2030 (Ray, 2017). This was reiterated by the Thai ambassador in India on March 13, 2019, at a seminar organized by Research and Information system for Developing countries in New Delhi. "India is on the rise and Thailand wants a positive engagement", he said.

Third, India–ASEAN trade and investment relations have been on a positive spin. Post the India–ASEAN FTA of 2010, bilateral trade between ASEAN and India crossed the US$80 billion mark in 2018. This embeds confidence into the two-way ASEAN–India partnership. India is also being viewed as an integral partner in the negotiations underway for the finalization of RCEP. The fact that RCEP negotiations have continued since 2013 with more than 27 rounds of negotiations implies clearly that the deal without India is not meaningful for the remaining 15 partners.

Fourth, India's influence in the maritime space and especially in and around the Indian Ocean makes India an important partner for SEA — from trade and logistics to tourism and leisure. India and ASEAN are working together on finalizing the Agreement on Maritime Transport. India's Project Sagarmala, launched 2014, aims to promote port-led development in the country. There is a need to connect the ports of India and ASEAN, for further building this partnership and to cooperate in harnessing marine resources as well as securing our seas. PM Modi visited Indonesia, Singapore, and Malaysia in the last week of May 2018, signaling to ASEAN countries India's commitment to rules and regulations and for the sustainable use of marine resources in the Indian and Pacific Oceans in accordance with international law, notably the United Nations Convention on the Law of the Sea (UNCLOS). Both ASEAN and India can contribute immensely in shaping the regional architecture in the Indo-Pacific region (De, 2018).

It is well known that India and Indonesia share several concerns, particularly those emanating from China's increasing footprint in and around the Straits of Malacca, close to Sabang.[3] Sabang itself, is only 100 nautical miles from the Southern tip of the Andaman and Nicobar Islands. Sabang has the potential to be a strategic port for India and Indonesia. The Indian Navy is equipped to monitor activity in the Straits of Malacca, Lombok, and Sunda. Indonesia is well aware that its dispute with China for the Natuna Sea can be handled through a strategic partnership with India (Panda, 2018).

Fifth, India's continental connectivity with Southeast Asia, through its Northeast is being provided a major fillip. Border trade as well as investment in the Northeastern region of India are becoming increasingly visible and vibrant. In particular, considerable progress has been made in implementing the India–Myanmar–Thailand Trilateral Highway and the Kaladan Multi Modal Transit Transport Project. India's relationship with Myanmar and Thailand at the bilateral level for further strengthening the connectivity projects is vital. The India–Myanmar–Thailand Trilateral Motor Vehicles Agreement (MVA) will play a critical role in realizing seamless movement.

---

[3]India is jointly developing the port of Sabang with Indonesia.

Sixth, the partnership with ASEAN has moved from merely an economic and commercial one to encompass more strategic areas. India is being engaged with ASEAN through as many as 30 sectoral dialogue mechanisms and seven ministerial-level interactions, in addition to annual summit meetings. In recent years, leaders from ASEAN countries are visiting India, just as Indian leaders are visiting these countries several times (De, 2018). In addition to the visits by heads of ASEAN states in the last week of January 2018, President Tran Dai Quang of Vietnam made another visit in the first week of March 2018. During this visit, the joint statement articulated the convergence of views on various bilateral and international issues, including the regional security situation in Asia. Both leaders reiterated the importance of achieving a peaceful and prosperous Indo-Pacific region. They desire an Indo-Pacific region where there is respect for sovereignty and international law, freedom of navigation and overflight, sustainable development, as well as a free, fair, and open trade and investment system.

India's positioning in the ASEAN-driven East Asia summits: As stated earlier, India has been a founding member of the East Asia Summits (EAS) and prime ministers of India have participated in all the 13 summits that have been held so far, the last one having been held in Singapore in November 2018. As Japan, USA, and Russia seek a larger role for India in the regional architecture, ASEAN countries underline that, "India has a big role to play". The ambassadors of Thailand and Japan in India recently underlined this at a seminar with both (Chutintorn and Hiramatsu) in favor of India becoming a member of the Asia-Pacific Economic Cooperation forum.

A manifestation of India's growing importance is that the grouping adopted separate declarations at the 12th East Asia Summit on countering terror financing and dealing collectively against radicalism and terrorism. According to Preeti Saran, two important statements were adopted on countering ideological narratives and financing of terrorism, which proved that India's concerns and sensitivities on the issue were well mainstreamed in the meeting. Further, a leader's statement was also issued articulating the need for effective steps to be taken to contain the use of chemical weapons.

Seventh, India's growing population as well as the growing number of technically skilled youth can power the growth of these countries. In a commentary published by the S. Rajaratnam School of International Studies, Senior Analyst with the Centre for Multilateralism Studies (CMS), Phidel Vineles, argues that the region — especially the ASEAN-5 (Singapore, Malaysia, Thailand, Indonesia, and the Philippines) — lack industry-ready skilled workers in spite of its vibrant demography. Malaysia and Thailand face challenges in equipping their respective work-forces with engineering and science skills. Besides that, Indonesia and the Philippines have high youth unemployment rates due to a workforce that is ill-equipped with skills and knowledge needed by key industries. With ongoing negotiations by India for achieving greater mobility for its work-force through the RCEP, there would be opportunities for India's skilled labor force to seek employment in these countries. This remains an area of concern as India seeks the commitment of partners to ensure easier movement of skilled Indian workers in the RCEP countries and greater access to local job markets (The ASEAN Post, 2018). In July 2019, despite Australia joining with the ASEAN countries to seek India's agree-ment on key issues, India continues to raise concerns about lack of access for Indian services in RCEP countries and flooding of the Indian market with Chinese goods, manufactured in or outside China.

Eighth, there are a plethora of areas in which India is recognized both in the region and at the global level. These include among others support from India for anti-piracy operations, anti-smuggling, and transnational crime. Building digital connectivity is another area where India leads and has already initiated projects as the Sustainable IT Infrastructure for Advanced IT Training at a cost of US$8.7 million, which involves setting up of the Centre of Excellence in Software Development and Training (CESDT) in CLMV countries, setting up of Information Technology Resource-cum-Study Centre for ASEAN coun-tries at C-DAC and assistance in IT curriculum development, teachers' training, provision of scholarships for ASEAN students, joint training programs and courses, e-learning, seminars, workshops, as well as exchange of visits of IT experts. Cybersecurity is another area for cooperation (De, 2018).

Ninth, innovation and the start-up culture is also helping India step up its growth rate. Initiatives as the Digi Locker and "Digital India" have the potential to contribute to the growth of micro, small, and medium industries in Southeast Asia. It is well known that Indian companies are running successful start-up ventures in Singapore.

Tenth, increasing trade and investment between India and ASEAN provides the scope for further collaboration in financial and economic areas. India and ASEAN can engage in Bilateral Swap Arrangements (BSA) in line with the Chiang Mai Initiative (CMI). India may be invited to join directly under the Chiang Mai Initiative Multilateralism (CMIM) initiative, helping ASEAN countries to enhance its leverage in gaining financial access in the event of a crisis. ASEAN countries have been uncomfortable with the CMIM's decision-making structure for some time. They are exposed to shocks distinct from those affecting China, Japan, and South Korea. These East Asian economies are not sensitive to the political and economic vulnerabilities that ASEAN countries face; therefore, their decisions may not adequately address the region's needs. ASEAN needs a regional financial arrangement that is fully under its control (Tan and Bhaskaran, 2019). In fact, India already has currency swap arrangements with some of the ASEAN countries including Singapore, Indonesia, Thailand, and Malaysia. Given that India has already BSA with four ASEAN countries, a regional swap arrangement between them would be easier to reach. With the swap arrangements, India and ASEAN can jointly strengthen their financial stability to address the short-term capital flows (De, 2018).

Some of these aspects of cooperation are discussed in the next section.

5.5 India's Act East Policy

Prime Minister Modi announced the upgrading of India's erstwhile "Look East Policy" (LEP), initiated in 1992 by then Prime Minister Narasimha Rao to a more action-oriented "Act East" strategy at the India–ASEAN Summit in Myanmar in November 2014. There have been several statements made by Prime Minister Modi at various ASEAN summits and meetings; the first of these was at the ASEAN Summit in November 2014 in Myanmar and the second was during his visit to South Korea in May 2014. This was further echoed in June 2015, by then External Affairs Minister (Ms. Swaraj passed away recently) when she went further and described Thailand as a significant partner during her visit to Bangkok.[4] The same year in August in Delhi, Indian President Pranab Mukherjee underlined India's Act East vision during the meeting with the Heads of States of the Pacific Island countries in Delhi in August 2015. A more comprehensive vision of the strategy was presented by Mr. Modi during his visit to Singapore in November 2015.[5] To Act East is imperative for India, embedded in the fact that India seeks to exert a greater influence in the global and regional geostrategic space.

India's relations with ASEAN have become multifaceted to encompass security, strategic, political, counterterrorism, and defense collaboration in addition to economic ties. Cooperation to curb terrorism, especially in the face of rising influence of Islamic State, has assumed priority. Defense partnerships with several ASEAN states have advanced.[6]

The India–ASEAN partnership, current issues, and potential for deepening this partnership are elucidated in the following sections.

5.5.1 *India–ASEAN Trade*

Economic engagement with ASEAN has been important for India. As India liberalized its economy, it also developed a strategic partnership with the ASEAN. The Framework Agreement on Comprehensive Economic Cooperation between ASEAN and India was signed in October 2003 and served as the legal basis to conclude further agreements, including Trade in Goods Agreement, Trade in Services Agreement, and Investment Agreement that form the ASEAN-Indian Free Trade Area (AIFTA). The ASEAN–India Trade in Goods Agreement was signed and

[4] Sushma Swaraj arrives in Bangkok to pay 2-day visit to Thailand. From https://www.business-standard.com/article/news-ani/sushma-swaraj-arrives-in-bangkok-to-pay-two-day-visit-to-thailand-115062700384_1.html.
[5] https://muse.jhu.edu/article/627452.
[6] https://thediplomat.com/2016/06/2-years-on-has-modis-act-east-policy-made-a-difference-for-india/.

entered into force on January 1, 2010.[7] Under the Agreement, ASEAN Member States and India have agreed to open their respective markets by progressively reducing and eliminating duties on 76.4% coverage of goods.

Economic cooperation activities under the AIFTA are also now being undertaken on agriculture, fisheries and forestry; services; mining and energy; science and technology; transport and infrastructure; manufacturing; human resource development; and other sectors such as handicrafts, small and medium enterprises (SMEs), competition policy, Mekong Basin Development, intellectual property rights, and government procurement.[8]

In 2017, ASEAN was India's fourth largest trading partner, accounting for 10.2% of India's total trade. India, on the other hand, is ASEAN's seventh largest trading partner. In 2018, intra-ASEAN trade had grown to more than 25% of its overall trade. Even as the ASEAN continues to trade with all major trade groupings in the world, with the share of extra-ASEAN trade being much higher than intra-ASEAN trade (around 75%), there is substantial scope for India to enhance trade relations with the ASEAN.

The following are evident from Figure 5.2, which depicts India–ASEAN trade:

a. India's imports from ASEAN have been higher that its exports to ASEAN over 2008–2015.

b. India's exports registered greater decline post 2013, in comparison to its imports.

c. Post 2010, the signing of India–ASEAN FTA, India's trade deficit has increased.

d. While India–ASEAN trade has grown on average by more than 13.6% over the period 2015–2018, in the April to December period of 2018–2019, trade grew by over 20.5%.

---

[7] Harsh Pant, Avantika Deb, India-ASEAN Partnership at 25; ORF Issue Brief No. 189, July 2017. From https://www.orfonline.org/research/india-ASEAN-partnership-at-25/; accessed on October 3, 2018.

[8] https://www.ASEAN.org/storage/images/2015/October/outreach-document/Edited%20 AIFTA.pdf.

Figure 5.2:   India–ASEAN Trade: 2008–2015

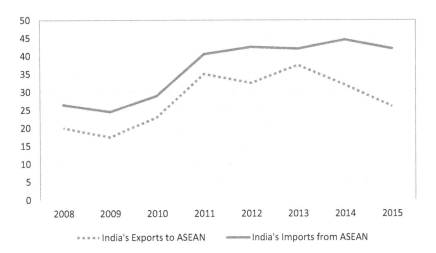

····· India's Exports to ASEAN   India's Imports from ASEAN

5.5.2 Issues in India–ASEAN FTA

As shown in Figure 5.2, India's trade deficit with ASEAN has widened after the India–ASEAN FTA in 2010, as imports have been increasing at 4.8% p.a. while exports increased at merely 3.3% p.a. This was because while tariffs by India were needed to be greatly reduced, reciprocal concessions from ASEAN countries were not secured. A closer examination of FTAs and their outcomes reveals a mixed picture. Though trade with the ASEAN has grown from $5 billion in 1992 to US$70 billion in 2016–2017 (US$40.6 billion in imports from ASEAN in 2016–2017 and exports to US$31.1 billion in 2016–2017), India's rising trade deficit remains a matter of concern, viz. US$11 billion in 2016–2017. This is while intra-ASEAN trade has remained steady over the period 2011–2015.

The ASEAN–India Trade in Services Agreement though signed in 2012 has yet not come into force pending ratification by all ASEAN countries. Other issues also need to be addressed in the context of trade between India and ASEAN countries. These include non-tariff barriers, dumping and business visas, as well as inefficient customs procedures. India also seeks greater market access for services.

Hence, the ASEAN–India FTA in goods should be revisited in view of the backlash against the current paradigm of global integration. Without a doubt, there is significant scope for ASEAN leaders to consider long-pending issues sought by India, especially the ratification process of the pending ASEAN–India Services and Investment Agreement. On the other hand, there are issues to be addressed within India as well. With manufacturing sector slowdown and the slow pace of India's integration into global value chains, India's export growth has been impacted. Even so, India's export of processed goods and components to the ASEAN has varied between 20% to 30% of India's exports to ASEAN. The automobile component industry is one area where India is entering global and regional value chains in a significant way.[9]

5.5.3 *India–ASEAN Investment*

The ASEAN–India Investment Agreement was signed in November 2014. The Investment Agreement stipulates protection of investment to ensure fair and equitable treatment for investors, non-discriminatory treatment in expropriation or nationalization, as well as fair compensation.

Inward FDI Investments from ASEAN to India are for construction of ports, townships, highways and shipping, processed food, automobile components, electrical machineries, hi-tech goods, etc. Indian investment in ASEAN is also growing fast. Out of 10 member countries of ASEAN, the TATA Group has presence in nine ASEAN countries.

In terms of ASEAN countries' share in FDI inflows to India in 2015, it was seen that the highest share was in services, viz. 21% of the total from ASEAN; second share was in computer hardware 14%, trading 9%, telecom 8%, pharmaceuticals 5%, others 43%. In 2015, ASEAN accounted for 22% ($18.4 billion) of the Outbound Foreign Direct Investment (OFDI) from India. If one considers the 8 years, i.e., from April 2007 to March 2015, total OFDI was about US$38.672 billion. In contrast, inward FDI from ASEAN was about US$49.40 billion over the 16 years spanning April 2000 to May 2016. Inward FDI from ASEAN countries increased by five times over the period 2010–2011 to 2016–2017, i.e., from US$1.8 billion to US$8.9 billion.

---

[9]http://www.delhipolicygroup.org/uploads_dpg/publication_file/india-and-asean-25-1082. pdf; accessed on December 11, 2018.

Overall increase in FDI equity inflows was about 3% in 2017–2018. Hence, there is a significantly higher outflow of FDI from India as compared to the inward FDI. Singapore remains the largest partner for India in terms of investment. To further enhance economic and strategic relations with the Southeast Asian countries, the Indian government has put in place a Project Development Fund to set up manufacturing hubs in CMLV countries through separate Special Purpose Vehicles (SPVs). In the past few years, India has significantly improved its ranking in Ease of Doing Business; in 2018, India was ranked 77 among 190 economies. These achievements have opened new opportunities for trade and investments with India.

Country wise details of investment inflows from ASEAN countries into India are provided in Table 5.2.

It is evident that Singapore, with the major share of FDI inflows into India, is at the number 2 position. For Indian investors too, Singapore has become the major investment and trading hub in the East (and also Indo-Pacific). Thailand's rank is 34.

Table 5.2:   Investment Inflows Cumulative 2000 (April) to 2018 (March)

Rank/All countries	Country	Amount of foreign direct investment inflows in USD million	Percentage share
2	Singapore	66,770.70	17.72
25	Malaysia	866.76	0.23
27	Indonesia	629.10	0.17
34	**Thailand**[a]	**380.87**	**0.10**
38	Philippines	235.93	0.06
81	Cambodia	10.34	0.00
84	Myanmar	8.97	0.00
98	Vietnam	4.92	0.00
125	Brunei Darussalam	0.40	0.00
	Laos	Nil	

Note: [a]More details of India–Thailand investment details as well as a comparison of investment flows from China and ASEAN are provided in Chapter 8.

Source: Department of Industrial Policy and Promotion; From http://dipp.nic.in/sites/default/files/FDI_FactSheet_29June2018.pdf.

India receives highest FDI in the services sector — overall inflows into services were US$6709 million in the year 2017–2018; second highest was in computer software US$6153 million, or 8 % of total; and third highest was telecom — also 8%, amount is US$6212 million. India's digital industry offers several investment opportunities for ASEAN due to (a) strong demand for smartphones and digital services, (b) booming start-up ecosystem, (c) increasing adoption of digital medium, (d) infrastructure development, and (e) abundant supply of IT workforce. Indian government is also providing financial services.

However, India needs to further improve and deliver an enabling environment for attracting inward FDI and retaining it too. Red tape and bureaucratic mismanagement can be a deterrent for investors. A recent case relates to that of the American company, the $26-billion Flex, one of the world's top contract manufacturer for electronics, which alleged that the government's functioning is entangled in "red tape" and threatened to move its production from Sriperumbudur in Tamil Nadu to Malaysia if promised concessions were not given.[10]

An India–ASEAN expo was held in New Delhi in February 2019, with the objective of bringing together Indian, ASEAN, and Global Multinational companies to work together. Despite interest in the Indian market being high, the participation was subdued. While as many as 200 plus exhibitors from India and ASEAN had initially been planned, the number had to be sharply revised downwards.[11]

5.5.4 *Defense and Strategic Cooperation*

Continentalism, marked by an obsession with land frontiers and a sea blindness, has deep roots in Delhi's political history. However, a neglect of the seas and maritime security cost India dearly on several occasions,

---

[10]Flex threatens to move production out of India due to red tape. From; https://www.moneycontrol.com/news/business/flex-threatens-to-move-production-out-of-india-due-to-red-tape-report-3054441.html; accessed on October 17, 2018.

[11] https://www.business-standard.com/article/economy-policy/despite-bilateral-bonhomie-business-remains-slow-at-india-asean-expo-119022201225_1.html; accessed on March 14, 2019.

the most horrifying being the terrorist attack on the Taj Hotel in Mumbai in 2008.

The Modi government's vision was articulated as SAGAR, or Security and Growth for All in the Region, in 2016. Although this concept was first unveiled by the Atal Bihari Vajpayee government in 2003 with the objective of rapid modernization and expansion of India's maritime sector, it is now extended to promote India's connectivity in the Indian Ocean, in both economic and security domains. During a visit to Mauritius and Seychelles in March 2015, Prime Minister Modi said, "We seek a future for Indian Ocean that lives up to the name of SAGAR". The statement envisions the criticality of security risks. With naval exercises and maritime capacity-building programs with navies of partner countries as well as regular warship deployments in the Bay of Bengal, the Indian Navy is enhancing capabilities to expand its footprint. In his keynote speech at the Shangri-La Dialogue in Singapore in June 2018, Prime Minister Modi articulated that India's vision for the Indo-Pacific was that of "a free, open, inclusive region". Adding that "Southeast Asia is at its center", the government's position was to highlight the importance of a rules-based order that is inclusive. India also indicated that it sought multilateralizing India's defense exercises with Southeast Asian countries and also including more of these countries in New Delhi's own defense initiatives, including those based in the Indian Ocean. The statement was also to nudge the ASEAN countries to seek rules-based solutions to the disputes in the South China Sea and for the restoration of strategic balance in India's maritime neighborhood.[12]

The Rim of the Asia Pacific (RIMPAC), the world's largest international maritime exercise, also brings together India and five Southeast Asian countries as well as several other countries. The exercise of 2018 included forces from Australia, Brunei, Canada, Chile, Colombia, France, Germany, India, Indonesia, Israel, Japan, Malaysia, Mexico, Netherlands, New Zealand, Peru, Republic of Korea, Republic of the Philippines, Singapore, Sri Lanka, Thailand, Tonga, United Kingdom, United States, and Vietnam. Participating nations and forces exercised a wide range of

---

[12] Modi's Vision: ASEAN and Indo-Pacific Security, Wilson Center. From https://www.wilson center.org/blog-post/modis-vision-asean-and-indo-pacific-security.

capabilities and demonstrated the inherent flexibility of maritime forces. These capabilities included among others disaster relief and maritime security operations, sea control, and complex warfighting. The relevant, realistic training program included amphibious operations, gunnery, missile, anti-submarine and air defense exercises, as well as counter-piracy operations and diving and salvage operations. This large grouping of allies and partners support advantageous regional balances of power that safeguard security and prosperity and advocate a free and open international order. RIMPAC 2018 portrays the combined capabilities of joint forces to deter and defeat aggression by major powers across the landscape of potential conflict or escalation of tensions. This biennial RIMPAC was conducted near Hawaii, USA, from June 28 to August 3, 2018 (Singh, 2018). There is a possibility that the next RIMPAC be held in the South China Sea. That would truly be a game changer and would push back China's unilateralism in those waters. If the Indo-Pacific concept gains traction, it would be a huge setback for China (Pham and Newsham, 2018).

India's Bilateral Engagement
According to Scott Cheney Peters, evidence of India's implementation of the Act East Policy comes from several firsts in bilateral engagement. The Indian Navy has helped conduct joint training and enforcement efforts with regional forces; examples include the coordinated patrols (CORPATs) with both Indonesia (since 2002) and Thailand (since 2005). The biannual Indonesia–Indo CORPATs are expected to develop into more comprehensive exercises in 2018. Malaysia has been keeping maritime cooperation with India at a low key, factoring in China's sensitivities.

New Delhi's strategic approach to other countries in Southeast Asia is also exemplified through its outreach to Vietnam. Despite the fact that through history, Vietnam has fought 17 wars against China (in contrast to one against USA), there is a joke among the Vietnamese that their country's coast line looks like a bent spine that reflects the crushing weight of China bearing down on them. A resurgent and nationalistic China is perceived by the Vietnamese as an existential threat. Vietnam, seeking to escape over-dependence on China, has expanded economic and strategic relations with India (Rachman, 2016: 108).

In addition to initiatives including the training of Vietnamese submarine crews and sale of interceptor boats, India may also sell its indigenously manufactured Akash "Surface to Air" missiles to the Southeast Asian state. Vietnam, in turn, has allowed Indian warships to access its port facilities. In addition, in 2018, the Indian ONGC Videsh has been given a 2-year extension to explore a Vietnamese oil block in an area of the South China Sea which is contested by both China and Vietnam.

Vietnam and India have strengthened their defense ties in recent years. PM Modi, during his visit to Vietnam in May 2016, offered a line of credit of $500 million to Vietnam for the import of defense equipment from India, which has been accepted. India also extended another credit line of $100 million to Vietnam for buying a number of naval vessels. India is already training the Vietnam Navy personnel in operating the Russian-origin Kilo-class submarine. In the past, defense assistance to Vietnam has included the refurbishment of military aircraft and transfer of naval spares. India's capacity-building programs have included submarine training for Vietnam and pilot training for Vietnam and Malaysia.

With Indonesia, India has beefed up its maritime cooperation, with increased military delegation visits and training exchanges. Given the geostrategic significance of the Malacca Straits, the Indian Navy has upgraded its coordinated patrols outside these to a comprehensive naval exercise and it is now an expanded version of the original format.

With Singapore, the Singapore–India Maritime Exercise (SIMBEX) has been the Indian Navy's most productive maritime engagement in Southeast Asia. In addition to upgrading the scope and complexity of individual exercises, India and Singapore have sought to enlarge the scope of SIMBEX beyond its traditional emphasis on anti-submarine operations. The 2017 exercise included other areas of operational cooperation, including advanced naval warfare drills and air defense exercises.[13]

India has an agreement with Singapore for the use of artillery and armor ranges and airbases in India for training purposes. On November 29, 2017, India and Singapore signed the "India–Singapore Bilateral Agreement for Naval Cooperation" during the Second Defense Ministers

---

[13]The Nautical Dimension Of India's "Act East" Policy. From https://www.rsis.edu.sg/wp-content/uploads/2018/04/PR180409_The-Nautical-Dimension-of-Indias-Act-East-Policy.pdf.

Dialogue held in New Delhi. The Agreement will enable increased cooperation in maritime security, joint exercises, temporary deployment from each other's naval facilities' and mutual logistics support. The agreement will increase the operational radius of the Indian Navy from the maritime domain near Singapore and the same option will be available to the Singapore Navy in the Bay of Bengal.

With Philippines, India has had enduring maritime relations. India also supported the Philippines case at the Tribunal in July 2016; however, a sea change in Philippines attitude toward China under President Duterte resulted in no further mention of the dispute. It is important to mention here that the Philippines seeks to bolster maritime relations with India and this was articulated by security analyst Chester Cabalza. In his view, once the Philippines had received the favorable verdict from the tribunal over the South China Sea case, India used its influence among Asian neighbors to push for peaceful resolution of maritime differences. India, a naval power, had a moral responsibility to push for freedom of navigation as a global interest, asserting that no state has a monopoly over the seas and oceans. India has always hoped that assertions of maritime and international laws will prevail in maintaining an equitable balance of powers in an evolving multipolar world (Cabalza, 2018).

India's bilateral defense cooperation with individual ASEAN countries has been institutionalized through the signing of bilateral defense Cooperation Agreements or MOUs. Three forms of cooperation have gained momentum — cooperation between Navies, the maintenance and supply of equipment, and assistance for training. India has regularly participated in discussions on non-traditional and hard security issues in the ARF, EAS, and the ADMM+. The Indian Navy has also participated in the ARF DIREx series of maritime exercises with Malaysia focused on disaster management (Nanda, 2018).

India has also strengthened bilateral defense and security cooperation with Vietnam, Malaysia, Singapore, and Indonesia at a time when these countries are seeing rising tensions and territorial disputes with China.

An outstanding example of India's efforts to build closer ties with regional navies is the MILAN exercise that has been held biennially since 1995 at Port Blair in India's Andaman and Nicobar Islands. Training and capacity-building assistance have been extended to all ASEAN countries.

India currently offers 400 training slots every year to ASEAN defense personnel in Indian defense training institutions, many of them on a *gratis* basis, under the Indian Technical and Economic Cooperation program.

The modes of capacity-building assistance found most effective by India have included MOD training courses and programs at military training establishments, provision of loaned service personnel, short-term training teams, civilian and military advisers seconded to foreign governments for extended periods, joint coordinated patrols, and joint exercises. Capacity-building has been accompanied by effective communication at different levels including inward and outward visits of defense ministers and military and civilian leaders and visits by ships, aircraft, and other military units; staff talks; conferences and seminars to improve mutual understanding; and to create interoperability and habits of cooperation and working together.

According to Swee Lean Collin Koh, instead of relying on national approaches to assist Southeast Asia's maritime security capacity-building, it would be better for the extra-regional powers to coordinate with each other. This would avoid the overlapping of efforts. The author further suggests that the Quad may serve as such a platform. A more robust "Act East" approach for India could well begin with initiating discussions within this set-up.[14]

5.5.5 *Other Areas of India–ASEAN Economic Cooperation*

In addition to the trade, investment, and strategic aspects of cooperation, India–ASEAN engagement has broadened to include various connectivity initiatives: India's Connectivity Vision is reinforcing the push toward economic integration with the ASEAN, and thus, a number of connectivity initiatives are under implementation or under consideration. These include the following: (a) the India–Myanmar–Thailand Trilateral Highway and the Kaladan Multi Modal Transport Agreement in Myanmar; (b) the

---

[14] K. S. L. Collin, "Book Review — *Maritime Security in the Indo-Pacific: Perspectives from China, India and the United States*, edited by Mohan Malik (Lanham, Maryland: Rowman and Littlefield, 2014)", *Contemporary Southeast Asia*, Vol. 37, No. 1 (2015), pp. 137–139.

proposed India–Thailand–Myanmar Trilateral Motor Vehicles Act; (c) the ASEAN–India Maritime Transport Cooperation Agreement, which is under negotiation; (d) an ASEAN–India Air Transport Agreement has been proposed to improve air connectivity. These initiatives are discussed in a subsequent chapter.

There has been an inclusion of several sectors as tourism, agriculture, forestry, food security, environment, renewable energy, telecom, science and technology, and IT. To facilitate progress and concrete achievements in these areas, a number of ministerial dialogue platforms for these sectors have been established.

On the occasion of the India–ASEAN Summit held in January 2018, PM Modi announced that India would offer 1,000 scholarships at Indian Institutes of Technology to PhD students from the Association of Southeast Asian Nations (ASEAN) (Sengupta, 2018). India has also established the Nalanda University, where students from ASEAN countries are enrolled. Measures to facilitate student and people mobility in the region have been undertaken.

India and the ASEAN have also worked on enhancing private sector engagement, which has been a key area of focus for both sides. The ASEAN–India Business Council (AIBC) was set up in March 2003 in Kuala Lumpur to provide an inclusive forum to major private-sector players from India and the ASEAN countries for business networking. AIBC organized the ASEAN–India Business Leadership Conclave in July 2016 in Kuala Lumpur, Malaysia. It is believed that for forging both digital and infrastructure connectivity, the private sector has a critical role to play through the Joint Business Councils as well as through the ASEAN–India Business Summit and India–ASEAN Business Fairs.

India has also made a significant commitment to assisting the Initiative for ASEAN Integration that aims to narrow the development gap between the relatively more developed maritime ASEAN and the less developed continental ASEAN countries, also referred to as the CLMV. Indeed, human resource training, whether in India under the ITEC program or through specialized institutions set up in CLMV countries, has been India's strength in overseas assistance programs.

To fund these programs, India has established the ASEAN–India Cooperation Fund, the ASEAN–India Green Fund, and the ASEAN–India

S&T Development Fund. To encourage cooperation in connectivity, India has set up a US$1 billion special facility to assist projects in physical and digital connectivity. India has also contributed US$77 million to develop manufacturing hubs in CLMV countries.

5.6 Conclusion

Maritime Cooperation has emerged as a significant priority area of cooperation. India organized the third EAS Conference on Maritime Security and Cooperation on June 7–8, 2018 in the coastal city of Bhubaneshwar, Odisha, as a follow-up to the EAS Summit of 2017. The conference focused discussions on issues including Maritime Safety and Security, Good Order at Sea, and Blue Economy. The 2018 India–ASEAN Summit that was held in January 2018 also focused on maritime connectivity and security.

The ASEAN region is becoming one of the preferred trade and investment regions for Indian businesses and Federation of Indian Chambers of Commerce and Industry (FICCI) as an apex Chamber of Commerce and Industry of India gives special focus to this region.

However, in terms of trade in goods and services, there exists tremendous scope for expansion. At present, India's exports of services is mainly in software and IT-enabled services. Technical education, financial services, and healthcare services are exported to a lesser extent (AIC & RIS, 2015:107).

The combined strength of the single ASEAN market is more than US$2.6 trillion and India's US$2.7 trillion economy creates an economic powerhouse that has the potential to become one of the strongest in the world.

It is evident then that India's foreign policy has assumed a more proactive stance toward India's neighbors in the East. While the Act East policy enunciated since 2014 also provides a fillip to India's relations with other countries on its Eastern flank including Japan, South Korea, and Australia, ASEAN emerges as India's natural partner. Both India and ASEAN countries have expressed their mutual desire of creating a free and inclusive regional architecture. For several reasons articulated above, including both economic and political, ASEAN's significance for India and the other global powers has increased in the past 10 years (Maini, 2017:39).

However, there are several challenges in India's relations with ASEAN; nevertheless, India must demonstrate that it is truly Acting East. Compared with China, India is clearly at a serious disadvantage in trade relations with ASEAN. For decades, trade in commerce in most ASEAN countries has been in the hands of ethnic Chinese who, even during the darkest periods of strict communism in China, maintained links with relatives and associates in their ancestral towns and villages. When China liberalized its economy following Deng Xiaoping's reforms in the 1980s, these "bamboo networks" fueled China's economy and vice versa, as Murray Weidenbaum and Samuel Hughes described in their 1996 study of overseas Chinese tycoons. While there are fairly well-established ethnic Indian business communities in Singapore, Malaysia, and even in Thailand, they are no match to the big, rich, and powerful ethnic Chinese equivalents in those countries (Lintner, FEER, 2006).

To Act East, what must India do? **First**, there is an imperative for India to Act on its commitments, especially in the economic sphere and for improving connectivity. Instead of talking about ASEAN-wide connectivity projects, New Delhi now needs to focus on more effective delivery of projects it is already committed to. In this context, prompt completion of the India–Myanmar–Thailand Trilateral Highway and the Kaladan Multi Modal Project are imperative. India also seeks to invigorate ties with its immediate neighbors as Myanmar and Thailand in SEA through building both air and port connectivity.

Second, this rising trade deficit has led to many economists in India cautioning the government on being too optimistic with trade agreements. RCEP negotiations hence are taking much longer and India is placing roadblocks in its path due to its apprehensions. Moreover, there is a low utilization of the India–ASEAN FTA. This indeed is a significant failure of outcomes with India seeking closer economic integration with the ASEAN.

Third, the cultural connect between India and ASEAN needs strengthening if more stakeholders are to be brought in. While India is offering scholarships to students from ASEAN states to study at the Nalanda University, this initiative should be broadened to include our front-ranking institutions such as the IITs and the IIMs. India needs to engage with the best and the brightest of ASEAN, who will drive the regional policy in the coming years. New Delhi is giving more attention to cultural diplomacy in ASEAN but still only three countries in the region — Indonesia, Malaysia, and Myanmar — have Indian cultural centers. Tourism can be further encouraged between India and ASEAN with creative branding by the two sides. While India and ASEAN have been very ambitious in articulating the potential of their partnership, they have been much less effective in operationalizing their ideas. The need now is for both sides to focus on functional cooperation and make the idea of India–ASEAN partnership more exciting (Pant, 2018).

Fourth, India's maritime concerns include the entire gamut of traditional and non-traditional threats to its security and sovereignty. While seas connect countries and bolster trade relations, there are increasing vulnerabilities too, which must be handled with superior naval capabilities, in their outreach for disaster relief, humanitarian assistance, and preparedness for war. Deployments of naval vessels and visits by warships as well as joint training exercises are essential components of India's revitalized navy. India has been consistent in its approach in seeking a positive and favorable maritime environment through combined and cooperative mechanisms with its neighbors in the maritime space.

India accords importance to issues as maritime domain awareness and would like to enter into White Shipping Agreements with ASEAN countries, implying that the agreement would allow the navies of countries to exchange information about ships in their oceanic territories. This will develop a common operating picture to assist India to deal with both traditional and non-traditional security threats and NTS issues in the Bay of Bengal, the Malacca Straits, and the Indo–Pacific region. With Myanmar, India signed an agreement for sharing white shipping information to improve data sharing on non-classified merchant navy ships or cargo ships.

It needs to be reiterated that ASEAN unity and strength are in India's interest. ASEAN countries are constantly being wooed by the major powers, but they are aware of their collective strength. This was articulated by Siswo Pramono, head of the Indonesian foreign ministry's Center for Policy Development and Analysis, when he said that rapid economic growth within the ASEAN has given member countries unprecedented leverage. "We don't have to 'choose' between [the US and China], because we have the pie", he said. "The pie is our strategic position and rapidly growing regional market. ASEAN has more confidence than before, because we are the fastest growing economic region in the world is East Asia. The market is here, people are here. We don't have to care what US or China says — it's up to us" (Panda and Basu, 2018).

Finally, in conclusion, India must continue to engage bilaterally with each of the Southeast Asian countries, in addition to the multilateral institutional mechanisms with ASEAN. Both Myanmar and Thailand are significant for India as land bridges to continental SEA; while Indonesia, Vietnam, Singapore, Philippines, and Malaysia share maritime concerns with India and are significant partners in India's Indo-Pacific positioning. It would be pertinent to share here a remark of Professor Khin Maung Nyo in Yangon: When India was looking Eastwards, it looked at Singapore; when it is Acting Eastwards, India looks beyond Myanmar.[15]

---

[15] Interview to the author, Yangon, May 1, 2019.

Chapter 6

Galvanizing India's Act East Policy: With a Focus on Northeast India and Myanmar

6.1 Introduction

As part of the Eastern Himalayan region, Northeast (NE) India is well known for its water resources, rich biodiversity, and unique culture and ethnicity as compared to the rest of the country. The eight states of Arunachal Pradesh, Assam, Manipur, Meghalaya, Mizoram, Nagaland, Tripura, and Sikkim make up this region. Geography ensures that the NE is a 'gateway' to the ASEAN region. The historical linkages and trade relations of NE India confirm the long-standing relationship that the region shares with the Southeast Asia (Momin, 2016).

Many communities in India trace their origin South of the Yarlung Zangbo, source of the Brahmaputra River, including the Tai-Ahoms or Ahoms, an offspring of the Tai people who are called Shan in Myanmar, Thai in Thailand, Lao in Laos, Dai and Zhuang in China, and Tay-Thai in Vietnam (Laishram, 2011). This has already been discussed in a previous chapter.

This chapter provides a discussion on the aspects of investment and infrastructure development in the NE for improved connectivity. India's border trade as well as India's connectivity linkages with Myanmar are included. About 98% of the NER's borders form India's international boundaries; on the one hand, it shares borders with South Asian countries like Bangladesh, Bhutan, and Nepal and on the other hand with Southeast and East Asian countries like Myanmar and China.

These lend both advantages and disadvantages. This chapter views not only the economic potential and its dimensions of the NE region but also delineates some of the strategic aspects which emanate as a result of the insurgencies. The latter has impacted the development of the NE region, besides resulting in several social and political upheavals.

6.2 Connectivity for Economic Enrichment of the Northeast

For decades, India's NE has remained neglected and deprived of development opportunities. The lack of development has been due to poor connectivity, negligence by the central government, and the presence of insurgent groups. However, recognizing the importance of connectivity for the development of this region, the Modi Government has prioritized taking the benefits of development to the Northeastern states and ending their isolation from the rest of India.

With this vision and the need for shared prosperity with the NE, an endeavor had been to enlist the participation of all the Chief Ministers at the India–ASEAN meetings, several of which were convened in 2018, in celebration of 25 years of India's dialogue partnership with ASEAN. At one such Center-led initiative, Delhi Dialogue X, the Chief Minister of Meghalaya, Conrad Sangma articulated, "Connectivity in the form of roads, railways and airways linking the State to the ASEAN countries is vital for development. These communication networks play dynamic roles as 'veins and arteries' for the flow of goods, services, and persons within and outside the country" (Sangma, 2018).

At the India–ASEAN connectivity summit in 2018, initiatives were outlined for boosting connectivity of the NE region with Myanmar and Thailand. Among those to be referred to **first**, the importance of the early completion of the India–Myanmar–Thailand Trilateral Highway was stressed upon, which would be a major infrastructural project toward development and economic growth in the region. The importance of stronger institutions and coordination for better regional cooperation as prerequisites for this to materialize were also underlined. (The IMT highway has been discussed in detail in another chapter.)

Second, a proposal was made for the implementation of the plan for reopening of the old Stilwell Road from Ledo, Assam, India, to Kunming, Yunnan Province of China via Myanmar covering a length of 1,736 km, as it would help boost cross-border traffic between India and ASEAN.

Third, the importance of air connectivity, the UDAN[1] vision of the Prime Minister, was highlighted and some examples listed — i.e., Shillong Airport at Umroi and Baljek Airport near Tura connecting Meghalaya with the neighboring countries — could play a vital role for connecting the region for the promotion of exports and imports. "This priority sector requires full-scale development for promotion of trade, tourism, cultural exchange, and technology transfer", he said. In the words of Conrad Sangma, "if air connectivity is improved beside movement of people for tourism, cultural exchanges students from other ASEAN nations would get an opportunity to take advantage of the educational facilities available in the region". The government has also proposed the UDAN (*Ude Desh ka har Nagrik*) scheme to ensure that even the common person can travel by air, to give a fillip to flights to the NE. Guwahati is being developed as a nodal city for connectivity within India and with Myanmar as well.

Fourth, it was affirmed that Meghalaya had accorded top priority in providing all-weather road connectivity and accessibility to market centers, border haats, tourist destinations, production centers, and rural settlements to incentivize farmers and producers. Other NE states are also taking such initiatives. The Ministry of Development of NE Region (DoNER) has been made responsible for the Northeastern Region (NER), which comprises eight states, viz. Arunachal Pradesh, Assam, Manipur, Meghalaya, Mizoram, Nagaland, Sikkim, and Tripura. In addition to the above, there are several other initiatives in the NE that have been accorded priority by the Modi Government.

---

[1] UDAN — Ude Desh Ka Aam Nagri; an initiative for air connectivity to make unserved/underserved airports in small cities operational with regular flights, and offer subsidized airfares to encourage more people to fly.

Fifth, the Kaladan Multi Modal Transit Transport Project, which would help to connect via sea, rivers, and road to Mizoram, has been prioritized. The route through Sittwe Port, located in the Rakhine state of Myanmar, would significantly lower the cost and distance of movement from Kolkata to Mizoram and beyond.

Sixth, there are two important bridges that have been completed in 2017 and 2018. In mid-2017, the 9.15-km long Dhola–Sadiya bridge to connect and bring closer the people of Assam and Arunachal Pradesh was inaugurated. It was named after the famous Assamese singer Bhupen Hazarika. The second is the 4.94-km Bogibeel on the Brahmaputra River, India's longest rail and road bridge, which was inaugurated on December 25, 2018, by PM Modi. This bridge will also help to connect Assam with Arunachal Pradesh.

Seventh, the NE Industrial Development Scheme was announced on March 21, 2018. The NE Industrial Development Scheme (NEIDS) encourages the setting up of micro, small, and medium enterprises (MSMEs) in the NE region. The central government has underlined the significance of not only building roads and highways but also providing access by sea and railway for the benefit of firms trading with neighboring countries. Several incentives are available under the NE Industrial Development Scheme (NEIDS) for new units that are being set up in the Northeastern states. An overall cap on benefits received via the NEIDS scheme has been fixed at ₹2 billion (US$29.7 million) per unit.

Some of the specific incentives for an initial period of 5 years include a reimbursement on the goods and services tax (GST) paid to the government as well as income tax benefits, 3% interest subsidy on working capital credit, incentives for capital investment, as well as transport incentives.

The next section discusses the following aspects of the Northeastern states:

a. potential for investment, with special reference to Assam, NER's largest state;
b. a brief discussion on Assam;
c. border trade.

6.2.1 *Northeast: Potential for Investment*

The Northeastern states exhibit several features, which could be harnessed for making them an attractive investment destination. These include the following:

- **Hydropower:** It has been estimated that about 90% of the region's hydropower potential remains unutilized.

Table 6.1 shows the state-wise hydropower potential of the NER. Arunachal Pradesh has the highest potential of hydropower not only in the region but also among the states and union territories of the country. The state of Sikkim is the second highest ranking in the potential of hydropower with a total potential of 4,286 MW. The Northeast region has achieved only about 3% of its hydro potentiality up to October 2013, whereas the national average is 23.53%. After completion of the different hydro schemes under construction, the potentiality will be achieved up to 4.84% only. The region has 42.54% of the hydropower potential of the country, which is estimated at 63,257 MW, natural gas reserves of

Table 6.1:   Hydropower Potential of Northeast India (2014)

States	Identified capacity (total MW)	Capacity developed (percentage)	Capacity under construction (percentage)	Unexploited capacity (percentage)
Arunachal Pradesh	50,328	0.81	5.41	93.78
Assam	680	57.69	0.00	42.31
Manipur	1,784	5.96	0.00	94.04
Meghalaya	2,394	8.62	5.39	85.99
Mizoram	2,196	0.00	2.82	97.18
Nagaland	1,574	5.17	0.00	94.83
Sikkim	4,286	13.42	56.99	29.59
Tripura	15	0.00	0.00	0.00
Northeast total	63,257	2.76	8.49	88.75

Source: Ministry of Power, Government of India; retrieved from Singh, Rajmani; https://www.easternpanorama.in/index.php/other-articles/3626-resources.

190 billion cubic meters, coal reserves of over 900 million tons, and oil reserves of more than 500 million tons. It also includes large mineral resources (Singh, 2017).

6.3 Marketable Surplus of Agro-Produce

The NER produces huge marketable surplus in a number of perishable commodities, such as banana, pineapple, orange, and tomato. For example, banana production in the region is estimated at 1.2 million tons a year, a fifth of which is consumed locally (APEDA, 2017).

Table 6.2 indicates the huge marketable surplus that exists for exports from the NER. This underlines the potential for the food-processing sector to attract US\$33 billion investment in the coming years and generate employment of 9 million person-days, according to a Grant Thornton report. The report underlines the agri-export zones in the NE, viz. Assam for ginger and Sikkim for orchid flowers as well as cherry pepper (Grant Thorton, 2017). In fact, Sikkim has achieved the status of being the first fully organic state in India. Moreover, the scope for

Table 6.2:   Top 10 Commodities with Marketable Surplus

Product	Production in NER (thousands of tons)	Consumption (percentage)	Marketable surplus (percentage)
Rice	6,755	94.60	5.40
Banana	1,208	20.20	79.80
Potato	113	82.40	17.60
Cabbage	912	25.80	74.20
Pineapple	777	5.00	95.00
Orange	590	14.70	85.30
Tomato	517	32.30	67.70
Jackfruit	493	16.70	83.30
Cauliflower	479	30.70	69.30
Brinjal	398	79.00	21.00

Source: Sathguru analysis, Ministry of Statistics and Program Implementation: Compiled by BS Research Bureau.

organic farming has been documented as an important source of income for NER farmers. This is because it reduces the vulnerability of the farmers to climate change and variability by comprising highly diverse farming systems as well as increases the diversity of income sources and the flexibility to cope with the adverse effects of climate change and variability (Babu, 2017).

6.3.1 *Harnessing the Marketable Surplus of Agro-Produce*

"A dedicated marketing and visibility campaign for products from the NER needs to be implemented, which will help in increasing the awareness in target customer segments. These could be large or small enterprises/start-ups or directly to customers", says the study. Further, the agricultural and horticultural produce value chains in the NER are marred by several challenges, such as inadequacy of infrastructure, unavailability of processing industries, production and aggregation issues, etc. All these need to be addressed according to the study by Sathguru Management Consultants, in their report published in September 2017 (IBEF, 2017).

In addition to hydropower and agro-produce, there are several other areas for potential growth. These include bamboo, rubber, tea, and coffee among others.

(i) **Bamboo:** It has been estimated that almost 50% of India's bamboo produce comes from the NE states. However, in comparison to the other countries, the yield per hectare is very low. Given the potential of bamboo to increasingly replace plastic, there is huge potential for bamboo cultivation for sustaining livelihoods as well as for environmental protection (Behera and Sahu, 2018). Four states of NE, i.e., Tripura, Assam, Mizoram, and Nagaland, have formulated their policies for the development of bamboo and conservation of bamboo forests.

(ii) **Rubber:** Rubber is another cash crop that can attract a lot of foreign investment — and given the fact that there is a burgeoning demand for rubber in India, the potential is huge. Moreover, the rubber industry is feeling the pinch of the US–China trade war as the Indian

Government raised tariffs to reduce the current account deficit. Tripura in the NE and Kerala in the South are our rubber-producing states.

(iii) **Tea and Coffee:** The NE produces India's best quality teas. Assam is the largest tea-producing state and accounts for more than 50% of the country's total tea production. In 2015, Bonhomia announced the launch "Boho" coffee machines. This company is the first one to manufacture coffee and tea capsule in India. With India being the largest producer of tea in the world, innovative branding of Indian tea would add further value for exports (Grant Thorton, 2017).

(iv) Some of the specific advantages and potential for investment are in the area of harnessing of crude oil and natural gas, development of petrochemicals, IT/ITeS, forest and mineral-based industries, engineering industry, chemicals, handicrafts and textiles, tourism and hospitality industries, as well as horticulture.

The greatest advantage is that NE states have a large and young labor force, a high number of traditional industries, and small and medium enterprises (SMEs). However, the technology used in these industries is outdated. With the completion of pending infrastructural projects, there will be more scope for further investment in such SMEs.

6.3.2 *Investors Summit — 2018 Advantage Assam: An Assessment*

As discussed, India is actively pushing for greater investments in its Northeastern states: Arunachal Pradesh, Assam, Manipur, Meghalaya, Mizoram, Nagaland, Sikkim, and Tripura. It is well known that the NE states of India share borders with China, Myanmar, Nepal, Bhutan, and Bangladesh. With a population of 3.12 crores, as per the Government of India Census 2011, Assam's population comprises 2.58 of India's total population (Government of India, 2011). Its largest city, Guwahati, is fast urbanizing and developing as the main connecting link for the NE as well as the neighboring countries.

Given the fact that Assam is not only producing 50% of India's total tea, it also has several other advantages in terms of organic produce, a major initiative taken in 2015 has been the setting up of a Mega Food Park in 50 acres of land at the cost of ₹76 crore. This park has facilities of fully operational industrial sheds for SMEs, developed industrial plots for lease to food-processing units, Dry Warehouse of 10,000 MT, Cold Storages of 3,000 MT, Common Effluent Treatment plant, Quality Control Labs, etc. The Food Park is expected to leverage an additional investment of about ₹250 crores in 30–35 food-processing units and generate a turnover of about ₹450–500 crores annually.

In February 2018, an Investors Summit was held in Assam, titled, Advantage Assam. During this 2-day summit, about 200 Memorandum of Understanding (MOUs) were signed, and investment proposals amounting to ₹1,00,000 crore had been committed (Economic Times, 2018). Also, the investment would be forthcoming from the World Bank for developing the inland water transport of the state. Developing small airports is also a priority of the central government under its UDAN scheme. Despite potential investors visiting the NE states and especially Assam during the Investment Summit it was learned through official sources that foreign investment was then committed, implying that the investors flocking to Assam were all from India.

In a survey conducted by NCAER, Assam, Jharkhand, and Bihar are ranked among the least favorable states for investment. However, in terms of individual pillars (which are six in number, others being labor, economy, etc.), they are ranked higher. Assam has a higher ranking in the land pillar of SIPI, which implies that the state ranks highest in having the least number of projects stalled based on land-related disputes and environmental clearances.[2] However, there are several weaknesses in terms of infrastructure, availability of raw materials, bank branches, etc., as a result of which the overall rank of the state has gone down from 17 in N-SIPI'17 to 19 in N-SIPI'18 (NCAER, 2018).

As has been well documented in the literature on Inward FDI (Hong, 2012; Jaumotte, 2004) and others, there are several institutional factors in addition to the economic and sector-related factors which are extremely important in not only attracting investment but also absorbing

---

[2] Six pillars, in that order from 1 to 6 are land, labor, infrastructure, economic climate, political stability and governance, survey-based responses.

investment. Among the institution factors, law and social norms, regulation enforcement, as well as FDI incentive-related policies are significant. Education and human skills, political stability, economic labor costs, and productivity as well as competitiveness are equally important. Hence, as indicated above, despite the improvement in infrastructure, the above ranking indicates that there exists a vast potential for Assam's ratings to be improved if it is to become a hub for attracting investment.

6.4 Economic Corridors: Linking to Myanmar

India's border trade with Myanmar stagnated in 2017 at US$50 million, while the China–Myanmar border trade hit the mark of US$6 billion, more than 10 times that of India's. India's border trade story with Myanmar has been in the nature of barter trade till recently. Despite the border trade agreement having been signed in January 1994, the value of trade remains abysmally small. The barter trade which existed till December 2015 was replaced by formal or zero trade or head load trade. As expressed by Priyoranjan Singh, "the present state is that formal trade, or normal official trade, stands at zero, and informal, or illegal trade — or head load trade — is going on" (*Ibid.*). A visit by the ASEAN–India Centre team led by Prof. Prabir De confirmed the difficulties due to the lack of information on duty structures and an ineffective integrated check post at Moreh during the RIS Seminar on May 27, 2019. He also asserted that the border has to be adequately safeguarded, in addition to improvement of the infrastructure.

A recent study conducted by the ASEAN–India Center at RIS on four corridors highlights the importance of NER and its centrality to India's Look East–Act East Policy (LEP) and acts as a land bridge between South and Southeast Asia. The study has considered four corridors of India — namely, East–West Corridor (EWC) (part of Golden Quadrilateral Project), Trilateral Highway (TH), Kaladan Multi Modal Transit Transport Corridor, and Bangladesh–China–India–Myanmar Economic Corridor (BCIM-EC) — to assess their likely impacts on economic development on the connected areas. Among these four corridors, EWC is the existing corridor and part of the Golden Quadrilateral Project, whereas the others are corridors proposed to connect India with neighboring countries in the Eastern neighborhood (De *et al.*, 2018).

This RIS study indicates that NER states are likely to gain more in terms of growth in freight from Kaladan corridor and Trilateral Highway than the BCIM-EC. Gains are robust and highly significant in case of NER states such as Assam, Arunachal Pradesh, Manipur, Meghalaya, Mizoram, Nagaland, Sikkim, Tripura, and Eastern Indian states such as West Bengal, Bihar, Jharkhand, and Odisha.

Finally, while Guwahati is a connectivity node in NER, cities like Nagaon, Jorhat, Dibrugarh, Guwahati, Tinsukia, Dhubri — all in Assam, Imphal, Gangtok, Itanagar, Agartala, Shillong, and Aizawl — are fast emerging as economic nodes in NER. These cities which perform secondary (manufacturing), tertiary (services), or quaternary (management, research, education) function of economic significance need to be connected through the corridors. This approach emphasizes the integration of infrastructure improvement with economic opportunities such as trade and investment and also includes efforts to address the social and other outcomes of increased connectivity (ADB, 2014, 2017).

Suthiphand Chirathivath has highlighted the huge potential of expanding trade between Thailand and India's NE, through the Greater Mekong sub-region (Chirathivath, 2010, pp. 190–193). This was further articulated by him to the author in an interview on May 30, 2018.

Table 6.3 provides an overview of the economic corridors connecting the regions.

The opening of the two land border crossings between India and Myanmar at Tamu/Moreh in the state of Manipur and Rihkhawdar–Zowkhawtar in Mizoram will help to provide access to cross-border markets and hence give a fillip to both trade and movement of people. According to a statement issued by the Indian Embassy in Myanmar, "the landmark Land Border Crossing Agreement between India and Myanmar, signed on May 11, 2018, has been brought into effect with the simultaneous opening of international entry-exit checkpoints at the Tamu–Moreh and the Rihkhawdar–Zowkhawtar border between Myanmar and India" (Borah, 2018).

Table 6.3:   Economic Corridors

Corridors	Corridors length (km)	Origin	Destination	Connecting regions
East–West Corridor	3,300	Silchar (Assam)	Porbandar (Gujarat)	India
Trilateral Highway	1,360	Moreh (India)	Mae Sot (Thailand)	India–Myanmar Thailand
Kaladan	539	Kolkata (India)	Sittwe (Myanmar)	India–Myanmar
MM	158	Sittwe (Myanmar)	Paletwa (Myanmar)	Myanmar
Transport Project	210	Paletwa (Myanmar)	Zorinpuri (India)	Myanmar–India
BCIM-EC	2,800	Kolkata (India)	Kunming (China)	India Bangladesh Myanmar–China

The *raison d'etre* for Acting East through the NE is significant for the following reasons:

(i)   First, Myanmar shares a ~1,600-km border with four NE Indian states: Arunachal Pradesh, Nagaland, Manipur, and Mizoram. There are close connections between people living on both sides of the border.

(ii) Second, Myanmar is crucial for New Delhi's connectivity initiatives in the region, specifically through the IMT highway, which is expected to be completed by 2020. The KMMTTP is another connectivity project to achieve better linkage with NER through Myanmar.

(iii) Third, there is tremendous scope for energy cooperation, given Myanmar's substantial reserves of potential hydropower and natural gas, in addition to its critical location as a gas pipeline corridor. The analysis in a report published by the Economic Research Institute for ASEAN and East Asia (ERIA) suggests that the benefits of greater energy market integration far outweigh the costs, especially since the benefits of economic development will spread to isolated areas of the NER. This will require cooperation at the sub-regional level (Anbumozhi *et al.*, ERIA, 2019).

(iv) Fourth, the opening of these land border crossings will aid the growth of trade and tourism in NE India and Myanmar. Both NER and Myanmar are replete with nature's bounty to be explored by the keen traveler. With Bangladesh, India has 26 Land Customs stations in the NE, of which 20 are functional. With Myanmar, two border crossings were opened in 2018, as stated earlier (De *et al.*, 2018).

(v) Fifth, this will help in the growth of medical tourism in the Northeastern states of the country. Manipur, especially Imphal, is being developed as a hub for medical tourism and it already attracts several patients from Myanmar for affordable treatment. Those who can afford higher costs prefer to travel to Bangkok because of the dearth of air connectivity with India. This was shared by Professor Khin Maung Nyo from Yangon with the author.[3]

(vi) Finally, the opening of these land routes is facilitating educational exchanges. It is enabling students, journalists, and research scholars to travel by road to each other's country and be enriched by their experiences. Moreover, the Myanmar Institute of Information Technology, in Mandalay, which was established in 2015 with India's support has faculty from India. This is a very popular institute for students from Myanmar.[4]

(vii) NER is in an advantageous position to help provide educated and trained manpower to Thailand and Myanmar like nurses, medical staff, and English teachers for schools.

Myanmar is India's land bridge to ASEAN, and hence, closer connectivity with Myanmar is *sine qua non* for the success of India's "Act-East Policy" (Borah, 2018).

6.5 Issues and Challenges

Although there exist several opportunities and possibilities for greater convergence of the NER with Myanmar and beyond to Thailand, in the

---

[3] Interview of Professor Khin Maung Nyo, Yangon, May 1, 2019
[4] Established in 2015, Myanmar Institute of Information Technology (MIIT) is an initiative under the friendship project between the Government of the Republic of the Union of Myanmar and the Government of the Republic of India. From https://www.miit.edu.mm/.

continental landscape, there are several challenges which must be addressed too. The most serious ones relate to security issues.

(1) The entire region in Western Myanmar bordering India and Bangladesh also faces new challenges, posed by the hundreds of insurgents of the "Arakan Army", who are moving into areas along Myanmar's borders with Mizoram and Manipur. The armies of India and Myanmar are mounting coordinated operations to deal with this threat. This area is of particular importance to India (Parthasarthy, 2019).

(2) The quantum and composition of border trade with Myanmar through Moreh/Tamu is of rising concern. In the past, when India and Myanmar allowed barter trade of up to $20,000 per transaction, there was a semblance of official statistics about the size of the informal trade. But with India switching to the formal trade regime, it's now free-for-all. According to Khin Maung Tin, Secretary-General of the Border Trade Chamber of Commerce at Tamu in Myanmar, over 300 shops at Namphalong sell goods worth over ₹2 crore to Indian buyers daily. Myanmarese buy roughly ₹50 lakh worth goods from India. Drugs and smuggling of gold continue, even as insurgency activities are somewhat controlled due to the combined actions of the Myanmar army and Indian forces. Moreover, without a doubt, the informal trade at Namphalong is a smokescreen for various illegal activities (Bose, 2018). This was also reiterated by India's former ambassador to Myanmar, Gautam Mukhopadhyay, at an RIS Seminar on May 27, 2019. It was also confirmed that Myanmar–China border trade is at least 10 times that which Myanmar has with India.

(3) The China factor is also impacting the development of our corridors for connectivity. In recent days, the Arakan Army, which has close links with China through the Kachin Independence Army, attacked Myanmar workers engaged in the construction of the Kaladan Corridor. China is not comfortable at the prospect of the Indian built port of Sittwe being located near to its economic corridor. China's larger strategic aim is to secure the unchallenged use of Myanmar's territory for access to the Bay of Bengal and the Indian Ocean (*Ibid.*).

(4) NER is becoming a conduit for the movement of drugs from Myanmar to Bangladesh. Consignments confiscated in the last 3 years reveal

that two routes are active in India's NE that transport a synthetic drug, known as Yaba, from Myanmar to Bangladesh. More prolific is the route through Mizoram originating at Champhai, which leads to different locations on the India–Bangladesh border (Bhattacharya, 2019).

(5) The lack of development of the NER and its neglect for several years have limited the region's capacity for realizing its potential in several secondary and tertiary sectors. The NER does not have the same level of economic development as the rest of the country. The people of the region often do not have access to basic social and infrastructure services. Moreover, the region suffers from several inadequacies, such as availability of electricity, physical infrastructure, and interstate and intrastate connectivity (road, telecommunications, railways, etc.) (De and Singh, 2018, p. 262).

(6) The literacy rate in the region is high, but there is also a high rate of unemployment and underemployment. The incidence of poverty in the region is high, and the official income poverty measure does not accurately reflect the deprivation (De *et al.*, 2018, p. 25).

(7) In terms of its investment potential, it has been seen that Assam, the largest state of NER, has slipped in its rankings from 19 to 17 (NCAER, SIPI Report, 2018). There is huge potential for the state to reap benefits through food processing, organic farming, and pharmaceuticals, as has been articulated in the state government's report. This has also been emphasized by a Thai Professor, Chayan Vaddhanuputi, in an interview to the author in Chiang Mai on May 23, 2018, when he spoke of the huge potential of collaborative ventures in food processing between NE India and Northern Thailand. In his words, "Despite the brotherhood between the Tais in India and the Tais in Thailand, there is virtually no trading relation".[5]

(8) Although the distance between NE India and the Thai border is about 1,400 km, there are several trade and investment bottlenecks. There is a need for greater coordination between the central and the local administration, which often causes uncertainty among the business

---

[5]Chayan Vaddhanuputi, Professor in Chiang Mai University, in an interview to the author in Chiang Mai on May 23, 2018.

sectors in both countries. In addition, poor infrastructure, red tape, bureaucracy, and insufficient information hamper ties between India's NER and Thailand (Chirathivath, 2010, p. 189).

6.6 China's Strategic Manoeuvres: Is There a Way Forward for India?

Myanmar is considered as an important land and sea bridge for India to Act East. This was reiterated during the visit of India's President Kovind in December 2018, when an MoU was signed on "the Kaladan Multi Modal Transit Transport Project" for appointing a port operator, which would enable the Sittwe Port and Paletwa IWT infrastructure to be used commercially.

Another project, which India had considered, a few years ago, was investing in a deep-sea port, i.e., Dawei Port in Southern Myanmar. However, at present, the $8 billion project is being developed jointly by Myanmar and Thailand. "The Dawei deep sea port, when complete, will provide India an alternative sea route to Southeast Asia and reduce dependency on the congested Strait of Malacca and cut transport time", according to an official. The Dawei Port is part of the Southern corridor of the Mekong India Economic Corridor (MIEC). India is concentrating on the Southern Economic Corridor, which would connect Ho Chi Minh City in Vietnam, Phnom Penh in Cambodia, and Bangkok in Thailand, to Dawei in Myanmar. "When Dawei port is ready, India is planning to connect it with Chennai. There will be no need to go through the Strait of Malacca then", said the official, unwilling to be named (Narayan, 2013).

Thailand has time and again approached India for joint development of the port. This was articulated to the author by Mr. Apirat Sugondhabhirom, Minister and Deputy Chief of Mission of the Royal Thai Embassy in New Delhi.[6] However, New Delhi has not shown much interest in the project. Experts in India do believe that India must invest in the Dawei project and also work on the Chennai–Dawei corridor (Gupta, 2013).

---

[6]Interview to the author at the Thai Embassy in New Delhi in May 2018 of Mr. Apirat Sugondhabhirom, Minister and Deputy Chief of Mission of the Royal Thai Embassy in New Delhi.

India is not keen (for obvious reasons) to join the North–South corridor in the Greater Mekong sub-region linking cities of the Mekong basin countries — Cambodia, Laos, Myanmar, Thailand, and Vietnam — to China. The fact that this corridor cuts across to China is the reason India is not very keen to join it.

Here, it is of significance to note that China's port-building activity in India's neighborhood, especially the Kyaukpyu Port, has been causing concern. Though the total China–Myanmar investment in this project has been scaled down to US$1.3 billion (initial phase) from the earlier US$7 billion figure, the port will be of great strategic significance to China as it navigates its way into the Bay of Bengal — and the Indian Ocean — considered within New Delhi's range of influence (Patranobis, 2018). Located on the Western coast of Myanmar in Rakhine state, part of a special economic zone (SEZ), the port when developed will not be far away from a submarine base India is developing on its East coast, close to Vishakhapatnam.

With Suu Kyi having been appointed in December 2018, chairperson of a Myanmar Government steering committee tasked with implementing the establishment of the Myanmar China Economic Corridor (MCEC), a venture under China's Belt and Road Initiative (BRI), i.e., the stalled Myitsone Dam project, may also see the light of the day (Lintner, 2019). There is no doubt, however, that there is tremendous opposition to the Dam project as 90% of the energy generated would be for China. India, of course, is watching this project to understand Myanmar's strategic priorities.

India must enhance its partnership with Myanmar, not only in areas outlined above but also in the field of Blue Economy. This would help to strengthen maritime safety at the operational level and help realize the vision of Security and Growth for All in the Region (SAGAR). Despite, the vast maritime domain of the Bay of Bengal, the resources have remained untapped for a long time span. Bangladesh is also an important partner. Public and private partnership is important to move the Blue Economy forward — from research to design, deployment, and operation. For Southeast Asian countries, the importance of protecting marine resources and strengthening regional ocean governance mechanisms to leverage and promote the Blue Economy in large marine ecosystems is not lost.

Given China's port-building activities in the Indian Ocean, India has boosted its military presence in the Indian Ocean. One such initiative was taken on January 24, 2019, with the commissioning of a full-fledged naval base, the Indian Naval Ship Kohassa, on North Andaman Island. The base, commissioned by Admiral Sunil Lanba, chief of the naval staff, is the fourth military airfield in the Andaman and Nicobar archipelago (the Andaman). The 572-island archipelago dominates the Malacca Strait that links the Indian Ocean with the South China Sea. PM Modi also stressed on the importance of India's Neighborhood First Policy and SAGAR, during his visit in June 2019 to Sri Lanka and Maldives.

Some pressing and urgent issues in India Myanmar relations are reiterated here as follows:

(1) To ensure that the trading environment is secure for safe trade, Myanmar–India cooperation is essential to tackle the threats of piracy, terrorism, as well as trafficking. This is in addition to cooperation in times of natural disasters. Speaking at the inauguration of the 3rd EAS Conference on Maritime Security and Co-operation held in Bhubaneswar, Odisha in June 2018, India's Union Minister for Oil and Natural Gas, Dharmendra Pradhan articulated that East Asian countries should work in unison to tackle the insecurities associated with maritime terrorism and crimes including trafficking of humans and drugs.

(2) It is also well known that illegal activities such as extraction of jade, gold, and timber have been going on near the China–Myanmar border. However, given that the Chinese now desire to be seen as peace-makers in the region, this could be an opportunity for India to stabilize the political situation on its side of the borders with Myanmar (Barany, 152).

(3) For India's connectivity by air with Myanmar, India already has a near-open sky arrangement. The Guwahati airport is being revamped for better access of SEA with India in the Northeastern states. Assam is also playing a critical role in the linkages and tourism for wellness and heritage and other reasons must be developed. Closer ASEAN–India air links will promote tourism and trade and enhance greater connectivity between ASEAN and India. However, India's air

connectivity with the major cities in Myanmar needs an urgent response from the government. In September 2019, as expected, daily flights have been resumed from Kolkata to Yangon.

(4) India's soft power outreach through initiatives in education and health as well as cultural and religious bonding is well recognized and appreciated in Myanmar. This was shared with the author by Professors Khin Maung Nyo and Khin Maung Soe. Although India does not intervene in the Rohingya issue, it hopes for the safe repatriation of the Rohingya refugees. Given that India had signed an agreement in 2017, under which it is obliged to spend $25 million over 5 years, India in 2019, handed over 250 completed pre-fabricated homes to the Myanmar Government for use by the refugees upon their return.

6.7 Conclusion

In conclusion, it can be confirmed that for India to truly reaffirm its position in the Asian region, it must continue and further strengthen cooperation with Myanmar and Thailand. Leveraging the potential of India's economic and strategic relationship with these three countries has the power to change the economy of NE India and also advance India's Act East vision.

However, the NER itself is a resource-rich region, whose vast potential remains largely untapped. The 2019 budget increase of almost 25% from the previous year to over ₹50,000 crores for NER will help to boost the much-needed infrastructure. This is the highest ever increase that the region has received. Moreover, an integrated Northeastern economy is in the country's interest.

NER itself is a resource-rich region, whose vast potential remains largely untapped. The region's pace of development has been constrained for several decades due to apprehensions of inroads by China. As reports suggest, there is some activity by China in the NE. To quote a state-run Xinhua News Agency, "India's Northeastern states — which also include Manipur, Mizoram, Meghalaya, and Nagaland are said to be the country's most neglected region". Through this sudden reference to the NE, even though in a report focusing on the elections in the region, Beijing appeared to remind New Delhi that the NE will continue to be in China's lens.

In the past years, a handful of reports in Indian and Myanmar media quoting unidentified Indian Government sources have directed attention to possible Chinese attempts to facilitate a revival of insurgency in the NE. These reports elaborate a range of short- and long-term objectives that China could be focusing on. These include providing active help to insurgents to carry out attacks on the security forces, setting up a united NE insurgent front as well as assisting the formation of a NE government-in-exile (Routray, 2017).

The Japanese have shown great interest in investing in India's NE. As stated by Kenji Hiramatsu, the Japanese Ambassador to India, while addressing the 3rd Cherry Blossom festival in Meghalaya, "We aim to support the development of this region by connecting not only the intra-regional links within the NE but also the links between the NE and neighboring countries such as Bangladesh and Myanmar", he said.

Moreover, in terms of peace and security cooperation, India's bilateral ties with these countries must be further strengthened, not only to keep terrorism at bay but also to prevent third-country intervention in subversive activities including smuggling and trafficking. These partners are key for India to expand its footprint, even as China seeks out a larger sphere of influence for itself. India–Bangladesh relations have received a fillip with the re-election of Prime Minister Sheikh Hasina, with Myanmar, the visit of the Indian President reaffirmed India's constant support both in terms of socio-economic projects as well as in terms of connectivity by land, air, and sea. Thailand, in 2019, has taken over the chair position of ASEAN and is a significant country for furthering its ties through culture, economics, and strategic affairs.

Bangladesh, Thailand, Myanmar, and India are all members of BIMSTEC, which has been reinvigorated, especially since 2018, with the Summit meeting and the military exercises in Pune, India. India–ASEAN ties have also witnessed a momentum in 2018 with several meetings, consultations, and decisions being conducted to take the partnership forward. As India seeks rules-based partnerships and maritime cooperation, much more remains to be done if we are to achieve our vision of shared values and common destiny through bilateral engagement with these countries within the multilateral forums (Marwah, 2019). With RCEP negotiations still ongoing, it is evident then that the bilateral relationship must not be sacrificed for the multilateral. Moreover, as India seeks to build a Bay of Bengal community as well as position itself as an Indo-Pacific power, maritime cooperation with these three countries bilaterally assumes its own significance.

ASEAN countries, if united, can effectively succeed in leveraging their position, even as China and USA vie for influence. Together, ASEAN and India can contribute immensely in shaping the regional architecture. India is seen as a benign power by SEA, and most countries are keen to expand strategic ties for a safe, secure, and peaceful environment, which is conducive for development.

Chapter 7

India–Thailand Connectivity Initiatives: Strategic Underpinnings

Adam Smith realized back in the 18th century,

Good roads, canals, and navigable rivers, by reducing the cost of carriage, put the remote parts of the country almost at a level with those in the neighborhood of the town. They are hence the greatest of all improvements.

These words hold even today. A study by the Asian Development Bank (ADB) and the Asian Development Bank Institute (ADBI) showed that improved physical connectivity fosters closer economic ties between South Asia and Southeast Asia.

7.1 The Context

India needs to rebrand itself and position itself as a significant player in galvanizing the Asian century. China, through its connectivity projects within the ambit of the Belt and Road Initiative, is building railway lines, roads, and ports at an unprecedented pace. India is also working on corridors of growth such as the Asia–Africa Growth Corridor (Japan, Indonesia, and African countries) and the Quad countries (USA, India, Japan, and Australia), in addition to projecting itself as the nucleus of the Indo-Pacific. For India to expand beyond the subcontinent and from being a sub-regional power to a global power in global politics, it must also prioritize its projects of connectivity. Connectivity is the new "Great Game", and forging of both continental and maritime connectivity between India and the ASEAN is a key priority area envisaged by the India–ASEAN multilateral partnership. Both India and ASEAN countries are connected through land and sea with a rich history of maritime trade (Moudgil, 2018). It is essential to revive and reinvigorate those old links as the driving force of Asia's naval resurgence. Improving connectivity is, therefore, imperative for the region's prosperity, continued growth, and reliability. India–ASEAN connectivity can become the main driver for lower trade costs, improved industrial transport, increased trade and investments, new production technology, and as a platform for vast opportunities deepening the regional integration process.

"Connectivity is the pathway to shared prosperity". These words were stated by PM Narendra Modi during the 13th ASEAN–India Summit held in Kuala Lumpur, Malaysia, in 2015. However, for India to take an ascendant position in Asia, it must assign greater importance to fast-tracking projects of national and geostrategic importance. The role of the State is vital to surmount the connectivity challenge. Physical connectivity through India's Northeast is the path for enhancing trade and commerce with SEA.

While India underlines the importance of its connectivity projects through the Northeast states with Myanmar and further Eastwards to Thailand, there are several issues which have to be addressed. This chapter focuses on the connectivity projects, including those by land and sea and will also highlight several endogenous and exogenous factors/issues which have impeded the progress of these major projects.

Undoubtedly, for India to truly Act East, India must invigorate the delivery of its infrastructure projects and it is the State which must provide the impetus.

7.2 It's All about Connectivity for Strategic Influence

The buzzword in Asia is connectivity: for forging people-to-people links, for infrastructure development, for strategic influence, and for generating opportunities for trade and investment. Ultimately, the goal is enhanced growth, development, and shared prosperity! Hence, both India and China are engaged in their trajectories to achieve enhanced connectivity with the ASEAN as well as other growing regions as Africa.

The focus here is on India's connectivity projects with Thailand, as a gateway to the ASEAN, in the backdrop of China's expanding footprint in the continental and maritime spheres. It is evident then that enhanced ASEAN–India land and sea connectivity will not only help realize the capacity of multilateral cooperation but can also help to eliminate constrictions and bottlenecks to development. Though shipping is considered to be the mainstay of ASEAN–India trade, without well-developed maritime connectivity devoid of constrictions and bottlenecks, optimum utilization of regional free trade and cooperation agreements will be rendered useless. Studies show that construction of road, rail, and ports will bring development and increase prosperity in and with India's neighborhood (*Ibid.*).

In 2010, the Act East vision got its first kick-start on connecting the NER with the release of the Master Plan on ASEAN Connectivity, which was adopted at the 17th ASEAN Summit. It was aimed at building physical infrastructure to bring India closer to ASEAN countries. Initiatives by India to connect with Southeast Asia include the India–Myanmar–Thailand Trilateral Highway, the Kaladan Multi Modal Transit Transport Project, and the Mekong–India Corridor — an initiative of India to connect with the CMLV (Cambodia, Myanmar, Laos, and Vietnam,) countries which is also referred to as the Mekong Ganga Cooperation (MGC) initiative.

7.3 Connectivity Projects

India hosted the ASEAN–India Connectivity Summit (AICS) on December 11 and 12, 2017, with the theme of "Powering Digital and Physical Linkages for Asia in the 21st Century".

This summit was held a month after the 15th ASEAN–India Summit, in which connectivity was one of the major issues for discussion. India is the third country after Japan and China to initiate a dedicated meeting with the ASEAN Connectivity Coordinating Committee (ACCC). The purpose of this mechanism on connectivity between ASEAN and India has been to explore possibilities as well as the ways to support the Master

Plan on ASEAN Connectivity (MPAC), and physically connect it with India (Desai, 2017). The major projects include those by road, railways, air, and sea. The ones discussed in detail here include the following:

a.　India–Myanmar–Thailand Trilateral highway;
b.　Kaladan Multi Modal Transit Transport Project.

(a) India–Myanmar–Thailand Trilateral Highway

It was at the Trilateral Ministerial Meeting on the subject of Transport Linkages in Yangon, in April 2002, that the idea of a trilateral highway from Moreh in India to Mae Sot in Thailand through Myanmar was conceived, and it is at present an essential component of India's AEP. The IMT route is shown in Figure 7.1.

With a total length of 1,360 km, the IMT Highway will link Moreh via Imphal in Manipur, India, to Mae Sot in Thailand via Myanmar. The route would be from Moreh (India) to locations of Tamu, Kalewa, Yagyi, Monywa, Mandalay, Meiktila, Nay Pyi Taw, Payagyi, Theinzayat, Thaton, Hpa'an, Kawkareik, and Myawaddy in Myanmar, further linking to Mae Sot in Thailand. The 25.6-km long Myawaddy–Thinggan

Figure 7.1:　The IMT Highway

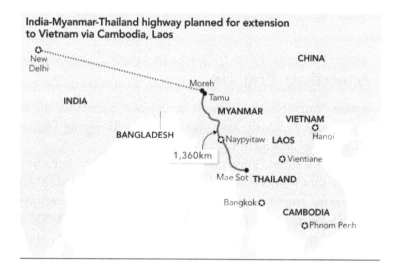

Nyenaung–Kawkareik section of the IMT Highway was put into service in July 2015, reducing travel time between Thinggan Nyenaung and Kawkareik by about 3 hours. This section also forms part of the East–West Economic Corridor of the Greater Mekong Subregion (Katoch, 2017).

IMT and Synergy with Thailand and CLMV countries: At the Third India–CLMV Conclave, in January 2016, India's Commerce Minister, Nirmala Sitharaman, had stressed the significance of connectivity between India and CLMV countries in sync with the Mekong–Ganga Cooperation Process. The IMT Highway will, as expected, facilitate trade, commerce, and other economic activities including tourism. It not only links India to Thailand in Southeast Asia but also provides for greater integration with Myanmar with whom India has had cultural, historical, ethnic, and religious ties.

Progress of IMT: The IMT highway starts from Moreh in Manipur on the India–Myanmar border and runs via Tamu (Myanmar) to Mae Sot (the Border Roads Organisation has completed 130 km connecting Moreh/Tamu to Kalewa). The project required about 78 km of new roads and the upgrading of an existing 400 km of roads. In Phase 1, India has the responsibility of building 78 km of missing links, upgrading 58 km of existing roads, and possibly improving a further 132 km. Most of this work has been completed. Thailand has taken on the responsibility of upgrading a total of 192 km in this phase and another 100 km under Phase 2.

The India–Myanmar Friendship Road, built with Indian Government assistance, running from the border at Tamu/Moreh to Kalemyo and Kalewa, was inaugurated in 2001. This road, which is the first segment of the IMT Highway, was resurfaced and handed over to the Myanmar Government in 2009. Though the road has benefited transportation between Tamu and Kalewa in Myanmar's Sagaing region (bordering India), traffic remains low because of poor road conditions from Kalewa to Mandalay, Myanmar's second largest city. However, since the end of 2018 and 2019, it was seen that from Imphal to Mandalay, there is now an increasing interest especially among NE residents to travel to Myanmar by road.

Timeline revised: The 1,360-km IMT highway was initially scheduled to be completed by 2015.

However, the work on the 69 missing links (bridges) is continuing as stated by India's Consul General in Mandalay, Mr. Bhaisora. On a visit to Myanmar in May 2019, it was learned that a new contractor has yet to be appointed by the Indian Government for completing the work (there was an issue with the previous contractor).[1] According to an official from India's Ministry of External Affairs, the completion of the project is now expected by 2020.[2]

(b) Motor Vehicles Act: Negotiations continuing

India, Myanmar, and Thailand need to hasten negotiations on a motor vehicles act and legal infrastructure before the scheduled completion of the trilateral highway so that there are no impediments to the route being opened for business.

This was articulated by the Thai Ambassador to India, H.E. Mr. Chutintorn Gongsakdi, "The nearly 1,400-km trilateral highway will boost trade in Southeast Asia and is an integral part of India's 'Act East' policy".

He suggested, (in an interview to the *Hindustan Times* in December 2018), that India, Myanmar, and Thailand address pending issues — including the motor vehicles agreement, domestic ownership caps on transportation firms, routes, customs, immigration, and quarantine — in their negotiations. "Those are some issues that require to be resolved through discussions. They are not unsolvable, they can be solved, but it requires sitting down and ironing out properly", H.E. Gongsakdi said.

Why the concern? The Thai Ambassador's concerns about the MVA stem from the fact that global transportation and logistics majors have a presence in India. India needs to engage with the Thai trucking industry which has reservations about the MVA and the Trilateral Highway. H.E. Gongsakdi expressed concerns about the "liberal" provisions in India that allow 100% foreign investment in the transport service sector. Thailand is concerned that Indian transportation firms may "wipe out" its industries because it has "no limit" on foreign ownership. Thailand would permit

---

[1] Interview of Mr. Nandan Singh Bhaisora by the author on May 28, 2019, at Mandalay.
[2] Preeti Saran, India–ASEAN Investment Summit, January 2018.

mobility to only domestically owned transport companies of the participating countries. This would protect the local players. In his words, "We are concerned in negotiating the motor vehicles agreement that if we don't set a limit that companies which participate in this agreement have to be 51% Indian, then these multinational logistics companies could wipe out our small logistics companies". There needs to be an agreement on the routes to be made available to the transport firms and issues such as whether trucks from Myanmar and Thailand will be allowed to come up to New Delhi. "Those things are the nitty gritty, though most of the media attention is on the completion. The legal infrastructure is also important, and we can work on this now. We don't have to wait until the road is completed", H.E. Gongsakdi said (Dutta and Laskar, 2018). It is believed that India's Ministries of External Affairs and Home Affairs are playing a key role in negotiating the protocol on the movement of goods and passengers. The Asian Development Bank (ADB), which is funding the project, is also keen to see this issue resolved. India is expected to handle issues through its External Affairs Ministry and the Home Ministry.

7.4 Imphal–Mandalay Bus Service

A project that was initiated in 2003 is a bus service between Imphal and Mandalay. India and Myanmar finally agreed to launch the service, covering a distance of 579 km, in 2012. A trial run of the bus was held on December 9, 2015.

2018: Moreh to Mandalay in 12 hours: The bus service has been available since 2018. The author met a group of 21 students, who had traveled with their professors from Imphal's Manipur University to Mandalay by bus. The total journey took about 12 hours. The students and faculty reported that their travel by bus was comfortable. Such exchanges have brought great momentum and vigor to India–Myanmar people-to-people exchanges. It has been notified and also experienced by the author herself that the road and transport infrastructure are reasonably well developed in Myanmar as she undertook a road trip from Mandalay to Yangon on May 30, 2019, covering a distance of 650 km in about 9 hours.

7.4.1 *India–Myanmar Kaladan Multi Modal Transit Transport Project (KMMTTP)*

Another major connectivity project is the Kaladan Multi Modal Transport Project. This project was initiated by the Indian Government in 2008 and is entirely funded by India. The purpose is to seek an alternative route through Myanmar for the transportation of goods to the Northeast region of India. This will connect Kolkata to Sittwe Port in Myanmar by sea (539 km), and link further to Paletwa jetty by Kaladan River (158 km) (see Figure 7.2). The road link from Paletwa to the Indo-Myanmar border is 110 km, and the road connecting the Indo-Myanmar border to Lawangtlai in Mizoram is 100 km. The road will continue further to Dabaka in Assam a distance of 850 km.

A road is also planned to connect Paletwa in Myanmar to Zorinpui on the India–Myanmar border. Alongside this initiative, India has contributed to building a sea link via Sittwe Port in Myanmar to enable an alternative transit route through Bangladesh. The port, which links India and Myanmar, was built by India to dock ships with a displacement of up to 20,000 tonnes. Ships with a displacement between 3,000 and 4,000 tonnes can be plied between Sittwe and Paletwa which is in the Chin State. The goods can then be carried via Paletwa to Northwest India by truck.

Figure 7.2:   Kaladan Multi Modal Transit Transport Project

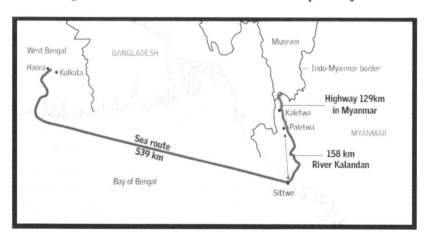

The project connects the people of Rakhine State with India. At one time, trade between India and Rakhine was vibrant with goods shipped between Sittwe and Kolkata. It is evident that the port would once again help to provide a fillip to the movement of cargo by both sea and road.

Progress of KMMTTP

In October 2015, the government revised the budget estimates by nearly six times to ₹2,904 crore and the State-owned Ircon Infrastructure and Services Ltd was appointed as a consultant to complete the project in 2019. The government also approved a revised cost estimate of 2.9 billion rupees (about US$450 million) for the project, under which it has built a deep water port at Sittwe. In 2016, the project was tendered twice but without success. It is believed that the stalled work was recommenced in early 2017 as the project was awarded to a Delhi-based firm C & C Constructions. This project is the one and only biggest development work undertaken by India in a foreign country. According to the Indian Ambassador, Mr. Vikram Misri, work on a 109-km road linking a terminal on the Kaladan River at Paletwa in Rakhine with Zorinpui on the Mizoram border was held up due to "some approvals" from the Myanmar side. India awarded a contract to build the road in June 2017 and work was due to have begun in October 2017. The prolonged delay in completing the road had affected the viability of the port at Sittwe (which was completed by India in early 2016 and had a 6-m assured draft). The port was handed over to the local government under the terms of the bilateral agreement on the project. In April 2017, the Sittwe Port and IWT Paletwa jetty were ready and operational and in June 2017, i.e., barely three months later, India handed six gas tanker cargo vessels worth US$81.29 million to the Myanmar Government to transport gas to Northeast India via Manipur.

India and Myanmar signed an MoU on October 29, 2018, to appoint a private Port Operator for the operation and maintenance of Sittwe Port, Paletwa Inland Water Terminal, and associated facilities included in the Kaladan Multi Modal Transit Transport Project in implementation of India's Act East Policy. Following this MoU, the process of identifying bidders to maintain these facilities will be initiated by floating a Request for Proposal (RFP). Once the port operations commence, it would offer new infrastructure for trade including between India and Myanmar, thereby contributing to job creation and development in the whole region, particularly in the Rakhine and Chin States of Myanmar.

7.5 Key Issues

(a) **Inordinate delay:** "Almost two years down the line, the port has lost its navigability as the draft is down to barely one meter", Business Line stated. "Sources in both India and Myanmar blame it on prolonged disuse and failure on the part of Myanmar to continue dredging activities", it said. "As a corrective measure, India is now trying to amend the agreement to bring the port under joint operations" (Bose, 2018).

(b) **Ethnic Conflicts in the Rakhine State, Myanmar:** The prolonged ethnic conflicts, i.e., the Rohingya issue in Rakhine State where the port is located, have affected smooth implementation of the project. The trust deficit between the center at Nay Pyi Taw and the peripheries has also created problems. Local rights groups, for instance, have alleged forced displacement and unfair compensation during the upgrading of the 66-km Karaweik to Eindu road in the Kayin State of Myanmar, for which the Asian Development Bank (ADB) approved a $100 million loan as part of the Greater Mekong Subregion East–West Corridor (Katoch, 2012).

(c) **The unofficial "China" factor:** Private actors within China and outside official control also contribute to conflict, including illicit cross-border trade and mercenary services. It is mostly illegal Chinese people that usurp Myanmar's natural resources often colluding with corrupt officials in the Myanmar Government, military, and others to fuel conflict in Kachin and Shan States. As a result, Chinese business actors provide revenue to conflict actors on both sides and help sustain Myanmar's civil war (USIP SSG Report 2018, No. 1).

This fact was highlighted in an interview with the author by Mr. Khin Maung Soe, in Mandalay in May 2019.[3]

---

[3] Interview of Mr. Khin Maung Soe in Mandalay on May 27, 2019.

(d) **Security of workers:** There have also been instances in recent days when the Arakan Army, which has close links with China through the Kachin Independence Army, has attacked Myanmar workers engaged in the construction of the Kaladan Corridor. China is not comfortable with the prospect of an Indian-built port being located near its economic corridor. China's larger strategic aim is to secure the unchallenged use of Myanmar's territory for access to the Bay of Bengal and the Indian Ocean (Parthasarthy, 2019).

(e) **Narcotics trade:** It is well known that the border area between Thailand, Myanmar, and Laos, the Golden Triangle, with weak borders is a drug smugglers' delight. Despite overall poppy cultivation having declined in Myanmar, the rise of conflicts has resulted in expanding narcotics trade. According to Tun Nay Soe, United Nations Office on Drugs and Crime (UNODC) program coordinator for East Asia, an estimated 90% of heroin produced in Myanmar ends up in China, with the remaining 10% going to other countries in Southeast Asia. This presents a huge challenge for India.

The above issues highlight the many endogenous and exogenous factors impacting the viability of the Sittwe Port.

7.6 Strategic Engagement: Highways and Corridors

The economic corridor approach emphasizes the integration of infrastructure improvement with economic opportunities such as trade and investment, and also includes efforts to address the social and other outcomes of increased connectivity (ADB, 2014, 2017).

Trade facilitation and logistics services are the main catalysts in the development of an economic corridor. A corridor helps strengthen industrial (or services) agglomeration over time through the establishment of industrial zones (or SEZs) and facilitates the cluster-type development of enterprises. As economic reforms dismantle the restrictions to cross-border trade, the cost of trade can be expected to decline with liberalization, thereby strengthening the commercial integration process. Hence, an economic corridor can be conceptualized as public capital summed over transportation networks, human resources, communication facilities, energy grids, and institutional infrastructure (De, Ghatak and Kumaraswamy, 2018).

7.6.1 *East–West and North–South Four-Lane Corridors: The Disruptions in Myanmar*

India shares a 1,643-km border with Myanmar, and it is inevitable that it seeks to deepen its engagement with Myanmar. India's decision in mid-2016 for the National Highway Authority of India (NHAI) to develop a grid of 27 East–West and North–South four-lane corridors, crisscrossing India to facilitate smooth travel, will help optimize connectivity with the IMT Highway even more. At the same time, Northeast India is also the land bridge to the Greater Mekong Subregion.

While economic cooperation with Myanmar needs to be directed mainly to Myanmar's Western region with these areas being adjacent to Northeast India, the IMT Highway passes through hotbeds of insurgencies, especially the Sagaing Division in Western Myanmar and Moreh in Chandel district of Manipur.

As stated earlier, China has been using proxy irregular forces against both Myanmar and India, lethally arming the United Wa State Army in Shan State of Myanmar and establishing the United National Liberation Front of Western Southeast Asia against India bringing nine militant organizations including The National Socialist Council of Nagaland– Khaplang, (NSCN-K) and United Liberation Front of Assam (ULFA) under a common umbrella (Katoch, 2017).

(a) China–Myanmar Communist Connection

That China has been a trusted friend of Myanmar, through Myanmar's decades of isolation, is well known. It is worthwhile to note here that China not only enjoys an edge in terms of closeness to the military junta, which it always stood by, but also signed a Memorandum of Understanding in September 2018 with Myanmar to establish the China–Myanmar Economic Corridor, which forms part of Beijing's Belt and Road Initiative (BRI). China has already constructed dual-carriage motorways connecting Kunming, the capital of Yunnan province, with towns on the Myanmar border; hence, its influence is well embedded in Myanmar. It is surprising that the Chinese Government perceives India as an economic rival in the long run.

(b) Japan and India: Trusted in Myanmar

The new National League of Democracy (NLD) Government in Myanmar together with the Modi Government can embark on a new phase of Indo-Myanmar relations through transparent and committed diplomacy, closer economic cooperation, and building the right politico-military environment. The issues that hope to be resolved are the complete demarcation of the unsettled border, and to together fight the menace of terrorism. Japanese investments in Myanmar and India's Northeast infrastructure projects would help to integrate the region, thereby helping its development. India already has a "legal assistance pact" with Myanmar and an MoU for joint border patrolling and information sharing. Optimizing on the IMT Highway and AEP has much strategic merit for India, Myanmar, Thailand, and the region as such (*Ibid.*).

With both India and Japan having interests in securing port and ocean access in Sittwe and Dawei, respectively, this has enabled Myanmar to secure beneficial agreements under the new China–Myanmar Economic Corridor (CMEC), particularly in ownership and loan finance arrangements. A good example is a recent agreement concerning the Kyaukpyu Port and Special Economic Zone. The Kyaukpyu Oil Pipeline (240,000 barrels a day with a capacity for 440,000 barrels per day) with its gas pipeline (12 billion cubic units a year) directly supplies feedstock to another, i.e., the Anning refinery which is 28 km Southwest of Kunming in China. Kyaukpyu is only one of the channels through which China's energy needs are met (Wheeler, 2018).

7.7 Maritime Connectivity: Acting East

Some of the important features of India–ASEAN maritime connectivity architecture include the following:

- First, India is committed to putting into action the Master Plan on ASEAN Connectivity (MPAC) that has been formulated by the ASEAN Connectivity Coordinating Committee (ACCC) in October 2010.

- Second, India's vision of Security and Growth for All in the Region (SAGAR) aims at connecting Indian ports (SagarMala) to transnational docks for more significant benefits to all in the region. For instance, the Asia–Africa Growth Corridor (AAGC) and Project Mausam can collectively facilitate cruise tourism between India and the ASEAN (Desai, 2017).

General V.K. Singh, as Minister of State for External Affairs, while addressing the ASEAN–India Connectivity Summit in New Delhi in December 2017 *(the author was a participant),* stated that the ASEAN and India are exploring the signing of an ASEAN–India Maritime Transport Cooperation Agreement. This initiative, according to Singh, will help to enhance cooperation and communication, eliminate barriers hindering maritime transport, and establish a regional maritime transport framework system.

Concerning Thailand, in particular, during the ASEAN–India Summit in January 2018, PM Modi in a bilateral meeting with the visiting Thai PM said, "The land frontiers of our two countries are not far apart. And we are also maritime neighbors. So, Prime Minister (Prayut Chan-o-Cha) and I have agreed to forge a closer partnership in the fields of defense and maritime cooperation. A partnership to meet our bilateral interests; and to respond to our shared regional goals. And a partnership, which will be shaped by sharing of expertise and experiences; greater staff exchanges and more exercises; Cooperation on counter-piracy on seas; Deeper engagement in naval patrolling; and Building linkages in the field of defense R&D and production".[4] In an earlier visit in June 2016, both sides agreed to work toward the completion of the negotiation for the signing of the White Shipping Agreement between the two countries (Chakraborti and Chakraborty, 2018, p. 210).

7.7.1 *Port Connectivity*

Given that ports and waterways help in the flow of merchandise trade, it is evident that this requires investment in quality infrastructure. According

---

[4] Joint Press Statement in New Delhi, June 17, 2016. From https://www.narendramodi. in/pm-modi-with-pm-of-thailand-mr-thai-pm-prayut-chan-o-cha-at-the-joint-press-statement-in-new-delhi-484563, accessed on May 10, 2019.

to the "ASEAN–India Maritime Connectivity Report" published by the AIC in 2014, in the list of top 25 ports by container volume, ASEAN countries have seven ports while India has only one. India's port infrastructure is an area of concern between the two regions. Introduction of the "SagarMala" project, through which India proposes to invest in port infrastructure for improved integration and connectivity through the seas, is an important development (Desai, 2017).

7.7.2 Maritime Connectivity: Port Infrastructure and Efficiency Hold the Key

If India is to be a maritime power, it is vital to understand the status of our ports. It has been seen that ports that the Indian Government runs have witnessed an improvement in a few of the key operational efficiency metrics such as turnaround time and berth productivity, coming in the wake of a series of benchmarking exercises initiated at these facilities.

7.7.3 Comparative Data: Indian Ports Lagging behind Asia's Major Ports

Some aspects are flagged here as follows:

a. The average ship turnaround time, measured as the time taken by a ship at a port, at India's 12 major ports has come down from 2.61 days to 2.08 days in the last 5 years (see Table 7.1). The turnaround time can be reduced by improving operations. Indian ports, however, continue to trail the turnaround time benchmarks at major global ports such as Port Klang, Singapore, and Rotterdam, where this is usually no more than a day (*Ibid.*).
b. It is worth noting that Thailand's Laem Chabang Port is the top 20th port in the world with a handling capacity of 7.227 million TEUs, i.e., 20-foot equivalent units, and has grown at a fast pace; in 10 years, its growth has been 156%, one of the highest growth rates. With another terminal D having been added, as a part of Thailand's Eastern Economic Corridor (EEC) under Thailand 4.0's efforts to modernize the economy, a new global standard of port operations is expected.

Table 7.1:   Ship Turnaround Time in Global Ports (2014)

	Time taken (days)	Number of ship calls per month (mega vessels)
Port of Kelang/Klang	0–1	1,000
Singapore	1–2	1,500
Shanghai	0–1	1,500
Yokohama	0–1	500
Hamburg	1–2	400
Rotterdam	1–2	600
Antwerp	1–2	400
Tangier	0–1	400

Source: (Merck. O/ Port benchmarking report: SA TERMINALS 2015/16) and https://seasia.co/2018/01/01/southeast-asia-s-largest-ports-in-container-handling.

This will aid the growth of container volumes at Laem Chabang Port, adding the much-needed capacity by 3.5 million TEU. (Malaysia has two ports in the top 20, while China has nine. In contrast, no Indian port is yet among the top 20. However, India does have two ports. JNPT at 33rd and Mundra at 45th positions in the top 50 ports.)[5]

From Table 7.2, it is evident that there has been a significant improvement in the handling capacity of Indian ports. While port capacity has increased by 50% over the period 2012–2017, average output per ship berth day has also increased by about 20%.

Trade volumes and decreased costs depend on port efficiency and connectivity. India has a long coastline of over 7,500 km with 12 major and about 205 notified non-major ports. Around 90% of the country's trade by volume and 70% by value was moved through maritime transport. With a substantial focus on capacity enhancement and infrastructure development, in 2017–2018, the cargo traffic handled at major ports was 679.36 MT, an increase of 5% from 2016 to 2017.

---

[5] https://seasia.co/2018/01/01/southeast-asia-s-largest-ports-in-container-handling.

Table 7.2: India's Major Ports — Handling Capacity

The metrics — India

Unit	At the beginning of the 12th plan (March 31, 2012)	2015–2016	2016–2017 (on January 31, 2017)
Port capacity (MTPA)	696.53	965.00	1049.45
Cargo traffic (MT)	560.14	606.47	535.35
Av turnaround time (days)	2.61	2.04	2.08
Av output/ship berth day (tonnes)	11,112.00	13584.00	14478.30

Source: Ministry of Shipping, Govt. of India.

Port-led development has been given a big push with the SagarMala project, involving an investment of US$14.06 billion covering 142 port projects. In India, the 12 major ports handle ~57% of total cargo traffic (DIPP, 2018). However, despite improvements, lower operational efficiency has traditionally impacted the ports' ability to utilize efficiently existing infrastructure and caused them to lose significant market share to more efficient ports such as Colombo and Singapore. Besides, less-than-optimal operations at ports impact the country's trade competitiveness. Currently, nearly 25% of India's cargo containers (amounting to 3 million 20-foot equivalent units or TEUs) are presently trans-shipped in ports outside India, mainly at Colombo, Singapore, Port Klang, and Jebel Ali.

According to a World Bank report on the operational efficiency of infrastructural facilities, India's current port capacity can be boosted by at least 35% (Sasi, 2017).

7.8 Port Connectivity and Short Sea Shipping: A Boost to India's AEP

India's Chennai Port, as well as other ports, have been beefed up to boost India's SagarMala project that encourages coastal shipping. Short sea shipping in the Bay of Bengal is embedded in India's Act East Policy

(AEP), and this helps in deepening economic linkages through maritime connectivity with ASEAN countries. It is well known that for robust and dynamic trade in any region, three important physical factors are at play: ships, ports, and cargo.

Among the many container terminuses in the Bay of Bengal, Chennai Port can handle fifth-generation (5,000–8,000 TEUs) container vessels, and several shipping lines make direct calls. In early 2017, a direct container shipping service from Chennai to the East Coast of USA was launched, which would result in voyage savings of 10 days. However, the other three major container terminuses — Kolkata, Chittagong, and Yangon — can handle limited container cargo due to limitations of being river ports, and as ships must travel up the river, this adds to travel time and costs (Sakhuja, 2017).

In the absence of any major container port, regional trade is intimately connected to Singapore, Port Kelang, Tanjung Pelepas, and Colombo, which have been labeled as global standard trans-shipment hubs and handle ships carrying 6,500 TEU to 12,000 TEU. In effect, every container entering or leaving the Bay of Bengal must be loaded/ unloaded at least once before it reaches any destination outside the Bay. For instance, nearly 70% of containers from Chennai are shipped on board feeder ships to trans-shipment hubs, and Colombo is a popular destination for Chennai.

Besides, there are geographic realities that the region must contend with, given that the major shipping route from the Indian Ocean to the Pacific through the Straits of Malacca is nearly 1,500 nautical miles. What emerges is the fact that intra-regional trade in the Bay of Bengal is low, which presents principal challenges for regional connectivity. A prime weakness is that the maritime infrastructure in the Bay of Bengal is inefficient. For instance, the ports of Chennai and Chittagong are bigger than the port of Penang in Malaysia, but the volume of cargo handled by this port is much larger. There is a need to enhance capacity utilization of the ports in the Bay of Bengal through the cooperation of India, Myanmar, and Bangladesh. This will enable them to be competitive. New deep water ports at Haldia, Chittagong, Dawei, Kyaukpyu, and Hambantota can add to maritime connectivity in the region, with a few caveats discussed below.

7.9 Ports for Connectivity or Collusion: The China Conundrum

Strategic navigations of China in the Bay of Bengal impact India's strategic interests of achieving port connectivity. Kyaukpyu in Myanmar is not far from the port being developed by India in Sittwe and Hambantota in Sri Lanka is already with China on a 99-year lease. China has already helped build the port in Gwadar in Pakistan and Hambantota in Sri Lanka. The Chittagong port in Bangladesh is also receiving Chinese money. Despite the fact that investment in the port has been scaled down to $1.3 billion (initial phase) from the earlier $7 billion figure, the port will be of great strategic significance to China as it navigates its way into the Bay of Bengal — and the Indian Ocean — considered within New Delhi's range of influence.

It is also interesting to note that power projection with aircraft carriers is adding a new strategic dimension to maritime engagement, anti-piracy operations, as well as humanitarian assistance and disaster relief. In recent times, China's ongoing rapid military modernization plans has already led to the operational deployment of its first aircraft carrier. The Liaoning provides the People's Liberation Army Navy (PLAN) with a new capability for its growing naval force by employing naval aviation assets to its fleet and further increasing the combat range of its maritime forces. Such a development has already raised concerns from both India and Japan, two regional powers who view China's rise as a military power as an external defense challenge (Bommakanti and Kelkar, 2019). As stated earlier, there is an expectation that China would use ports as military bases in and around the Indian Ocean.

As a result, both Japan and India also began developing their aircraft carriers. India is also currently constructing a new carrier while proposals to build another are ongoing. All Indian carriers are used for fixed-wing combat aircraft like China's aircraft carriers.[6] The aircraft contingent of the Indian carriers is mostly made up of MiG-29K fighter jets purchased from the Russian Federation, as well as a handful of helicopters for

---

[6] https://www.defenseindustrydaily.com/ins-vikramaditya-may-hit-delay-cost-increases-03283/, May 6, 2019, accessed on May 27, 2019.

anti-submarine warfare (ASW) and maritime surveillance. An assessment and study should be further pursued regarding the development of various naval and airpower capabilities among the regional powers in the Indo-Pacific, particularly weapon platforms or defense systems that may have strategic effects on the regional security architecture.[7]

7.10 Conclusion

After the 1962 war against China, the Indian leadership chose not to develop infrastructure in the Northeast as a defense against Chinese penetration, especially in Arunachal Pradesh. However, the lack of infrastructure development has cost India on both the domestic and foreign policy fronts. Domestically, the disconnect of the Northeast from the mainland was one of the many reasons for the rise of insurgencies in this region. On the foreign policy front, India missed out on opportunities to diversify its energy needs with regard to Myanmar and enhance its economic relations with Southeast Asia due to modest connectivity infrastructure.

The geostrategic landscape of the region can be changed only by providing actuality to ASEAN–India relations through connectivity. Connectivity projects will not only curtail existing insurgencies but will also help India's Northeast states develop their economic potential. These projects will also help India remove physical impediments to trade with ASEAN countries and further integrate the two regions for better economic and security relations (Desai, 2017).

There is no doubt that despite the geographical proximity to Myanmar and further to Thailand through our Northeast region, India has been no match to the Chinese buildup of connectivity projects, including the China–Myanmar Economic Corridor. Moreover, the infrastructure along Myanmar's border region with China is very well developed, giving a major boost to its border trade, which in value terms is at least ten times more than that of India.

---

[7] https://appfi.ph/resources/commentaries/2670-carrying-power-projection-aircraft-carrier-development-in-the-asia-pacific, accessed on May 10, 2019.

The urgency with which India is endeavoring to complete the IMT, which has suffered from delays, time lags, and consequent shifts in the date of completion, is creditable. The Trilateral Highway and Kaladan Multi Modal Transport project are the major projects that facilitate India's engagement with ASEAN members. Both the projects are being executed by the Ministry of External Affairs.[8] The delays in project completion are not merely endogenous or related to finance/appointments of contractors, they are also due to the changes in government in participating countries. There is no doubt that India's Act East Policy has had a transformative impact on how the projects are now being pursued.

Both the land route as well as maritime connectivity between India and ASEAN members are crucial for the realization of the full potential of India–ASEAN trade. Maritime connectivity is the pathway to facilitate production networks as well as create global and regional value chains. India and China are actively competing to gain hold of strategic points of economic and geopolitical interest throughout Southeast Asia. India's Act East Policy has the potential to somewhat balance China's One Belt, One Road initiative. China is already the leading source of infrastructure funding in Southeast Asia, but now India is positioning itself as a balancing factor; in fact, SEA countries have welcomed India's resurgence in this regard. This was reiterated by experts who were interviewed by the author in Bangkok, Mandalay, and Yangon during her visit in May–June 2019.[9]

Several experts have underlined the importance of building up India's naval capabilities. To successfully counter Beijing's maritime expansion, there is an imperative to partner with other countries. India is building up its navy, but it currently does not have the capabilities to patrol sea lanes alone.[10] The lesson for India, time and again, remains the same — to have influence in Asia and influence in the larger geopolitical theater, India first and foremost needs to assert its place in the immediate neighborhood.

---

[8] Report: Maritime connectivity crucial to India-ASEAN trade, By: FE Bureau | Published: August 31, 2017, 5:23:40 AM. https://www.financialexpress.com/economy/report-maritime-connectivity-crucial-to-india-ASEAN-trade/833913/, accessed on May 10, 2019.

[9] Interviews of Khin Maung Nyo, Khin Maung Soe, and Surat Horaichakul.

[10] For India and China, Southeast Asia Is a Battleground. By Kamran Bokhari — December 12, 2017, https://geopoliticalfutures.com/india-china-southeast-asia-battleground/.

"If you cannot integrate with your region, you cannot integrate with other regions", former Foreign Secretary Shyam Saran said at the 2016 Raisina Dialogue.[11]

7.10.1 *Emerging Synergy and Opportunities: The Way Forward*

It is important also that private sector engagement is encouraged, as the State cannot be expected to be the only actor in expanding a country's influence. A case in point is the initiation of the Adani Port terminal at Yangon in May 2019. It has been learned that the Adani Yangon International Terminal Co. Ltd. has received approval from the Myanmar Investment Commission for an investment in a new container port in the Yangon Region; the amount invested is US$290 million.[12]

To further catalyze investments from the Indian private sector as part of the AEP, there is a proposal for a Project Development Company through separate Special Purpose Vehicles for setting up manufacturing hubs in Cambodia, Myanmar, Laos, and Vietnam (CLMV) to cultivate extensive economic relations with Southeast Asia. The India, Myanmar, and Thailand Motor Vehicles Agreement (IMT MVA) also needs to be fast-tracked, as once it is realized, it will become the first ever cross-border facilitation agreement between India, Myanmar, and Thailand, hence permitting easy movement of cargo, passengers, and personal vehicles along the roads linking these three countries.

On the issue of air connectivity, while there are more than 300 flights every week from India to Thailand, air connectivity with Myanmar infrequent, with only two flights per week from Kolkata to Yangon and one flight from Bodhgaya. Most people need to fly via Malaysia or Thailand. It is hoped that direct flights will be launched so that tourists and business people can travel easily. The e-visa facility is excellent, implying that one

---

[11] Suhasini Haidar. From https://dailytimes.com.pk/93120/why-india-must-heed-geography/, accessed on March 11, 2016.

[12] PTI. From https://www.thehindubusinessline.com/economy/logistics/adani-group-to-develop-container-terminal-port-in-myanmar/article27124926.ece, accessed on May 14, 2019.

can get a visa for Myanmar in one day. The author experienced this herself during her travel to Myanmar in May–June 2019.

Improved air connectivity will facilitate people-to-people exchanges and make it easier for student and faculty exchanges. Already, in Mandalay, the Myanmar Institute of Information Technology has well-renowned faculty from India. MIIT is ranked at a high position as it imparts quality IT knowledge to students in Myanmar and is much sought after. There is tremendous scope for medical tourism as well.

Hence, improved connectivity with India's neighbors in the East has the potential to catalyze lasting partnerships for mutual prosperity and advancement. Only then will India truly Act East!

Chapter 8

Thailand–India Economic Relations

8.1 Introduction

India–Thailand economic relations in the present times have their genesis in our linkages with SEA, through the seas. This historical proximity has been reiterated by several leaders. One such articulation was on February 4, 2016 when the then Vice President of India, Shri Hamid Ansari, in an address at Chulalongkorn University, Bangkok, stated, "Our economic progress and well-being is intimately linked to the growth and prosperity of the entire Asian continent, especially of our friends across the Bay of Bengal and Andaman Sea".[1] In his address, he also highlighted how India had emerged as a "bright spot with the highest economic growth amongst the larger emerging countries".[2]

Hence, both India and Thailand view this bilateral relationship with great interest and understand the potential to take forward economic engagement bilaterally. This chapter focuses on aspects of trade and investment within the context of India–Thailand bilateral relations.

Through a comparison of India with investment from the rest of ASEAN and China, into Thailand, the study indicates that India–Thailand economic relations are at an incomparable low level.

---

[1] From https://www.india.com/news/world/india-places-asean-at-the-core-of-act-east-policy-hamid-ansari-917595/.

[2] From https://www.business-standard.com/article/government-press-release/vice-president-of-india-shri-m-hamid-ansari-addressing-the-banquet-116020400585_1.html.

A discussion of Thailand's macroeconomy provides the context.

After the end of the Cold War, India and Thailand have seen their relations grow in all spheres. The 1990s is viewed as the "golden age" in Indo-Thai relations. It was in 1996 that Thailand initiated the "Look West" Policy aimed at exploring new markets, sources of energy and new investments flows. Thailand's "Look West" Policy has been the perfect complement to India's "Look East" Policy of the early 1990s, which has been instrumental in promoting bilateral relations between the two countries as well as in strengthening India's relationship with the region in general. India is considered to be one of the most important and influential actors in Asian as well as global interactions.

It is inevitable then that India and Thailand are important members of sub-regional groupings and partnerships. India was welcomed as an ASEAN sectoral dialogue partner in 1993, and the status was later upgraded to full dialogue partner in 1995. Subsequently, India joined the ASEAN Regional Forum (ARF). Thailand and India also have a strong relationship of cooperation in the East Asia Summit (EAS), the Bay of Bengal Initiative for Multisectoral Technical and Economic Cooperation (BIMSTEC), the Mekong–Ganga Cooperation (MGC), and the Asia Cooperation Dialogue (ACD) and more recently, the Regional Comprehensive Economic Partnership (RCEP). These mechanisms have been discussed in Chapter 4.

8.2 Thailand's Macroeconomy: A Brief Outline

Thailand in fact has set a classic example of rapid economic growth in less than a generation. A low-income country in the 1980s, Thailand was upgraded in status to an "upper middle-income economy" by the World Bank in 2011 (World Bank, 2011). The transition of this Southeast Asian economy happened not only in a short period but also against a backdrop of domestic political turmoil. The Thai economy, tagged as a tiger economy, grew at a fast pace of 8–9% during the latter part of the 1980s and the early 1990s. Thailand enjoyed some sort of an economic renaissance in the 1990s, driven by foreign investments along with an infusion of fresh technology in Thai agriculture and industries before it got caught up in the Asian Financial Crisis of 1997–1998 (Laplamwanit, 1999).

Thailand is one of the most prosperous countries in Asia. Although the Thai economy grew at 9.6% between 1986 and 1996 (mainly a result of its industrialization program), i.e., just before the East Asian crisis, it suffered huge losses on account of a massive capital flight that had been preceded by short-term capital flows and dependence on imports. The recovery of the Thai economy was aided by the International Monetary Fund, the World Bank, and the Asian Development Bank. In 1998, signs of recovery were imminent. Exchange rates began to recover, and interest rates had declined to below pre-crisis levels by mid-1998. Economic activity then began to turn as well.

The economy recovered from the crisis in the following years with moderate growth, before encountering the global financial crisis of 2008–2009. Since then, the economy of Thailand has encountered several economic, natural, and political events. In 2011, one of the worst floods to hit the country resulted in an economic loss of approximately $45.7 billion. Political uncertainty and tension arose in 2010 and yet again in 2013–2014 (Bajpai, 2015). Prime Minister Prayuth Chan-o-Cha has been in power since his predecessor, the then Prime Minister of Thailand, Ms. Yingluck Shinawatra was overthrown in a coup in 2014.

In analyzing Thailand's GDP, it is to be noted that agricultural development has played a major role in the transformation of Thailand's economy. The primary sector in the country has witnessed two phases. The first was characterized by growth in the agriculture driven by the utilization of unused labor and land. This phase lasted from the early 1960s to the early 1980s, during which time the economy was heavily dependent on agriculture as the main economic driver. Agriculture employed around 70% of Thailand's active working population. During the second phase, while labor shifted to urban areas, and no new land was utilized, there was nevertheless an increase in agricultural productivity. The agricultural sector continued its growth, although at a slower rate, led by productivity through mechanization and availability of formal credit.

With the growth in the other sectors of the economy, the dependence of Thailand's GDP on agriculture has gradually declined over the years, but this sector still accounts for about 12% of GDP and employs 32% of the population. Thailand's main agricultural output is rice, rubber, corn, sugarcane, coconuts, palm oil, and fish products. Thailand's industrial sector, comprising manufacturing as the major segment along with mining, construction, electricity, water, and gas, contributed 35.03% in 2017 to Thailand's GDP. The service sector accounts for 56.31% in 2017 of Thailand's GDP while employing 51% of the labor force. Within services, transportation, wholesale and retail trade, and tourism- and travel-related activities have been the prominent contributors to the GDP and employment generators. Per capita income was US$6,125.66 in 2017.

Thus, the economy of Thailand is built on a strong agricultural sector, a developed manufacturing sector, as well as a stable service sector. Also, the growth of the Thai economy is highly dependent on its export sector, which contributes 75% to the GDP; this exposes the Thai economy to global macroeconomic conditions and currency volatility in addition to economic fluctuations within the region.

It was the shift in Thailand's policy orientation from import substitution to export promotion during the 1980s that resulted in a major increase in the contribution of exports to the GDP. Thailand's major export destinations are China, Japan, the US, Indonesia, Malaysia, Australia, Hong Kong, Singapore, and India. Thailand's main exports are manufactured goods, with electronics, vehicles, machinery and equipment, and food items being the major components. With inflation in control and a strengthened financial system, the Thai economy has been able to attract foreign investments, mainly from Japan, Korea, and China.

8.3 Burgeoning Industrial Sector: Post-2014

Thailand has an ever-expanding industrial sector and has seen a period of steady growth since 2014. The present government has brought in sweeping reforms aimed at both modernization of the farm sector as well as the industrial sector.

Although Japanese and Korean investments in manufacturing plants had given Thailand a comparatively modern industrial base and the country continues to be the major tourist destination and source of foreign capital, there exists scope of further growth and development in Thailand (Mehta, 2002).

Based on the data of 2017, the National Economic and Social Development Board (NESDB) report has stated that the Thai economy in

2018 grew at 4.1%, supported by (i) the improvement of the global economy, (ii) the favorable expansion of government consumption and public investment, (iii) a recovery of private investment, and (iv) improvement of household income conditions. Given the above, it was expected that export value would increase by 10.0%, and private consumption and the total investment will grow by 4.1% and 4.4%, respectively. The headline inflation was forecast to be in the range of 0.9–1.4% and the current account would record a surplus of 8.4% of GDP.[3] However, the Thai economy slowed down to about 3.5% in 2018, mainly due to the uncertainties in the global economy and trade protectionism.

8.4 Thailand: Setting Economic Priorities

Given the slowing down of the Thai economy in 2018, at the macro-level and for the short term, the NESDB report suggests that economic management for 2019–2020 should focus on the following aspects: (1) promoting key commercial sectors by (i) fostering export sector, (ii) sustaining the expansion of the tourism sector, and (iii) supporting private investment expansion by facilitating and pushing up investment projects approved by the Board of Investment; (2) supporting small farmers and low-income households as well as strengthening SMEs and local economies; (3) expediting key public investment, together with driving infrastructure projects under the transportation action plans and the EEC; (4) arranging labor force both in terms of quantity and quality of labor to facilitate expansion of economic and investment activities (*Ibid.*).

The above sectors are being focused on by Thailand through the following:

(a) By developing the Thailand 4.0 model, the key manufacturing sectors are being prioritized for development in the Eastern Economic Corridor.

(b) Exports are to receive a boost with several concessions being offered to manufacturers and exporters in terms of tax concessions and other

---

[3] NESDB economic report, Press Release, 9.30 a.m., February 19, 2018, http://www.nesdb. go.th/nesdb_th/ewt_dl_link.php?nid=5169, accessed on October 9, 2018.

facilities in the Export Processing Zone. Thailand has been increasing its exports to India, and this growth has been faster than its imports from India.

(c) Tourism income is a major earner for the Thai economy, and in this context, India holds a very special position.

(d) The Board of Investment has been inviting and facilitating foreign direct investment through its investor-friendly policies. This was confirmed to the author by senior officers/interviewees of Indian business houses in Rayong.

The above are further discussed and elucidated in the Indian context in the subsequent sections that deal with bilateral trade, investment, and tourism.

8.5 India–Thailand Bilateral Trade

Thailand has been an important trading partner of India. Thailand ranked 20th in terms of India's exports (during 2000), while its rank was 24th in terms of India's import basket. In 2018, Thailand had a rank of 22 in India's exports. The amount of India's total exports to Thailand, in 1999, amounted to US$547 million while the corresponding value of India's imports from Thailand was US$622 million. Thailand's total exports had been concentrated in electronics, textiles, gems and jewelry, and agricultural products. Among commodity groups, "rubber and articles thereof", "electric machinery and equipment and parts thereof", "other footwears with outer soles", "other articles of plastics", "articles of jewelry and precious stones", and "articles of apparel and clothing not knitted or crocheted" have been important. Among the agricultural sector, it has been primarily exporting "crustaceans, whether in shell or not" and "rice" (Mehta, 2002).

Toward the end of the 1990s, specifically in 1999–2000, India has imported commodities of 82 groups (out of 99 commodity groups defined by different chapters of HS classification) from Thailand. Among the major imports from Thailand, it was commodities of the following groups, i.e., "sugars and sugar confectionery", "plastics and plastics products" and "electric and non-electric machinery", "textile articles", "natural and cultured pearls and precious metals", etc., which comprised the major share of India's imports from Thailand. A list of top 20 commodities (at four-digit HS level) of Thailand's total imports shows that Thailand's import is concentrated in a few specific commodities of petroleum oil, iron and steel, machinery, and transport equipment. The study by Rajesh Mehta shows that India has exported commodities of 85 groups out of the total 99 commodity groups. However, India's exports to Thailand have been concentrated in one commodity group "precious metals and stones", etc., which constituted around 38.2% of India's exports to Thailand. Other commodity groups of importance included "organic chemicals" and "residues and waste from the food industries — prepared animal fodder".

8.6   India–Thailand FTA

It was on August 31, 2004, that India signed an FTA for setting up a free trade area covering goods, services, and investment, making Thailand the first country in the ASEAN to sign such an agreement with India. (The India–Thailand FTA provided for ASEAN-plus tariff concessions once trade negotiations were completed.) In 2004, negotiations were held for selected products for the Early Harvest Scheme (EHS), under which both countries simultaneously and gradually eliminated tariffs on 82 common items between September 1, 2004 and August 31, 2006.

The process of negotiations has since continued from 2004 till date. Under the EHS, the 82 items include products like fruits, processed food, gems and jewelry, iron and steel, auto parts, and electronic goods. It was the initial phase of the proposed comprehensive FTA, which is to be upgraded to a full-fledged arrangement for reduction and elimination of duties on about 90% of goods traded between the countries. The FTA would also cover opening up of trade in services, an area of interest to India. Issues like significant cuts in duties on the number of products and movement of professionals are yet to be resolved by both sides.

By 2017, 29 rounds of India–Thailand Trade Negotiations Committee (ITTNC) meetings had taken place. During the last two rounds, several issues were discussed, including trade in goods, trade in services, investment, and SPS (sanitary and phytosanitary) and technical barriers to trade.[4]

India–Thailand bilateral trade increased from US$1.15 billion in 2000 to US$6 billion in 2007–2008 and further crossed US$10 billion in 2017–2018. The target is to increase this to US$16 billion by 2021. IT, pharmaceuticals, biotechnology, automotive, and tourism are some of the identified areas for cooperation (Sen, 2018).

More details are provided in the following section.

8.7 India–Thailand Trade: Recent Trends

India had a trade surplus *vis-à-vis* Thailand continuously during 1995–2004. With the growth in Thailand's exports to India, this turned into a trade deficit in 2005 and has remained so since. Since 2010, the trade deficit has amounted to almost US$2 billion a year.

Overall bilateral trade has multiplied eight-fold since 2000 to reach US$8.69 billion in 2013. Although it was expected that the upward trend would continue to reach about US$16 billion by 2014, with the Northeastern region as a major hub for investment, this did not happen (Rana, 2013). Two-way trade in 2014 was only US$8.66 billion, with about US$5.62 billion in Thai exports to India and US$3.04 billion in Indian exports to Thailand. In percentage terms, while imports from India comprise only 1.4% of Thailand's total imports, the share of India in its exports is 2.6% (it may be noted here that India's exports declined in 2014–2015 mainly due to a fall in commodity prices and devaluation by some of India's trading partners). Tables 8.1 and 8.2 provide the data for the period 2010–2014 and 2013–2014 to 2017–2018.

From Tables 8.1 and 8.2, it is evident that while exports from Thailand to India were higher than its imports, the increase over the 4 years in Thailand's exports and imports was 28% and 35%, respectively. This implies that if the trend in rate of growth of exports from India had continued, India's trade deficit could have shrunk.

---

[4]Personal Interview of Mr. Shirish Jain, Indian Counsellor in Thailand to Reena Marwah, May 24, 2018.

Table 8.1:   India–Thailand Bilateral Trade, 2010–2014 (USD Billion)

Description	2010	2011	2012	2013	2014[a]
Thai exports	4.39	5.18	5.48	5.19	5.62
Thai imports	2.25	3.01	3.20	3.50	3.04
Total trade	6.64	8.19	8.68	8.69	8.66

Note: [a]Embassy of India in Thailand website; accessed on December 28, 2017.
Source: Ministry of Commerce and Industry (2014), Government of India.

Table 8.2:   India–Thailand Trade, 2013–2014 to 2017–2018

Trade (USD Billion)	2013–2014	2014–2015	2015–2016	2016–2017	2017–2018
Exports to Thailand	3.70	3.46	2.98	3.13	3.65
Imports from Thailand	5.34	5.86	5.51	5.41	7.13
Total	9.04	9.33	8.49	8.54	10.78

Source: Commerce-app.gov.in/eidb/ieent.asp; accessed on October 16, 2018.

Table 8.3:   Overview of Bilateral Trade Value and Product Composition

Trade (USD Million)	2010–2011	2017–2018	Commodities
Exports to Thailand	2.25	3. 65	Gems, pharma, vegs, HH appliances
Imports from Thailand	4.39	7.13	Auto parts, iron and steel, chemicals, rubber
Total	6.64	10. 78	

Source: Commerce-app.gov.in/eidb/ieent.asp; accessed on October 16, 2018.

However, the post-2014 situation saw a decline in exports from India, rather than an increase, while imports from Thailand grew at a pace higher than the preceding discussed period. The increase over the 4 years was 34%. Hence, the trade deficit grew from about US$2 billion to almost US$3.5 billion in 2017–2018 (see Table 8.2).

Table 8.3 provides an overview of the trade value and composition for the years 2010–2011 and 2017–2018.

The Indian export basket to Thailand mostly comprises gem and jewelry, metal ores, chemicals, machinery, vegetables, electrical household appliances, and pharmaceutical products. Major imports include chemicals, polymers of ethylene, auto components, rubber, iron, and steel.

There is evidence that the bilateral FTA between India and Thailand has led to some production restructuring by both Indian and East Asian MNCs, leading to the emergence of FDI-led trade integration between India and Thailand. The India–Thai FTA's EHS has thus had a major impact in changing the composition of bilateral trade between India and Thailand.

Tables 8.4 and 8.5 provide details of India's exports and imports from Thailand over the period 2011–2012 to 2017–2018.

From Tables 8.4 and 8.5, it is interesting to note that India's basket of exports and imports to and from Thailand includes similar items (though there would be variations in the specific items), viz. pearls and stones, vehicles, nuclear reactors, iron and steel, and organic chemicals. India's imports of almost all these commodities (except pearls and iron and steel) are much larger than its exports. Hence, the low complementarity in India–Thailand trade.

India's exports to Thailand increased in 2017–2018 by 16% over the previous year. Thailand's share in India's exports rose from 1.1% in 2016–2017 to 1.2% in 2017–2018; overall, India's exports grew by 10%.

However, a detailed review of the data for the period 2011–2012 to 2017–2018 reveals the following:

(a) India's exports over the period 2011–2012 to 2017–2018 have increased from about US$3–3.6 billion, which is rather insignificant.

(b) In terms of commodities exported, it can be seen that while there was a decline in the exports of meat and residues, there were marginal increases in exports of organic chemicals, iron and steel, as well as vehicles.

(c) Imports of nuclear reactors, boilers, etc., increased by over 50%; however, the increase was registered in 2017–2018.

(d) The only major increase (more than double) is visible in the case of fish exports.

Table 8.5 provides details of India's imports from Thailand over the period 2011–2012 to 2017–2018.

Table 8.4:   India's Exports to Thailand 2011–2012 to 2017–2018 (USD Million)

S. No.	Commodity HS code 2	2011–2012	2012–2013	2013–2014	2014–2015	2015–2016	2016–2017	2017–2018
1.	Meat and Edible Meat Offal	90.48	265.96	296.66	393.97	108.68	34.72	21.46
2..	Fish and Crustaceans, Mollusks and Other Aquatic Invertebrates	119.46	101.73	149.70	111.67	124.7	223.88	256.20
3.	Residues and Waste From the Food Industries; Prepared Animal Fodder	201.31	310.48	201.95	114.87	32.54	24.35	52.01
4.	Mineral Fuels, Mineral Oils and Products of Their Distillation; Bituminous Substances; Mineral Waxes	89.88	44.01	115.38	59.23	44.89	44.99	93.46
5.	Organic Chemicals	224.77	190.20	162.66	199.91	233.24	176.50	244.48
6.	Natural/Cultured Pearls, Precious/ Semiprecious Stones, Precious Metals, Clad With Precious Metal and Articles, Imitation Jewelry; Coins	605.74	631.72	756.13	664.50	627.81	607.30	654.11
7.	Iron and Steel	191.44	421.86	382.35	264.77	121.86	223.32	250.31
8.	Nuclear Reactors, Boilers, Machinery and Mechanical Appliances and Parts Thereof	214.13	359.12	267.35	274.35	251.53	259.68	355.25
9.	Vehicles Other Than Railway or Tramway Rolling Stock, and Parts and Accessories Thereof	244.20	299.09	211.72	245.84	224.53	217.46	264.68
10.	All other 87 Items	1,393.90	1,109	1,159.37	1,135.72	1,218.08	1,321.24	1,461.87
11.	Total	2,961.01	3,733.17	3,703.27	3,464.83	2,987.86	3,133.44	3,653.83

Source: Ministry of Commerce, Government of India; http://commerce-app.gov.in/eidb/ecntcom.asp.

Table 8.5:   India's Imports from Thailand, 2011–2012 to 2017–2018 (USD Million)

S. No.	Commodity HS code 2	2011–2012	2012–2013	2013–2014	2014–2015	2015–2016	2016–2017	2017–2018
1.	Animal or Vegetable Fats and Oils and their Cleavage Products; Pre. Edible Fats; Animal or Vegetable Wax	62.15	31.70	159.41	81.63	5.0	0.17	282.32
2.	Organic Chemicals	527.11	438.78	409.20	495.93	357.67	412.70	635.46
3.	Plastic and Articles	546.65	582.80	613.36	716.94	720.5	727.33	975.74
4.	Rubber and Articles	525.36	313.71	372.24	371.41	310.31	290.09	373.45
5.	Natural or Cultured Pearls, Precious/Semiprecious Stones, Precious Metals, Clad with Precious Metals and Articles, Imitation Jewelry; Coin	299.49	270.15	221.33	102.23	102.28	97.64	118.93
6.	Iron and Steel	92.48	98.05	120.64	163.27	137.79	131.51	136.97
7.	Articles of Iron or Steel	138.11	138.66	103.30	166.28	166.63	155.06	155.89
8.	Aluminum articles	134.31	93.39	106.59	101.88	95.08	71.85	96.52
9.	Nuclear Reactors, Boilers, Machinery and Mechanical Appliances; Parts Thereof	1,136.04	1,384.43	1,228.82	1,382.71	1,328.39	1,184.73	1,341.78
10.	Electrical Machinery and Equipment and Parts Thereof; Sound Recorders and Reproducers, Television Image and Sound Recorders and Reproducers Parts	483.39	534.50	515.41	709.59	704.98	770.91	981.86
11.	Vehicles Other than Railway or Tramway Rolling Stock, and Parts and Accessories	244.17	297.70	303.95	409.29	434.28	410.87	535.00
12.	All other 83 Items	1,094.58	1,168.74	1,185.95	1,164.07	1,145.25	1,162.54	1,500.54
13.	Total	5,283.84	5,352.61	5,340.20	5,865.88	5,510.16	5,415.40	7,134.46

Source: Ministry of Commerce, Government of India; http://commerce-app.gov.in/eidb/Icntcom.asp.

From the above discussion, the following can be inferred:

(a) Imports from Thailand increased by 32% in 2017–2018 over the year 2016–2017; the overall increase in imports for India was about 21% over the 7-year period as shown in Table 8.5.
(b) The largest increases in imports by India have been in animal or vegetable fats (four times) as well as electrical machinery (doubled) and vehicles (doubled).
(c) In the imports of nuclear reactors, iron and steel, plastics, and organic chemicals, the increase in import value has been between 10% and 40% over the stated period.
(d) More than 50% of the imports in terms of value are a result of imports of plastic items, nuclear reactors, electrical machinery, vehicles, etc.

It is evident then that India's dependence on imports as given above can be reduced by aligning manufacturing of these items with our Make in India vision, as well as integrating with joint ventures based in India and Thailand.

8.8 Scope for Enhancing Bilateral Trade

Given India's growing balance of trade deficit with Thailand, there is an imperative to assess the potential for India to increase its exports to Thailand. Tables 8.6 and 8.7 provide data on Thailand's 15 imports from the world and India for the years 2016 as well as for the years 2017 and 2018, respectively.

It can be seen from Table 8.6 that India is a major source of fruits, reactive dyes, as well as ferro silicon manganese for Thailand (in bold). Gear boxes and parts of vehicles, etc., are also exported under the EHS (82 items). Medicines and groundnuts are also commodities for which there exists tremendous scope for India to expand its export. Given that Indian pharma and wellness products are in great demand in Thailand, there is great scope in this sector. However, Thailand applies a 10% tariff on imports of pharmaceuticals.[5]

---

[5]From http://www.eximguru.com/framework-agreement-with-thailand-lo82iutehs.aspx.

Table 8.6:   Thailand's Top 15 Imports from the World and India (2016) (Thousands of USDs)

S. No.	HS code	Commodity	From world	From India	Percent (India/world)
1.	710239	Others	82,819.71	NA	
2.	30354	Mackerel frozen	132,663.85	93,099.89	70.18
3.	90421	**Fruits of the genus capsicum**	1,151,951.98	40,074.22	3.48
4.	8708999	Other parts and accessories of vehicles of HDG 8701–8705	338,195.71	47,251.86	13.97
5.	30749	Other cuttlefish and squid fresh, chilled and frozen	1,246,703.90	85,095.32	6.83
6.	300490	Other medicine	67,763.87	6,356.55	9.38
7.	120242	Groundnut	2,387,931.03	67,190.14	2.81
8.	870840	Gearboxes	116,764.52	13,024.05	11.15
9.	720110	Non-alloy pig iron containing ≤0.5% phosphorus	69,002.11	43,795.57	63.47
10.	320416	**Reactive dyes and preparations based thereof**	28,899.99	23,738.81	82.14
11.	720230	**Ferro–silico–manganese**	35,430.24	1,392.87	3.93
12.	20230	Boneless	1,159,275.49	25,829.74	2.23
13.	271019	Other petroleum oils and oil from bituminous minerals, etc.			
14.	720711	Products containing by weight <0.25% CRBN of rectangular (including square)	591,065.25	13,333.00	2.26
15.	520100	Cotton, not carded or combed	433,431.13	15,542.28	3.59

Source: Ministry of Commerce, Government of India and adapted from RIS & AIC (2017).
Bold entries indicate India's high share.

Table 8.7: Thailand's Top 15 Imports from the World and from India, 2017 and 2018

S. No.	HS code 2	Description (chapter)	Thailand's imports from the world			India's exports to Thailand			India's percentage of share in Thailand's import	
			2017	2018	Percentage of growth in 2018 over 2017	2017	2018	Percentage of growth in 2018 over 2017	2017	2018
1.	85	Electrical, electronic equipment	42.30	45.61	7.84	0.15	0.24	65.32	0.35	0.53
2.	27	Mineral Fuels, Oils, etc.	31.64	42.73	35.07	0.11	0.08	−25.41	0.35	0.20
3.	84	Machinery, Nuclear Reactors, Boilers, etc.	27.35	29.56	8.07	0.36	0.63	77.88	1.30	2.15
4.	71	Pearls, Precious Stones, etc.	15.25	15.95	4.55	0.84	0.88	4.25	5.52	5.51
5.	72	Iron and Steel	10.65	12.53	17.72	0.26	0.27	4.72	2.44	2.17
6.	87	Vehicles, Other than Railway, Tramway	9.17	10.24	11.61	0.26	0.26	−1.07	2.84	2.52
7.	39	Plastics and Articles thereof	8.69	9.65	11.04	0.08	0.09	5.96	0.96	0.92
8.	73	Articles of Iron or Steel	7.12	7.50	5.31	0.12	0.09	−26.64	1.75	1.22
9.	90	Optical apparatus, Photo, Technical apparatus, etc.	5.60	6.02	7.44	0.03	0.04	15.56	0.58	0.62
10.	29	Organic Chemicals	4.33	5.05	16.49	0.22	0.41	83.74	5.12	8.07
11.	74	Copper and Articles thereof	3.99	4.43	11.05	0.02	0.02	13.65	0.54	0.55
12.	38	Miscellaneous Chemical Products	3.90	4.14	6.30	0.10	0.12	13.85	2.64	2.83
13.	76	Aluminum and Articles Thereof	3.43	3.86	12.65	0.06	0.13	139.06	1.64	3.47
14.	3	Fish and Crustaceans, etc.	3.22	3.53	9.46	0.27	0.34	24.80	8.37	9.54
15.	88	Aircraft, Spacecraft, and Parts Thereof	3.91	2.97	−23.86	0.00	0.00	—	0.01	0.00

Source: ITC Trade Map, July 2019.

Concerning groundnuts, as India produces about 15% of the world's production, there is a possibility of increasing exports to Thailand, given that less than 10% of Thailand's requirement is sourced from India. China produces almost 40% of the world's production. Hence, that would be the largest source for Thailand. Also, marine exports are being increasingly viewed by the Commerce Ministry as a source of foreign exchange. This was reflected in the 2018 Economic Survey of India, which showed that the share of marine products in India's export basket rose by the highest margin among all goods at 29.5%.[6] The government is taking measures to strengthen aquaculture production in states, potential collaborations, and marketing and integration of supply chains, with a focus on the inland fishery.

Table 8.7 reveals the following:

(a) Commodity groups in which India's percentage share in Thailand's imports is more than 5% are fish and crustaceans (India's share improved in 2018 over 2017), organic chemicals, as well as pearls and precious stones.
(b) Mineral oil imports increased from the world, but declined from India in 2018.
(c) In the categories of organic chemicals and aluminum imports, these increased from the rest of the world and from India.
(d) In the electricals category, Thailand's imports increased and India also improved its share in Thailand's overall imports.
(e) Machinery, nuclear reactors, boilers, etc., is another area for India to expand exports.

Hence, enhancing India's competitiveness, especially in sectors such as fish and crustaceans, electricals (in this sector, India needs to reduce its imports too), as well as organic chemicals, as elucidated above, can help to ease India's import deficits.

---

[6]Marine Exports — Modi Government sets firm eyes on the sea as a new source of major exports. *Business Standard*, February 1, 2018.

8.9 Thailand: A Favored Investment Destination

For years, Thailand has been among the most successful countries in Asia for attracting Foreign Direct Investment (FDI). The private sector in Thailand has been the main facilitator of growth and the government has played a promoting and supporting role. The Thai government has taken a consistently favorable stance toward foreign investors, recognizing their importance to Thailand's economic and technological development. Government approval to invest in Thailand is not even needed unless the special incentives offered by the Board of Investment are being applied for, and most sectors of the Thai economy are open to foreign investors. The combination of factors and the continued efforts of government agencies to reduce "red-tape" and facilitate investors have led to Thailand being among the highest-ranked countries for FDI by independent observers, as well as by foreign investors.[7]

Given that Thailand is considered as an attractive investment destination, Thailand has secured much higher rankings among most ASEAN countries as well as India. According to the World Economic Forum's "The Global Enabling Trade Report 2016", Thailand has a rank of 63, while that of India is 102.[8]

In terms of ranking in the Best Country Report of 2018, in which 80 countries were ranked in 9 categories, Thailand was at 15th rank in the "Open for Business" category.[9] In 2019, Thailand improved its rank from 15 to 10, while India was at rank 27.[10] This is evidenced by the fact that Thailand's Board of Investment has been very receptive to foreign investment. In an interview with the author, Munish Rathi, of the Aditya Birla group, stated that the BOI had been extremely facilitating and encouraging for Indian private-sector investment in the Map Tha Phut industrial estate.[11]

---

[7] BOI: The Board of Investment of Thailand. From https://www.boi.go.th/index.php?page=thailand_rankings.

[8] From http://reports.weforum.org/pdf/eti-2016-scorecard/WEF_ETI_2016_Scorecard_ETI.pdf.

[9] From https://www.usnews.com/news/best-countries.

[10] Best Countries 2019. From https://media.beam.usnews.com/55/57/eb2338c7493eadf38e29db4b8dca/190116-best-countries-overall-rankings-2019.pdf.

[11] Interview to the author, during her visit to Rayong on May 25, 2018.

Ease of Doing Business 2018 moved Thailand up to 26th rank from 46th in 2017 (from 190 countries worldwide). This brought Thailand to the top three in ASEAN.[12] India too has significantly improved its ranking in ease of doing business to 77 in 2018; yet, there are still bureaucratic delays, and the federal structure itself presents a complex landscape of rules and regulations for foreign investors. In terms of the rankings of the Global Innovation Index 2019, which assesses countries on 80 indicators, Thailand ranked 44, while India was at 57 (both countries improved their rankings).

8.9.1 *Thai Companies in India*

Several Thai companies are also engaged in India, since the 1990s — in the fields of agro-processing, construction, automotive, engineering, and banking. These are C P Aquaculture (India) Ltd., Italian Thai Development Public Ltd. Company (PCL), and Charoen Pokphand (India) Private Limited, one of the first groups to invest in India. Its shrimp raising investment at Chennai was a success (Chinwanno, 2009, p. 23). Krung Thai Bank PCL., Stanley Electric Engineering India Pvt. Ltd., Thai Summit Neel Auto Pvt. Ltd., Thai Airways International, PCL Precious Shipping (PSL) of Thailand, the Dusit Group, Pruksa Real Estate PCL, and Sirithai Superware PCL are other businesses set up in India. It can be noted that these businesses were set up for the production of items that used to be imported from Thailand.

8.10 Indian Investment in Thailand

Data on Indian Investments in Thailand are provided below, for the period 2001–2013 and then for the period 2014 till 2018.

8.10.1 *The Period 2001–2013*

Indian FDI into Thailand is estimated at being US$2 billion approximately since it started investing in the 1970s. In 2012, 25 investment

---

[12]You can find more information about the Ease of Doing Business 2018. From http://www.doingbusiness.org/reports/global-reports/doing-business-2018.

proposals from India, with an aggregate value of US$200 million, were approved, and in 2013, 16 new investment proposals worth US$53 million were approved. Thailand, for its part, has invested US$179.20 million in India (from April 2000 to September 2014).

The Tata Group is the major Indian company operating in Thailand. Tata Steel and Tata Consultancy Services have also had a presence in Thailand for several years. Other major Indian companies doing business in Thailand (reflecting the diverse sectors of interest) are the Aditya Birla group, Dabur, Lupin, Polaris, Kirloskar, Punj Lloyd, and NIIT. Mr. Sandeep Kumar, of the Aditya Birla Group which has established several companies, in an interview to the author has shared that the group had not established many companies in Thailand, but that the company had been recognized for its corporate social responsibility initiatives, including providing community service through vocational training.[13] The author also interviewed Mr. Rajeev Narang of SRF Industries and learnt of the company's growth in Thailand, an outcome of the facilitative business environment (*Ibid.*).

Tables 8.8 and 8.9 provide details of the Indian investment projects approved by the Board of Investment of Thailand over the period 2001–2013 and in the post-2014 period, respectively.

A closer look at India's investments in Thailand over the period 2001–2013 (i.e., prior to India's Act East Policy) shows the following:

(a) More than 50% of India's approved investment projects in Thailand were below 50 million baht or INR 10 crore and only 4% had investments of over 1,000 million baht (INR 200 crore).

(b) The major share of investment by Indian industry has been in the chemicals and paper sectors, closely followed by metal products and machinery. The latter was overtaken by the chemicals and paper sectors only in 2012.

(c) Investment in the services sector was nearly 10% of the total FDI investment; however, as can be seen in Table 8.9, share of services declined in the post-2014 phase.

---

[13] Interview to the author in May 2018 in Rayong, Thailand.

Table 8.8:   Indian Investment Projects Approved by BOI, 2001–2013

Sector	Number	Percentage	Amount (Million Baht)	Percentage
Agricultural products	26	12.3	2,024.40	4.7
Minerals and ceramics	9	4.3	6,272.40	14.7
Light industries/textiles	46	21.8	4,171.70	9.7
Metal products and machinery	20	9.5	11,441.40	26.8
Electrical and electronic products	38	18.0	775.00	1.8
Chemicals and paper	43	20.4	14,001.80	32.7
Services	29	13.7	4,093.90	9.6
Total	211	100.0	42,780.60	100.0

Source: Board of Investment, Thailand; http://www.boi.go.th/upload/content/TINDIA13_40907.pdf.

(d) India's investment over the period amounts to 0.45% of the total investment in Thailand, and India similarly receives only 0.06% of its inward FDI from Thailand. In 2014, approved Indian investment in Thailand amounted to US\$63.45 million; in contrast, FDI from Thailand to India was US\$23.72 million.

8.10.2 Post-2014: India's Investment in Thailand

The following investment trends are discernible from Table 8.8, which shows the investment from India to Thailand in the years 2015, 2016, and 2017. The data for 2018 are shown in Table 8.10, where a comparison for India has been provided with ASEAN and China.

From Table 8.9, the following trends can be seen:

(a) In 2015, chemicals and paper sectors were invested in, while in 2016, metal products and machinery recorded the highest investment.

(b) Investment in 2017 has fallen, possibly due to the low levels of private investment in India and the overall uncertainty in the global environment. Thailand itself experienced FDI inflows of about US\$2 billion only in 2016, with a significant improvement in 2017 to US\$7 billion.

Table 8.9: Indian Investment Projects Approved by the BOI Classified by Sector (Investment in Million Baht) (2015, 2016, and 2017)

No.	Sectors	2015 (Jan–Dec)		2016 (Jan–Dec)		2017 (Jan–Dec)	
		No. of projects	Investment	No. of projects	Investment	No. of projects	Investment
1	Agricultural Products	2	92.50	0	0.00	3	357
2	Minerals and Ceramics	3	183.60	1	165.00	2	446
3	Light Industries/Textiles	1	256.00	3	42.61	2	158
4	Metal Products and Machinery	3	140.50	5	697.00	0	0.00
5	Electrical and Electronic Products	2	3.18	7	40.80	4	9.0
6	Chemicals and Paper	2	579.30	3	174.00	1	36.0
7	Services	2	29.81	2	34.00	5	86.0
	Total	15	1,284.89	21	1,153.41	17	1,092
			US$ (35.8 million) approx.		US$ (32.1 million) approx.		US$ (33.5 million) approx.
	Exchange Rate*	US$1 = THB – 35.9		US$1 = THB – 35.9		US$1 = THB – 32.6	

Source: https://freecurrencyrates.com/en/exchange-rate-history/USD-THB/(different years).

(c) In terms of relative shares of different sectors in 2017, it is evident that while 40% of India's investment in Thailand was in the areas of minerals and ceramics, a third of outward FDI to Thailand was for agricultural products.

This shows that India has been able to take advantage of the liberal FDI policy. Moreover, with the capacity to export in agro products being limited as Thailand has bound its agricultural tariffs at an average of 39.9% *ad valorem*, the FDI route is the only feasible option.

Also, while investment in the services sector increased to more than double in 2017, in comparison to the previous 2 years, investment in chemicals and paper saw a major increase in 2015 (see Figure 8.1). This fact was corroborated by Mr. Rathi, in an interview to the author, in May 2018.

Table 8.10 provides a detailed view of Investment Projects approved by the Board of Investment for the year 2018 for India, ASEAN, and China.

It is evident that the investment projects approved for India are a minuscule of those for both ASEAN and China, reflecting clearly that Indian investment in Thailand has remained stable between 2015 and

Figure 8.1: Indian Investment Projects Approved by the BOI Classified by Sector

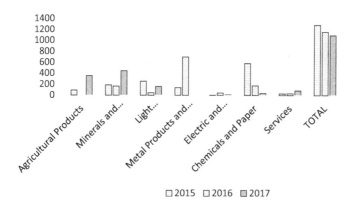

Table 8.10:   Investment Projects Approved by the BOI Classified by Sector for 2018 (January–December) (Million Baht)

Sectors	India		ASEAN		China	
	No. of projects	Investment	No. of projects	Investment	No. of projects	Investment
1 Agricultural Products	0	0.00	8	1,984.17	7	722.00
2 Minerals and Ceramics	0	0.00	4	503.34	4	3,132.35
3 Light Industries/Textiles	1	5.5	1	99.00	3	529.00
4 Metal Products and Machinery	1	20.0	23	19,060.35	27	17,944.17
5 Electrical and Electronic Products	7	48.8	23	10,485.88	21	760.18
6 Chemicals and Paper	2	276.9	10	1,071.05	15	2,632.39
7 Services	1	80.0	75	32,505.72	20	7,091.11
8 Technology and Innovation Development	0	0.00	0	0.00	0	0.00
TOTAL	12	431.2	144	65,709.51	97	32,811.20
Exchange Rate on 07/01/2019 (US$1 = 31.91)	US$13.5 million		US$2.058 billion		US$1.028 billion	

Note: Investment projects refer to projects with capital of at least 10% from investor country.

Source: International Affairs Bureau, BOI, Thailand.

2017, with a substantial reduction in 2018. Indian investment shrunk to a mere US$13.5 million in 2018, compared to US$33.5 million in 2017.

To understand how investment from India compares with that from the rest of ASEAN as well as China, the sectorwise data for 2018 have been collated and presented in Table 8.10. This would enable us to understand the potential sectors for India to expand investment in Thailand.

In 2018, in terms of percentage share, India's investment to Thailand was a mere 0.0065 of that provided by ASEAN collectively and a mere 0.013 of that provided by China.

Given China's BRI projects in SEA, Thailand continues to receive inflows of funds for investment.

From Tables 8.8–8.10 and Figure 8.2, the following can be inferred:

(a) India's overall investment in Thailand ranged from about US$32 to 35 million over the years 2015–2017. In 2018, it declined to about US$13.5 million. In contrast, FDI from ASEAN and China was about US$2 billion and US$1 billion, respectively. India's share is hence a miniscule in comparison.

(b) Thailand's inward investment from ASEAN countries for services alone is almost 50% of the entire investment from ASEAN.

(c) Investment in metal products and machinery also comprises almost a third of investment from ASEAN.

(d) Investment in metal products and machinery comprises more than half of the total investment from China, reflecting the requirement for foreign investment in this one sector, providing an impetus to Thailand's manufacturing sector.

(e) Investment secured for electrical and electronic products is also significant from ASEAN countries. Although the number of projects in this sector is almost similar to the ones from ASEAN, in terms of investment, China provided only about 8% as compared to ASEAN. This probably reflects the demand for building superior quality manufacturing capabilities and becoming a hub in this sector in the region.

(f) Investment in chemicals and paper is secured from India, and this compares favorably to that secured from the rest of ASEAN (Indian investment is about a fourth of that received from ASEAN).

Figure 8.2: **Investment Projects Approved by the BOI Classified by Sector for 2018 (January–December)**

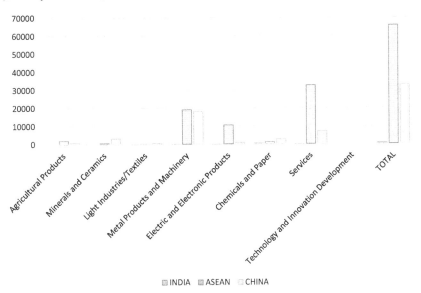

This would probably imply that scope for Indian investment in chemicals and paper remains significant in all ASEAN countries. The major source of investment in this sector is China (from Table 8.10).

(g) In agricultural products and ceramics sectors, Indian investment was significant in 2017; in 2018, there was no additional investment.

(h) Technology and innovation development is a new area that has been added by the BOI. This is another area where Indian investment should seek avenues for mutual benefit.

It is worth underlining that inward FDI to Thailand has been encouraged in sectors, which have the potential to catalyze its manufacturing capabilities.

Given India's growing aspirations not only in the region but globally too, it is important to understand the issues constraining India's trade and investment with Thailand, an important country for realizing India's Act East vision.

8.11 India–Thailand Bilateral Trade and Investment Issues

There are several bilateral issues related to both trade and investment, which are elucidated below:

(i) There has been a slow progress on the bilateral trade and investment front, as even after more than 30 rounds of the ITTNC, issues remain unresolved. This could be the result of India's increasing trade deficit with Thailand and its rethink on whether FTAs are beneficial. It is believed that some of the trade liberalization measures and rules of origin could provide a boost to Indian investments in Thailand. Moreover, Thailand has been demanding unconditional access to India's multibrand retail space, across the country, but India's stance is that this decision has to be taken by individual state governments, a confusing position which amounts to a refusal.

(ii) In terms of the commodities that the two countries trade in, it has been noted that there is limited trade complementarity, with both countries exporting similar goods. Thailand and India are exporting nuclear reactors, semi-precious stones, and non-metallic minerals, among others (see Tables 8.4 and 8.5).

(iii) A study by Indian and Thai economists had pointed out that mere trade liberalization is not sufficient for generating substantial trade flows unless broad-based trade facilitation measures are also set in place (Das *et al.*, 2002, p. 33).

(iv) Thai exporters have often cited India's complex duty structure as one of the reasons for the low economic engagement with India. It was also mentioned by the concerned officer at the Thai trade center, Mr. Nanthapol Sudbanthad, Royal Thai Consulate, Mumbai, on August 20, 2018,[14] that there are multiple tariff and non-tariff barriers in India. It is to be noted that while tariffs for agricultural products are high in India, as in other countries too, the situation with non-agriculture tariffs is different. For non-agriculture products,

---

[14] Interview of Mr. Nanthapol Sudbanthad on August 20th at the Thai Consulate office in Mumbai, India.

most tariff lines for India are between zero and 10%. Tariff lines with tariffs above 10% have a total import share of less than 4.6%. Most of these high-tariff categories have import shares of less than 0.1% (Singh, 2017).

US expert Mr. Ross, who was in New Delhi in May 2019, said that "India's average applied tariff rate of 13.8%, remains the highest of any major world economy. The very highest".

(v) The officer at the Thai Trade office in Mumbai, Mr. Nanthapol Sudbanthad, who spoke to the author, also cited issues in investing in India, given that each of India's states had very different policies and this was confusing for the Thai investors as also investors from other Southeast Asian countries.

(vi) For Indian exporters, there are issues too. They face restrictions in terms of NTBs in Thailand. Moreover, India has been demanding greater access under Mode 4 of trade in services, which is related to the movement of professionals. However, Thailand reserves employment in a large number of services like engineering, accounting, law, and architecture, for Thai nationals, and for others has a restrictive visa policy. India has also been pushing Thailand to sign the mutual recognition agreement, which will do away with the need for Indian professionals to secure additional qualifications from Thailand before being allowed to work there under Mode 4. Thailand, on the contrary, has been asking for freer movement of Thai workers, but India is hesitant as this might lead to an influx of semi-skilled workforce into the country. According to the Thai ambassador in Delhi, Mr. Gongsakdi, there is a shortage of IT professionals in Thailand. Their country is willing to grant visas for the workers and their families for 5 years; however, the demand for India is for a 10-year visa. This continues to limit the movement of professionals. However, Indians in Singapore have been increasingly successful in the start-up initiatives as well as other businesses. The foothold in Singapore is helping them to access other countries in Southeast Asia. This was stated by Chandrima Das, founder of Bento (a robot advisory firm), who stated that they were working toward building clientele in Hong Kong, Thailand, Malaysia, Indonesia, and other countries (Singh, 2017).

Specific investment barriers have been identified, which are responsible for the low level of investment. Indian investors are constrained by information gaps on policy guidelines, potential sectors, and prospective collaborators, as well as the difficulty of locating a reliable counterpart. They are not allowed to hold more than 49% share in Thai businesses and are hampered by the need to recruit skilled staff. A minimum daily wage policy of the Shinawatra Government raised wages to 300 baht per day, resulting in greater dependence on cheaper immigrant labor from Cambodia and Myanmar (Alexandra, 2013), but this labor is largely illegal, and the government is clamping down on their entry.

(vii) Thailand also has a strict protectionist quota system in place, where sponsoring companies must ensure the employment of four local workers for every foreign worker they wish to sponsor. This quota system can prove particularly difficult to manage, given the unpredictability of employee attrition rates.

While India and ASEAN countries signed an agreement for trade in goods in 2010, conflicts and delays have emerged, critically in the agreement on services and investment. The reason is that India has a bigger stake in the services agreement as it is a major provider of information technology services and a source of engineers and education and medical professionals, among others. However, liberalization of trade in services is highly sensitive in Malaysia and Thailand, where professional licenses are legally mandated to preserve national interests (Thuzar *et al.*, 2016).

(viii) For Thai businesspeople, doing business in India is not easy either, although India has significantly improved its rank in Ease of Doing Business, in fact from a rank of 142 out of 189 countries in 2014 (*Doing Business Rankings* of countries by the World Bank), its rank in 2019 was 77. Thailand is ranked at 26. Despite the improved ranking, some of the issues identified with doing business in India are the lack of standardized procedures and intra- and inter-state harmonization of rules, difficulty in loan approvals for foreign projects, and inadequate information. Construction permits are easily obtained in Thailand (rank 6), while this is still most challenging in India. For the Make in India vision to be realized, India must also ease procedures, as has been pointed out by several Indian business-persons settled in Thailand.

(ix) In terms of the "Strength of Investor Protection" Indicator, while Thailand has a strength of 0.77, India's strength is measured at 0.57. This is based on the indicators of financial freedom of the World Bank for 2016.[15]

8.12 Importance of India–Thailand Economic Relations

8.12.1 *A Perspective from Thailand*

(a) India is already the third largest economy in the world in terms of GDP and is one of the fastest growing economies too with a growth rate of more than 6.5% in 2018–2019. Moreover, it is a large market with a growing middle-class population of more than 650 million.

(b) Physical connectivity is improving and this holds the promise of reducing trading costs with India.

(c) India, with a large labor force is emerging as a low-cost production base in Asia.

(d) Over the decades, nearly 30 Thai companies are engaged in the field of infrastructure, real estate, food processing, chemicals, and hotel and hospitality sectors in India.

The above was further reiterated by Thai Trade Center executive director and Consul Suwimol Tilokruangchai, in an interview to PTI when she said, "The Thailand based companies see a good opportunity here and are looking to invest around US$ 3 billion by 2020. The fast-growing Indian market remains attractive for Thai investors given the opportunities in green and brown field projects including energy, infrastructure, and metals". "We are looking towards India with great interest from the last seven decades and plan to enhance the bilateral trade thanks to the positive approach of both the Thai and Indian governments", she added. The

---

[15] Financial Freedom Index, The World Bank, 2016. From http://www.financialfreedomindex.com/investor_protection.php.

Department of International Trade Promotion Ministry of Commerce, Thailand, and the Thai Trade Centre, Mumbai, had organized a 3-day Thailand Week in June 2018, Suwimol said (Economic Times, 2018).

An exhibition titled *Namaste Thailand*, with a display of products made in Thailand, was held in New Delhi in early 2019. The event not only underscored the cultural connections between the two countries but also showcased opportunities for trade and investment.

8.12.2 *A Perspective from India*

(a) India is keen for access to the services sector in Thailand. The exports of services would help to reduce the adverse balance of trade between the two countries.

(b) India would be able to transform its production networks by linking up through Thailand to Global Value chains, hence being able to access the networks of other Southeast Asian economies too.

(c) The Thai government has also invited Indian companies to invest in the growth of Thailand. At present, around 40 Indian companies have made an investment of around US$2 billion in the areas of software, agricultural chemicals, and electric car development in Thailand. Leading Indian companies to invest include Tata Motors (Thailand), Tata Steel Thailand, TCS, The Aditya Birla group, Mahindra Satyam, Lupin, NIIT, Kirloskar Bothers, Punj Lloyd group, Ashok Leyland, Jindal group, and Usha Siam Steel Industries.

(d) Thailand's Special Measures Investment Year 2019.

The key objective for 2019 to be designated as the investment year is to stimulate investment in targeted industries, especially large-scale projects with a positive impact to the country's economy. All eligible projects can locate in any area except Bangkok. The total period of all procedures must not exceed 43 months (Thailand Board of Investment, 2019).

(e) According to S.S. Phool, of the India Thai Chamber of Commerce, as well as other Indian businessmen in Thailand, India also wants Thailand to take part in the development of sectors like infrastructure, electronics, automotive, hospitality, health care, and consumer goods by availing the opportunities provided by Make in India, Digital India,

Skill India, and other initiatives.[16] Amid this developing scenario, India–Thai Chamber of commerce (ITCC) is trying to culminate excellent business relations between the two countries. Since its inception in 1974, ITCC has been playing a substantial role in strengthening the bilateral relations. The foundation of ITCC rests on the pillars of business growth between the two nations.

(f) The Indian diaspora can also be catalyzed for bridging the business-to-business and people-to-people contacts not only between Thailand and India's Northeast but all of India as well. This is an area that holds tremendous promise.

Hence, barriers to trade and investment between the two countries must be reduced through (a) liberalizing their trade in services; (b) reforming their regulatory frameworks; (c) gaining knowledge about each other's markets; (d) greater involvement of the stakeholders, industry bodies, as well as sector experts; and (e) gaining greater market access for service providers (Goyal & Mukherjee, 2018).

8.13 Tourism

Tourism is another sector that not only provides the space for cultural linkages and enhanced understanding between the people of India and Thailand but also facilitates a greater civilizational bonding and connects with Buddhism, Brahmanism, and Hinduism. Thailand is well known as a major tourist destination for Indian people, due to its tourist-friendly policies. Not only is Thailand with its scenic beaches a haven for Bollywood, but the locales also invite young couples for destination weddings and theme parties. It is no doubt then that Thailand has the fourth largest tourism receipts in the world (UNWTO, 2018). Its percentage share was 4.32 of the entire world's earnings from tourism in 2017.

In contrast, India, with a population and land size several times larger than that of Thailand, did not feature in the top 10 countries in terms of earnings from tourism. Thailand's earnings were US$57.5 billion, while that of India's was US$27.3 billion in 2017 (*Ibid.*).

---

[16]Interviews with Mr. S.S. Phool, Mr. Kitti Limskul, and Mr. Raj Sachdev by Reena Marwah, July 21, 2014.

Indian tourists are increasingly being preferred to Chinese tourists, who at present do outnumber the 1.6 million tourists who traveled from India to Thailand in 2018.Thai ambassador Gongsakdi seeks to increase this number to 2 million in 2019. In his words, "Indian tourists are preferred as they help the Thai economy by spending almost INR 10,000 per family per day. In contrast, Chinese tourists are increasingly staying in hotels owned by the Chinese and are also using Chinese tourism companies. In this way, Thailand does not benefit very much in terms of revenue".[17]

In terms of e-visas availed by Thai citizens traveling to India, the number was 32,179, which is 1.9% of the total visitors to India in the year 2017. It is heartening to note that the figure for the period January to June 2018 was 31,290, indicating a share of 2.8% in tourist arrivals from Thailand (*Ibid.*).

It is also significant to note here that while India seeks to boost travel and tourism from Thailand to its Northeast, the Thais would like to travel to all parts of India, including the cities of South India, through which India has age-old links through the Cholas, also the temples in Thailand and South India have much in common. This was highlighted to the author by the Thai ambassador. There is no doubt that India, despite its improved infrastructure, still carries an image of low safety for tourists as well as possibilities of naïve customers being overcharged for services. Moreover, the tourism circuit connecting places of worship for Buddhists needs to be publicized.

To be viewed as a tourist destination, the importance of image building for India is significant. As Faizal Yahya questions, "Is India's image undergoing a rebranding process into something more positive and dynamic? Given the myriad of images and complexities of Indian society, could India be marketed as a single brand by the government?" (Yahya, 2008, p. 137).

According to the Indian Ambassador Mrs. Durai, "There are around 17 Indian cities directly connected to Bangkok with around 330 flights per week. One can reach any city of India in 3–4 hours. We have excellent

---

[17]Interview of Thailand ambassador to New Delhi, India to the author on March 14, 2019 at Namaste Thailand, New Delhi.

people-to-people contacts and air connectivity, which complement our trade and investment relations. We have all elements necessary for doing business between India and Thailand". She also added that Indian coffee had a huge potential in Thailand as young Thais are increasingly consuming more coffee. In her words, "I welcome coffee companies in Thailand to look at Indian coffee and engage with Indian companies and Coffee Board" (Durai, 2019).

Thailand has been offering free visas for Indian travelers, and this too has greatly enhanced the footfalls of Indians in Thailand. The connect through the Indian diaspora could be beefed up; this would help Indians to travel to cities in the North of Thailand including Chiang Mai and Chiang Rai as well, where there are several Indian families.

8.14 Conclusion

India and Thailand are increasingly seeking out each other in terms of economic and business engagement. Over the period 2004–2015, there was stagnancy in India–Thailand bilateral trade, despite the Early Harvest Scheme covering 82 items signed on August 30, 2004. Post-2010, the ASEAN–India FTA was signed and India sought to increase trade with countries in Southeast Asia. However, both with ASEAN and specifically with Thailand too, India's exports have not risen as fast as the latter's exports to India, giving rise to an increasing trade deficit for India. Hence, the delay in signing of the India–Thailand free trade agreement and its consequence of India being perceived as overcautious and unwilling to take forward the bilateral relations. Without a doubt, economics is the overarching concern for countries today, even as they yearn for higher standards of living in a global environment that is unpredictable and increasingly nationalist.

During the visit of the Thai Prime Minister to India in June 2016, at the joint press statement, PM Modi said,

> "We encourage them, and the other business-sector stakeholders, to take the lead in tapping the emerging business opportunities in both our countries. Alongside trade, there are also ample avenues for greater manufacturing and investment linkages. We see a synergy between Thai strengths

in infrastructure, particularly tourism infrastructure, and India's priorities. Information Technology, pharmaceuticals, auto-components, and machinery are some other areas of promising collaboration. We also see early conclusion of a balanced Comprehensive Economic and Partnership Agreement as our shared priority".[18]

Thailand's PM Chan-o-Cha, who visited India in 2016 and in 2018, also agreed that while India and Thailand had already been negotiating an FTA, the talks should be made all-encompassing by taking the trading relations beyond just goods to include services and investments (*Ibid.*).

As discussed, there are huge opportunities for India and Thailand to promote trade, investment, and tourism. Thailand is seeking India's cooperation in several sectors, such as aerospace, automation, medical devices, pharmaceutical, bio-technology, and IT/ITeS, as it strives to transform into a value-based economy.

The Thailand Board of Investment, flagging the importance of overseas investment in the Eastern Economic Corridor, held a seminar titled Opportunity Thailand in 2017. "According to the government's Thailand 4.0 model, ten target industries have been identified as the new engines of growth to transform the country into a regional innovation hub through the use of creativity, advanced technology, research and development and human resource development. Indian companies can contribute in all these sectors", Kanokporn Chotipal, Director and Consul (Investment), Thailand Board of Investment, told *BusinessLine.* "A full-fledged FTA can play a vital role to boost trade for both sides and will lead to investment as well. Trade volume has increased significantly after the Early Harvest Scheme of Thailand–India was put in place and the ASEAN–India FTA was implemented. An FTA can complement each other's economy in the long run", she said. "Both the governments have to draw the attention of businesses from both sides to the benefits that each can get from the FTA, so that they can utilize the privileges offered", she added.

---

[18] Joint Press Statement in New Delhi, June 17, 2016. From https://www.narendramodi.in/pm-modi-with-pm-of-thailand-mr-thai-pm-prayut-chan-o-cha-at-the-joint-press-statement-in-new-delhi-484563; accessed on May 10, 2019.

She further added, "India should consider Thailand because our infrastructure is excellent, transparency of rules and regulations and, of course, costs are still low compared with other developed countries in ASEAN" (Sen, 2018). Through 5 years of reforms, Thailand has facilitated the setting-up processes and reduced the time to start a business from 27.5 days to 4.5 days (Nordea, n.a.). Medical tourism and pharmaceuticals are areas where Indian companies could have significant opportunities, both here in India and for investment in Thailand.

The Indian diaspora in Thailand, which number about 250,000 can also play an instrumental role in furthering economic engagement between our two countries. Migrants from India include people from Punjab, Uttar Pradesh, and South India, who established themselves in various businesses including textiles, hotel business, gems and jewelry, travel agencies, etc., in Bangkok, Chiang Mai, Chiang Rai, and other cities.[19]

There are several opportunities both through the bilateral and multilateral forums to engage with Thailand. Thailand and India are closely cooperating in BIMSTEC, ASEAN, MGC, as well as the East Asian Summit. Finally, it is the Regional Comprehensive Economic Partnership, which, for Thailand as the chair of ASEAN, is a pressing issue. ASEAN and Thailand in particular seek India's cooperation in concluding the RCEP negotiations in 2019 as, without India, the scope for increasing economic partnerships in Asia would be quite hollow. This was articulated by Chulalongkorn University's ASEAN Studies Centre's Director of Academic Affairs, Piti Srisangnam, "Free trade agreements will be beneficial to Thailand and ASEAN as a whole. With a shrinking export sector, Thailand needs RCEP more than ever".[20]

---

[19] Details revealed by Mr. Ranjeet Singh (owner of Ga Boutique), President of the Indian diaspora in Chiang Mai to the author on April 24, 2019.

[20] Patpon Sabpaitoon, 'Challenges in store as Thailand assumes ASEAN chair'. From https://www.bangkokpost.com/news/general/1603614/challenges-in-store-as-thailand-assumes-asean-chair, January 1, 2019; accessed on May 8, 2019.

Chapter 9

Reimagining India–Thailand Relations: The Way Ahead

This last chapter underlines and reiterates Thailand's place in Southeast Asia and its immense relevance for India, not merely because it is a land bridge to SEA but also because of the immense opportunities which are within it.

Hence, here, the discussion is focused on the following aspects:

1. Economic aspects and positioning Thailand as a manufacturing hub in ASEAN: Possibilities for India
2. Repositioning Thailand in India's geostrategic construct
3. Potential for India to deepen relations with Thailand

The effort here is to avoid repetition of the aspects discussed through the multilateral and bilateral perspectives in the previous chapters.

From India's standpoint, it is imperative to understand Thailand for purposes of expanding economic engagement, which is the precursor for commercial, strategic, diasporic, and people-to-people relationships. It is also not without reason that Thailand's leaning toward China must be balanced by a resurgent India, even as the former continues to be politically in the grip of military generals, whose affinity to China is a given.

A major section of this book has been devoted to India's soft power influence and reach; yet to be truly considered a regional power, India must also project its hard power capabilities in terms of delivering on projects as well as committing to its role as a security provider and dependable ally for its neighbors. Several foreign policy experts, including former Foreign Secretaries Shyam Saran and S. Jaishankar, have asserted that unless India is viewed (in its neighborhood) as being a strong and reliable partner, its influence will not be perceptible beyond it. This has also been echoed by interviewees in Thailand including one of their eminent strategic affairs experts Professor Panitan Wattanayagorn.

9.1 Economic Aspects and Positioning Thailand as a Manufacturing Hub in ASEAN: Possibilities for India

Thailand is well established as an export manufacturing hub among ASEAN countries. It is also a hub for companies of global powers such as Japan and the USA. The imperative for an interest in developing alternatives to China as a production base has resulted in Thailand's importance as it provides a strategic gateway to ASEAN and the rest of the Asia Pacific. With the increasing growth in CLMV countries, as well as stable rates of growth in ASEAN-5, this region is drawing investors from across the world.

Thailand's ability to source low-cost labor from its neighboring countries, especially Myanmar and Laos, as well as its well-developed logistics infrastructure, abundant natural resources, and well-established industrial base make it an attractive manufacturing hub, especially for the CLMV countries. In addition, government incentives are helping the manufacturing sector move up the value chain. This evolution has been spurred by the wider adoption of high-tech equipment, the development of cluster structures, and the establishment of special economic zones along its borders. Thailand's manufacturing sector in 2015 contributed 27% to its GDP; this rose to 35.03% in 2017.[1] Export surpluses have been the outcome of its capacity to export food and beverages, metal products, construction materials, electric appliances, as well as vehicles and machinery.

---

[1] From https://www.statista.com/statistics/331893/share-of-economic-sectors-in-the-gdp-in-thailand/.

With this, futuristic outlook of Thailand's economic situation, there are several aspects that need to be considered for placing Thailand in a pivotal position.

9.1.1 *India, Thailand, and the ASEAN Economic Community*

Thailand's membership to the ASEAN economic community and free trade area and its developed infrastructure make it an ideal base for import/export enterprises. Since the introduction of the e-Customs system in December 2016 (an online system that centralizes all customs and licensing procedures), and promotion of export-processing zones, the costs of running a cross-border trading operation in Thailand were further reduced. For the AEC, it still needs to move toward a freer and more connected economic region. In addition to practical tax concerns and cooperation as well as harmonization of Permanent Establishment rules, there are several other hurdles in the way of cross-border collaboration. Indian companies are also integrating with East Asian production networks, especially in critical, knowledge-based parts of the value chain (Kumar *et al.*, 2006).

Although India and ASEAN countries signed an agreement for trade in goods in 2010, conflicts and delays have emerged, critically in the agreement on services and investment. The reason is that India has a bigger stake in the services agreement as it is a major provider of information technology services and a source of engineers, education, and medical professionals, among others. However, liberalization of trade in services is highly sensitive in Malaysia and Thailand where professional licenses are legally mandated to preserve national interests. Other concerns stem from India's manufacturers, whose profit margins have already been severely impacted by imports from China. However, even as the trade war with the United States continues unabated, Beijing is vigorously pushing ahead with negotiations on the Regional Comprehensive Economic Partnership (RCEP). ASEAN countries and Australia too are keen for India to relent. Indian industrialists from several sectors, especially such as steel, auto, textiles, and engineering goods, have been apprehensive about taking on commitments to eliminate tariffs for RCEP members, especially China. Even as India continues to negotiate, there can be no dilution of the interests of industry, which is already struggling with a volatile global economy.

9.1.2 Thailand in the "Mighty Five": Aligning Economic and Strategic Interests

The five Asia-Pacific nations of Malaysia, India, Thailand, Indonesia, and Vietnam (MITI-V or the "Mighty Five") are expected to be included in the top 15 nations on manufacturing competitiveness over the next 5 years. This is as per the Global CEO survey, conducted by Deloitte, published in its 2016 Global manufacturing competitiveness index report. In its rankings by country, Thailand is at a high rank of 14 globally and is expected to retain the same position in 2020, even though its index score is expected to improve from 60.4 to 62.0 over the period 2016–2020 (Deloitte, 2016). In the IMD World Competitiveness report of 2019, which assesses 63 economies on 235 indicators, Singapore topped at number 1, Thailand was at a rank of 25, and India at 43 (Jamrisko, 2019).

These five countries (Malaysia, India, Thailand, Indonesia, and Vietnam) can further synergize their development priorities and technical cooperation in the coming years. It is well known that India's relations with Malaysia, Vietnam, and Indonesia have been prioritized by the Modi government. Among several initiatives, India is also developing the port of Sabang in Indonesia.

While articulating Thailand's view on ASEAN centrality, Professor Chinwanno in an interview to the author remarked, "In ASEAN we do not have a unified position on many issues, we should find a common goal and common strategy and this can be led by any of the Mighty Five, viz. by Thailand or Indonesia. The original members should be the core group. In terms of security we are all concerned with the unreliability of USA and assertiveness of China; we can talk both of the traditional issues and the non-traditional issues, for the traditional issue is the border issue, the South China Sea and Taiwan Straits. Whatever China does, it does to deter USA; however, we have to make the Chinese realize that whatever they do to deter USA, adversely affects the smaller countries in ASEAN".[2] This statement amply reflects Thailand's concerns of collateral damage, a fallout of USA–China trade war.

9.1.3 *Catapulting Growth of CLMV*

In addition to infrastructure projects, both India and Thailand can help the CLMV countries by providing them assistance in smaller and deliverable projects in agricultural and energy-related cooperation such as production and processing of agricultural products, renewable energy, sustainable hydropower development, and development of joint research in the field of agriculture, fishery, forestry, livestock, aquaculture, and energy. In doing this, Thailand can cooperate with Japan, India, and the Asian Development Bank to help the CLMV with their existing projects.[3] The leaders of Cambodia, Vietnam, Laos, Myanmar, and Thailand agreed on a shared vision to push for the region's true potential and increase connectivity between the five countries. The CLMV countries have consistently approached Thailand for enhancing connectivity in the region. Thailand 4.0 brings renewed hope to the region.

It was at the ASEAN World Economic Forum in Vietnam 2018 when this was echoed by Aung San Suu Kyi, Myanmar State Counsellor. "I think we could work together and not just make this a commercial region, but a region that could be a lesson on how we make our complementarities strong", Ms. Suu Kyi said. "By keeping things together, and even making our competition healthy, we will progress".

Thailand desires India's cooperation for the development of CLMV countries; India on its part is taking forward several mechanisms for collaboration, under the MGC process, especially with Cambodia, Myanmar, and Vietnam. The Thai Ambassador in New Delhi shared this with the author. The Ayeyawady-Chao Phraya-Mekong Economic Cooperation Strategy is a political, economic, and cultural organization among Thailand, Laos, Vietnam, Cambodia, and Myanmar (ACMECS). ACMECS

---

[2]Professor Chulacheeb Chinwanno, Department of Political Science, Thammasat University, in an interview to the author on May 29, 2018 in Bangkok.
[3]From http://www.nationmultimedia.com/news/opinion/kavi/30311843.

provides one such opportunity for close development cooperation and coordination between Thailand and India. Thailand is taking the lead to creating a regional fund with its neighbors to back infrastructure and other development projects and to lessen their reliance on Chinese investment (Macaes, 2019, p. 132). Here lies the opportunity for India.

9.1.4 *Thailand's EEC: A Catalyst for Regional Integration*

It can be inferred that Thailand's EEC will grow into a modern metropolitan, a hub of trade and investment, a center for regional transportation and logistics, a significant source for human resources, a tourist attraction, and most importantly the most modern Gateway to Asia. This is based on the assumption that Thailand — and, indeed, ASEAN region as a whole — will evolve into a sophisticated network production base for key industries such as automobiles and electrical manufactures.

While Thailand's industrial policies are in a phase of transition and reform, they need to be even more attractive for bringing investments in R&D and high-tech industries, especially from India and Japan. According to several Indian manufacturers, the incentives offered under Thailand's industrial policies are attractive, yet the data on investment, as given in an earlier chapter, from Indian companies do not show any major increase. Moreover, in comparison to investment received by Thailand from ASEAN and China, it is insignificant. According to the Thai ambassador in New Delhi, "no Indian company has yet come forward to take advantage of the facilities under the Eastern Economic Corridor". However, sources say 1 in 7 startups in Southeast Asia are started by Indians or Indian-origin CEOs; moreover, there is keen interest in expanding into Thailand as a means of risk diversification and as a stepping stone to the ASEAN market.

9.1.5 *Potential of Thailand's Tourism Industry*

In 2016, 32.6 million foreign tourists visited Thailand. In 2018, tourist arrivals were 38.27 million; 39 million tourists visited in 2019. Tourist arrivals are expected to remain high in the coming years with improved connectivity through and within Thailand. Despite the baht having strengthened, overseas travelers continue to visit Thailand. Also, industries related to tourism, including hospitality, food service, and recreational activities, will once again be prime targets for potential investors. Indian tourists have, time and again, been provided free-visa entry to take advantage of the burgeoning growth of the capacity to spend of India's large middle-class population. Thailand received about 1.9 million tourists from India in 2019.

9.2 Repositioning Thailand in India's Geoeconomic and Geostrategic Construct

First, with regards to an outlook for economic revival, Thailand is expected to grow manifold in the coming years. For India, its AEP has become one of the most important cornerstones of its foreign policy. Possibly then, encouraged by Thailand's Look West policy, the two countries could seek out newer areas of convergence to compel greater economic cooperation.

Second, with Thailand being viewed as a bridge to the East, India needs to develop and link itself to its production networks in manufacturing and services. Given that more than two-thirds of the world trade for inputs and products is through global value chains (GVCs), for boosting manufacturing, it is imperative for India to link up with these through its Southeast Asian partners, especially Thailand. This hinges on India's ability to improve infrastructure in the Northeast and link to Thailand through Myanmar. Two key projects, the KMMTTP and the 3,200-km Trilateral Highway connecting India with Myanmar and Thailand, have suggested ways in which the connectivity corridors can be boosted and point out comparisons with how China is going about building connectivity with Southeast Asia. Greater connectivity with the East is expected to enhance India's trade with the ASEAN to US$100 billion. The development of physical infrastructure for connectivity also requires other conditions as appropriate logistics and transportation policies, reduction of tariff and non-tariff barriers as well as one stop customs clearance among other measures. However, security concerns at our borders must be calibrated, even as the aspiration is for efficient connectivity.

Third, India should take definite proactive measures to engage in trade, investment, and economic opportunities with Thailand. The key in the short run is not to sign more agreements, but to first implement those already in place so that concrete changes can be seen. From a more long-term perspective, India must take measures to increase its exports to Thailand, not only to reduce its trade deficit but also to boost Indian manufacturing. Despite more than 33 rounds of ITTNC trade negotiations and talks on investment, issues remain unresolved, resulting in a perception that there is a lack of seriousness in India's willingness to Act East.

Even as India seeks to integrate with the global economy, it ranks 74 out of 169 countries (according to the DHL Global Connectedness Index Report of 2018). Thailand, in contrast, ranks 25th globally (DHL, 2018). Concerning opening up retail space for inward FDI from Thailand, it has been argued that much of India's fear is exaggerated, because even with full liberalization, foreign retailers would find it difficult to dominate the Indian market. However, in the retail food business, 100% FDI is permitted. This presents an opportunity for foreign investors in India.

It may be true that both countries face various bilateral issues, as detailed in the earlier sections of this chapter. It is also true that the possibilities for further collaboration are manifold, not only in trade and investment but also in tourism, corporate partnerships, and institutional connections. These multifaceted areas would eventually help develop the entire region, especially if there is a conscious harnessing of the potential of India's Northeastern states.

Fourth, Thailand–India relations are strategically pivotal when it comes to combating terrorism, crime, drugs, and human trafficking and enhancing peace in the region. In May 2013, a Memorandum of Understanding (MoU) for Extradition was signed in addition to the Treaty on the Transfer of Sentenced Persons. Thus, as Ambassador Shringla stated in an interview, "the bilateral framework for legal and security cooperation has also been strengthened with an MoU on cooperation in the exchange of intelligence related to money laundering and financial terrorism. India and Thailand also need to work together to combat piracy, to ensure the security of sea lanes as well as for safety and security of navigation in the Indian Ocean" (Parashar, 2014).

Fifth, despite India's huge advantage in the maritime space, it has not leveraged this to strengthen relations with countries in the Indian Ocean, while China has fast-expanded its footprint both on the continental shelf and in the seas. India has realized it cannot ignore its maritime interests in the Indian Ocean (as evidenced by Prime Minister Modi's 2015 visit to three island countries in the Indian Ocean and investment in marine infra-structure, as well as his 2019 visit to Sri Lanka and the Maldives), and here it requires cooperation from Thailand. Without Thailand as a partner, India's position as a dominant power in the Indian Ocean may be compromised. India needs to strengthen its influence and control over Indian Ocean choke points through security relationships with Thailand and other key littoral states such as Singapore, Mauritius, and Oman. India had set up the Andaman and Nicobar Command in 2001 in the Bay of Bengal (its only triservice command), which serves as a focal point for the engagement of its navy with the navies of Thailand and Indonesia, to secure its strategic interests.

Sixth, with Thailand as the current Chair of ASEAN, there is the expectation that India's ties with the ASEAN will grow. Thailand desires to expand its ties with India, not only in the economic and strategic spheres but also in people-to-people exchanges.

Seventh, India presents itself as a large market for Thailand and other SE Asian economies. With a large middle class and strong macro-economic fundamentals, boosted by the anticipated reforms by Modi Government 2.0, India can add further dynamism to the East Asian region.

Thus, while the ASEAN countries are banding together in response to the China challenge, as many among them fear China too, India suffers from no such trust deficit at present with any of the ASEAN countries. However, although India has been mainly inward looking in the past, its regional initiatives and mechanisms are becoming integral to an outward strategy in response to China's grand BRI.

It is surprising then that Thailand moved into India's strategic lens only 10 years ago. Given India's concerns of securing the sea-lanes of communication through the Northwest and Northeast corners of the Indian Ocean, Thailand's geostrategic location must not be lost sight of. This has been amplified by Brahma Chellaney: "If China were to gain the upper hand in the Indian Ocean region, it would mark the end of India's great-power ambitions. India after that will be seen as merely a sub-regional power whose clout does not extend across South Asia, with

Pakistan challenging it in the West and China in the North and South" (Chellaney and Singh, 2015, p. 38).

As Rachman states, post the 2014 coup, Thailand which had been historically regarded in the Western camp, began to tilt toward China. USA downgraded its relationship with the Thai military and called for a return to democracy. In response, the Thais moved closer to Beijing — announcing the purchase of submarines from China in 2015. Such weapons sales have a more profound impact (Rachman, 2016, p. 109). However, there are concerns among the Thai people, and one such articulation is Thailand's difficult position *vis-à-vis* USA and China, for the past at least two decades. Thailand, in fact, has pursued a strategy of hedging and comprehensive multilateral engagement in its relations with the United States and China, since 2001 (Busbarat, 2016).

Concerns have been articulated regarding Thailand's ability to balance the big powers. There has been a concern regarding the Kra Canal or the Kra Isthmus, which will cut Thailand's South from the mainland. This project, which is seen by China, as helping to reduce travel time for its ships, is being considered under its BRI. The canal, when built, would permit the East–West passage of ships from the South China Sea to the Indian Ocean without having to detour all the way South around Singapore island at the bottom of the Peninsula. India is hopeful that Singapore would continue to oppose this.

Moreover, there is anxiety among the Thai people, and one such articulation is Thailand's difficult position *vis-à-vis* USA and China, both of which are jostling for influence. "Once the US pushes back against China's grand strategy, Thailand may become just another pawn between two powers. The *junta* is betting Thailand's future without sufficient public scrutiny. The detailed cost-benefit analysis of Thailand's participation in BRI has not been made public, which has a right to more transparency" (Panyaarvudh, 2019). Macaes has also envisioned that in a few years China would have built the Kra Canal, thus linking the Indian and Pacific Oceans, as it lies within its BRI vision. Moreover, there is a Chinese construction company that has in 2018 expressed interest in the project (Macaes, 2019, p. 65). Thailand, as chair of ASEAN, must help the grouping to strike a balance between the existing and rising powers, for it to remain united and strong.

9.3 Potential for India to Deepen Relations with Thailand

It was during the Republic Day Parade 2018 that India presented its indigenous defense capabilities before the heads of all 10 ASEAN nations and on the sidelines of Republic Day Parade, Prime Minister Modi concluded six bilateral meetings with the Vietnam, Philippines, Myanmar, Thailand, Brunei, and Singapore in which defense and security cooperation was one of the key focus areas.[4]

This underscores the strategic lens through which India is viewing key bilateral relationships with countries in SEA and especially with Thailand. The way forward is discussed in what follows.

9.3.1 *Historical and Cultural Linkages*

India can leverage its strong historical and cultural linkages with Thailand to build partnerships. Moreover, India's large business community and diaspora in Thailand, with some families settled for more than three generations, could contribute in strengthening the bonds of friendship. Friendship associations, cultural centers, and social organizations such as the Thai Bharat Cultural Lodge (TBCL) and others could be further strengthened through the Indian embassy. There is a strong common interest in promoting sub-regional, regional, and international tourism in the Bay of Bengal space and the Buddhist tourist circuits, and in showcasing similar cultural and historical sites. While Indian tourists to Thailand exceed 1 million a year, Thai tourists to India number only about 100,000, leaving tremendous scope for expanding tourism along with the Buddhist sites.

9.3.2 *Linkages through the Indian Diaspora*

India must take advantage of the fact that its large diaspora is well integrated in the Thai society. Thailand's experience leads us to the fact that

---

[4]From https://www.vifindia.org/article/2019/january/04/india-s-gradual-transition-from-defense-market-to-export-hub.

Indians, as traders, merchants, and investors, have exercised their expertise and skills as businesspersons throughout history. Through more than 60 associations and business councils, there are several levers to build linkages in business, education, tourism, and investment. The Indian diaspora has contributed significantly in enhancing India–Thailand relations. As India's External Affairs Minister, Dr. S. Jaishankar has stated, "As far as the Indian government is concerned, we value the diaspora enormously because we think in many ways they are the image of the country in the world. The success of the diaspora in different parts of the world leads to stronger connections with other societies"[5] (Santosdiaz and Mehta, 2019).

9.3.3 *Education and Science and Technology Linkages*

Human resource development, education, science and technology, information technology, biotechnology, etc., are areas in which the two countries have a common interest (Sudhit, 2003). Agreements have been signed between the Indian Council for Cultural Relations (ICCR) and Thammasat University for the establishment of the ICCR Hindi Chair of Indian Studies (Hindi Languages) and to encourage work on the translation of Thai literature into Indian languages. Thammasat University and Chulalongkorn Universities have established Indian study centers to help catalyze social science research in the areas of mutual interest. Silpakorn University also has a center for Sanskrit Studies. Chiang Mai University, on April 24, 2019 also launched the India Study Center in the Department of Social Sciences. A seminar titled, India–Thailand relations: Beyond Boundaries was also organized on the occasion. The author also spoke of India's multidimensional linkages with Thailand and the imperative for strengthening these. Ambassador Suchitra Durai also highlighted the significance of forging understanding between our two countries through people-to-people contacts. In this context, learning the Thai language in India through centers of Thai studies in Indian Universities must also be

---

[5]Santosdiaz, R. & Mehta, R. (2019). Potential for India's USD 80 billion remittances economy. https://www.msn.com/en-in/news/other/potential-for-indias-usd-80-billion-remittances-economy/ar-AAHjOlp; accessed on September 15, 2019.

underlined. Moreover, scholars of Sanskrit and Hindi may be encouraged to learn the Thai language.

To build connections in science and technology, Thailand's Geoinformatics and Space Technology Development Agency (GISTDA) has signed two MoUs. Another project aims to publish an archaeological atlas in a book and digital form jointly by India's National Atlas and Thematic Mapping Organization (NATMO) and Thailand's GISTDA, with thematic plates using high-resolution satellite data and geospatial technology to highlight the spread of Buddhism from India to Southeast Asia. The proposed project will include other ASEAN countries that will be participating in the AEC, along with India and Thailand (Bhattacherjee, 2013).

9.3.4 *An Expansion of Two-Way Trade*

On the trade front, the two countries have decided to increase bilateral trade to more than US$12 billion in 2020, from US$8.6 billion in 2017–2018. Concerning the AIFTA and Thailand, some of the product categories of export interest to India on which tariffs are being gradually eliminated are processed food, organic chemicals, pharmaceuticals, fish and crustaceans, and machinery. Thailand expects this will help foster multilateral relations with India. Trade in services has been a neglected area in India–Thailand relations. A survey of Indian and Thai companies conducted in 2014 showed that investors in both countries gave precedence to stable political and social conditions as well as market growth potential, prior to undertaking any investment (Mukherjee and Goyal, 2015).

Potential for Indian military equipment exports: Thailand has more than doubled its military spending from under US$3 billion to US$6.07 billion in 2014. Its per capita defense expenditure at US$86.4 is two and a half times that of India's. The Thai junta leader declared, soon after the coup in August 2014, "If we don't increase the budget and purchase new weapons, then nobody will fear us" (Lefevre, 2014). Military generals being given permission to increase defense budgets, it is plausible that US$7.1 billion is the budget for military purchases for the fiscal year 2019–2020. This could be an opportunity for India to leverage its Make in India vision and enter into defense export deals with Thailand and also achieve a more balanced trade.

9.3.5 *Investment and Infrastructural Alliances for Connectivity*

China has been (since at least 2013) engaged in extensive infrastructure building of Belt and Road projects in Southeast Asia; in contrast, India's projects have been experiencing unprecedented delays. While China's investments in the CLMV countries on connectivity projects have progressed well, Thailand presents another story. Despite China's closeness to the Thai Prime Minister, its Sino-Thai rail project, which is a part of the Kunming–Singapore project, has also witnessed delays. When the junta seized power, negotiations on the Sino-Thai rail project intensified, but the timely construction of the line has been far from assured. The delays are primarily due to civil society protests over a lack of transparency (Lauridsen, 2019, p. 22). Post-2014, India has expedited the connectivity projects including the IMT Highway as well as the KMMTP. Once these projects are completed, the potential for flow of goods and capital from and to Myanmar and Thailand will receive a boost. According to the report on private equity by Bain and Co., India's economy is poised for growth in the coming year with capital markets on an upswing. However, high rates of interest are a dampener (Bain and Company, 2019).

9.3.6 *Balancing Chinese Strategic Influence*

In the strategic sphere, Thailand, upbeat about India's potential as the world's fastest growing economy, is keen to expand ties as a balancing power to China in ASEAN. India's relations with Thailand have largely been propelled by soft areas rather than strategic areas. However, since 2005, when the first Coordinated Patrol (CORPAT) was held between the Indian Navy and the Royal Thai Navy, joint exercises are being conducted by the two countries. The subsequent series of patrols with joint exercises and exchanges to enhance inter-operability have increased confidence levels between the two navies and contributed to the effective implementation of the Law of the Sea to prevent illegal activities. For example, the

17th cycle of CORPAT, conducted in the Andaman Sea from November 13 to 18, 2013, was to counter piracy, poaching, and arms smuggling. A recent interaction of Indo-Thai CORPAT was held in January 2018. During the exercise, one ship and one aircraft from both navies participated. From June 6 to 22 June, 2018, both sides held the 26th edition of the Indo-Thai CORPAT. The engagement occurred along similar lines and involved a series of interactions between the two sides, including high-level meetings as well as activities including ship visits and cultural events.

In addition to joint maritime patrols, India–Thailand defense cooperation includes training of officers at each other's armed forces training institutions and exchange visits at various levels. India and Thailand had also initiated joint army exercises called "Exercise Maitrayee" at Ramgarh in Bihar in 2010. The drill in 2017 was held in the Indian state of Himachal Pradesh for 15 days. In 2018, this exercise commenced on August 9, 2018, in Thailand's Chachoengsao Province to enhance interoperability between forces from both countries. This time the two armies met for 10 days. Exercise Maitrayee had focussed on increasing interoperability between the countries and involved joint training, planning, and execution of a host of tactical drills designed to offset likely threats that may be encountered in urban warfare scenario.

Given China's extensive border trade and the role of non-state actors in Myanmar, India must expand its engagement with this immediate neighbor in the East. It is the only ASEAN country that shares a land border with India. India has also cooperated in helping Myanmar with technology crucial for maintaining internal security and coastal maritime patrolling capabilities (Ram, 2018). Yet, the strategic component of the policy will always remain underutilized until there is proper formalization and coordination between agencies and an operational policy in place. India should now work toward operationalizing a policy that will propel it toward being recognized as a major power in the world (*Ibid.*).

9.3.7 *Advantage Thailand: Learnings for India*

Thailand has a rich and unique experience in the development, maintenance, modernization, and upgradation of infrastructure, particularly roads, airports, ports, power, telecommunications, and communications. It has excelled in the social services and other sectors, particularly health-care, population control, hospitality, tourism, ecological management, and poverty alleviation. In addition, *One Tambon, One Product* model of sustainable development provides learnings for India's growth story.

9.3.8 *Advantage India: Learnings for Thailand*

In Asia, where democracy is in retreat, India's vibrant democracy — the election processes as well as its capacity to provide a multicultural setting for over a billion people — has lessons for Thailand. India's experience in managing a pluralistic, diverse, and heterogeneous society is noteworthy, and there is much that Thailand can learn in these and other areas. India's technical and management institutions as well as its advances in software development continue to awe Thailand.

9.3.9 *RCEP: The Mega Trade Deal*

27 rounds of RCEP negotiations have been held since 2013. Despite all efforts of the RCEP countries, the mega trade deal was signed in 2019, without India. In early November 2019, at the third RCEP Summit in Bangkok, PM Modi announced that India was not going ahead with signing the deal, due to India's concerns over potential adverse consequences on its agricultural and industrial sector. In a sudden development, Japan (ahead of the India–Japan Foreign and Defence Ministerial Dialogue (2+2) in Delhi), on November 30, 2019, signaled that it would not join RCEP, without India as a partner. It is also accepted by most ASEAN countries that a mega deal without India does not hold much merit for ASEAN. Hence, negotiations are expected to continue, and if India's key concerns are addressed, there may yet be a possibility of RCEP with India in 2020!. This is despite 26 rounds of negotiations having been held since the first round was held in 2013. Thailand, as the ASEAN coordinator, is keen to see the conclusion of this mega trade deal in 2019. A mega deal signed without India does not hold much merit for ASEAN.

9.3.10 *India's Indo-Pacific Vision*

As India puts its weight behind an Indo-Pacific vision, where a rules-based regional architecture is being envisaged, it must prove that it can continue to secure the trust of key partner countries in ASEAN. Even as Thailand and the rest of ASEAN balance their own relationships between China and USA, India must realize that its own proximity with USA is not the only guarantor of an *India-style Indo-Pacific* that excludes China. Moreover, an *ASEAN style Indo-Pacific* does not epitomize "balancing" China, but in contrast, being all-inclusive. Australia and Japan are also stakeholders in the vision of a free and open Indo-Pacific. Can ASEAN be insulated from the big power rivalry? A difficult question indeed.

9.3.11 *BIMSTEC and MGC*

Without a doubt, Thailand is a key partner in the MGC and BIMSTEC. Currently, it is also the coordinator for India–ASEAN relations. ASEAN countries being mainstreamed in this geopolitical construct is essential for India and Thailand to play a dominant role. This was articulated to the author by Dr. Panitan Wattanayakorn when he said,

> "In my thinking, as adviser to deputy PM, we are interested in cooperation under this concept. It is under the already existing framework which includes BIMSTEC, MGC and the Indo-Pacific. Thailand is in the middle of this region and we can push ourselves to be more important with the development of smart cities and digital connectivity. Thailand and India can work together to link South and South East Asia. With the master plan of BIMSTEC, ACMECS and IMT we can link up; this connectivity can bring down transnational crime and Thailand looks forward to more cooperation with India".[6]

---

[6]Dr. Panitan Wattanayakorn, Advisor to the Deputy PM of Thailand for security and Institute of Strategic and International Studies, Chulalongkorn University, in an interview to the author on May 27, 2018, in Bangkok.

Given the significance of the seas, and the imperative for maritime cooperation, India can provide "distance support" in the form of information on possible threats as well as technological inputs, through its bases on the Andaman and Nicobar islands, i.e., in the Sea Lanes of Communication in the Indian Ocean and this could be useful for the navies of Thailand and other Southeast Asian countries (Devare, 2005, p. 107).

9.4 Conclusion

Thus, as has been discussed earlier, the competitive advantage of Thailand's manufacturing sector lies in its abundance of natural resources and its existing supply chains. Many of the global manufacturers who utilize Thailand as a production base rely on the country's logistics infrastructure, which connects it to a broader production network across other ASEAN countries. Indian companies located in Thailand commend the conducive investment climate.

Some, for instance, produce in Thailand to distribute products locally and within the neighboring CLMV countries (i.e., Cambodia, Laos, Myanmar, and Vietnam). Many of these are seen as having considerable market potential, especially with the formal launch of the ASEAN Economic Community.

However, at the micro level, Thailand needs to improve its ranking in its perception of corruption. It was ranked at 101 in the 2018 KPMG report (KPMG, 2018). There are other micro-level challenges, too, which may thwart its growth momentum. These include the high household debt, which has weighed on consumer spending in recent years and the slow growth in public expenditure. Despite its stable foreign exchange reserves the ultimate test is political stability.

Political stability is important for Thailand. This is because the country has experienced more than a century of centralization and interrupted democratic struggles. It is evident, according to Tanet Charoenmuang, that the struggle for democracy will be ongoing, for a closed political regime cannot co-exist with an open, liberal economic system (Charoenmuang, 2006, p. 229). Thailand held its elections on

February 29, 2019, but the verdict continued to be unclear till mid-2019. It is inevitable that the monarchy will be the nucleus of power. On July 16, 2019, the 36-member Cabinet of Thailand's elected government was sworn in. Although this marked the end of 5 years of military rule, power will continue in the hands of the same allies of the army. India's relations with the Royalty have a long history; it is expected that India will continue to be considered an important partner by the Thai political stalwarts.

It is likely that Thailand's King Vajiralongkorn or Rama X (who was crowned in a 3-day grand ceremony, in the first week of May 2019) will continue to wield power along with influence (*The Economist*, May 11, 2019). India's relations with the Royalty have a long history; it is well known that Princess Sirindhorn is a regular visitor to India, especially to Bodh Gaya and cities in India's Northeast states. It is expected that India will continue to be considered an important partner by the Thai political stalwarts.

In the ultimate analysis, the India–Thailand relationship needs to be repositioned from one of economics alone to a geostrategic one as well. The onus is on India to lift the relationship not only for enhancing engagement with the ASEAN but also for reducing the influence of China in the region, both on land and in the maritime space. As Edmund Downie, writing about India's Look East policy stated, "A half-hearted commitment to the policy has severely restricted India's footprint in these regions, even as Chinese influence destabilizes Indian hegemony in South Asia" (Downie, 2015). Despite India's bilateral strategic overtures with Thailand or defense pacts in the multilateral ambit with ASEAN, it cannot hope to contain China on Southeast Asia's continental or maritime shelf; at best, it can hope that as long as ASEAN's significance does not dwindle for Asian regionalism, India will be a country of significance for regional security.

Given Thailand's pivot toward China, it is even more significant for India to scale-up the level of its cultural, economic, and strategic engagement with Thailand, if it truly wants to Act East. A waning Look West policy of Thailand is not in India's best interest. It is, therefore, no surprise that the Modi Government had invited leaders from the BIMSTEC countries, which includes Thailand and Myanmar from ASEAN, for the swearing-in ceremony on May 30, 2019. A resurgence and dynamism in our ties with these countries is merited, ensuring that this regional grouping does not go the SAARC route! While gestures add meaning to bilateral and multilateral relationships, the real value is in an India that is a reliable, dependable partner, whose active diplomacy, visibility, and outreach are aligned with its capacity to elicit loyalty of its neighbors.

Bibliography

ADB Annual Report (2014). https://www.adb.org/sites/default/files/institutional-document/158032/adb-annual-report-2014.pdf.

ADB Annual Report (2017). https://www.adb.org/documents/adb-annual-report-2017.

Abuza, Z. (2019). *Thailand's Stolen Election*. https://thediplomat.com/2019/05/thailands-stolen-election/.

Acharya, A. (1997). Ideas, identity, and institution-building: From the 'ASEAN way' to the 'Asia-Pacific way'? *The Pacific Review*, 10(3), 319–346.

Acharya, A. (2013). *The Making of Southeast Asia: International Relations of a Region* (Cornell Studies in Political Economy). Ithaca, NY: Cornell University Press.

Albert, E. (2017). ASEAN: The Association of Southeast Asian Nations. Council on Foreign Relations. https://www.cfr.org/backgrounder/asean-association-southeast-asian-nations.

Alexandra, S. (2013). 'Human trafficking: The case of Burmese refugees in Thailand' International Journal of Comparative and Applied Criminal Justice 279, 283; see also, Mekong Migration Network & Asian Migrant Centre, Migration in the Greater Mekong Subregion: Resource Book 82.

Allingham, P. V. (n.a.). England and China: The Opium Wars 1839–60. Victorian Web. Thunder Bay, Ontario: Lakehead University. http://www.victorianweb.org/history/empire/opiumwars/opiumwars1.html.

Anand, V. (2017). ASEAN centrality and the South China Sea dispute. https://www.vifindia.org/article/2017/august/08/asean-s-centrality-and-the-south-china-sea-dispute; accessed on August 8, 2017.

Andaya, L. Y. (1994). Interactions with the Outside World and Adaptation in Southeast Asian Society, 1500–1800. In *Cambridge History of Southeast.* Nicholas Tarling, Volume 1, 345–401. Cambridge, UK: Cambridge University Press.

ASEAN (2019). ASEAN conception and evolution by Thanat Khoman. https://asean.org/?static_post=asean-conception-and-evolution-by-thanat-khoman; accessed on January 15, 2019.

Babu, S. (2017). *Organic Farming: Problems and Prospects in North East India.* Meghalaya, India: ICAR.

Bain and Co. Boston, USA. (2019). *Private Equity Report.*

Baker, C. J. & Phongpaichit, P. (2005). *A History of Thailand.* New York: Cambridge University Press.

Baruah, S. L. (2012). *A Comprehensive History of Assam.* India: Munshiram Manoharlal.

Basu, P. K. (2017). *Asia Reborn: A Continent Rises from the Ravages of Colonialism and War to a New Dynamism.* New Delhi, India: Aleph Book Company.

Behera, R. S. & Sahu, R. K. (2018). Bamboo — The poor man's green gold. *Indian Periodical.* http://indianperiodical.com/2018/12/bamboo-the-poor-mans-green-gold/; accessed on December 16, 2018.

Beng, O. K., Basu Das, S., Chong, T., Cook, M., Lee, C., & Ming, M. Y. C. (2015). *The 3rd ASEAN Reader.* Singapore: ISEAS-Yusof Ishak Institute.

Bhattacharyya, R. (2019). India's Northeast emerges as a drug-trafficking corridor between Myanmar and Bangladesh. *The Diplomat*, May 2, 2019. https://thediplomat.com/2019/05/indias-northeast-emerges-as-a-drug-trafficking-corridor-between-myanmar-and-bangladesh/.

Boisselier, J. (1975). *The Heritage of Thai Sculpture.* New York: Weatherhill Briggs.

Borah, R. (2018). The opening of an India Myanmar land border: Crossing a boon for Northeast India. *The Diplomat*, August 13, 2018. https://thediplomat.com/2018/08/the-opening-of-an-india-myanmar-land-border-crossing-a-boon-for-northeast-india/.

Bose, P. R. (2018). At Moreh, trade with Myanmar borders on informal. *The Hindu Business Line*, November 12, 2018. https://www.thehindubusinessline.com/news/at-moreh-trade-with-myanmar-borders-on-informal/article25478894.ece.

Bain and Company, Global Private Equity Report 2019, Boston, USA. https://www.bain.com/insights/topics/global-private-equity-report/.

Bajpai Prableen, Investopedia, August 18, 2015. https://www.investopedia.com/articles/investing/081815/emerging-markets-analyzing-thailands-gdp.asp; accessed on October 6, 2018.

Baker, C. J. & Phongpaichit, P. (2005). *A History of Thailand.* NY: Cambridge University Press.

Baruah S. L. (2012). *A Comprehensive History of Assam.* Munshiram Manoharlal.

Basu, P. K. (2017). Asia Reborn: A Continent Rises from the Ravages of Colonialism and War to a New Dynamism, Aleph Book Company.

Beng, O. K., Basu Das, S., Chong, T., Cook, M., Lee, C. Yeo Chai Ming, M. (2015). *The 3rd ASEAN Reader.* ISEAS-Yusof Ishak Institute. https://muse.jhu.edu/book/42016.

Bhatt, P. (2016). India-Myanmar-Thailand Trilateral Corridor: Understanding the aspects of economic diplomacy. *International Journal of Diplomacy and Economy* 3(1).

Bhattacherjee, A. (2013). India and Thailand: Bilateral Trajectory after the Indian Prime Minister's Visit, IPCS, New Delhi, June 16, 2013, http://www.ipcs.org/comm_select.php?articleNo=3993.

Boisselier, J. (1975). *The Heritage of Thai Sculpture.* New York, USA: Weatherhill Briggs.

Bommakanti, K. & Kelkar, A. (2019). China's Military Modernisation: Recent Trends, ORF Issue Brief No. 286, Observer Research Foundation.

Brookings India (2017). India-Singapore security relations in an evolving Asia: Address by Singapore Defence Minister. https://www.brookings.edu/wp-content/uploads/2017/11/transcript_india-spore_20171211.pdf.

Brown, Robert L. (1999). The Dvāravatī Wheels of the Law and the Indianization of South East Asia, Leiden: Brill (Originally published in 1996).

Buang, S. (2017). Revisit the consensus rule. https://www.nst.com.my/opinion/columnists/2017/05/242494/revisit-consensus-rule; accessed on February 20, 2019.

Busbarat, P. (2016). Bamboo swirling in the wind: Thailand's Foreign Policy imbalance between China and the United States. *Contemporary Southeast Asia*, 38(2), 233–257.

Butwell, R. (1964). *Southeast Asia Today and Tomorrow: Problems of Political Development.* New York: Praeger.

Cabalza, C. (2018). The Philippines strategic relationship with India. *The Diplomat,* January 27, 2018. https://thediplomat.com/2018/01/the-philippines-strategic-relationship-with-india/.

Caporaso, J. A. & Levine, D. P. (1992). *Theories of Political Economy.* New York, NY: Cambridge University Press.

Casparis, J. G. de & Mabbett, I. W. (1992). Religion and Popular Beliefs of Southeast Asia before c. 1500. in (eds.), Tarling, N. *The Cambridge History of Southeast Asia*, Volume 1, Cambridge, UK: University of Cambridge Press.

Census (2011). Government of India, Population of Assam. https://www.census2011.co.in/census/state/assam.html.

Chakraborty, T. & Chakraborty, M. (2018). Foreword. In *Expanding Horizons of India's Southeast Asia Policy: Look, Move and Act East.* New Delhi, India: Knowledge World.

Chandran, N. (2018). Southeast Asia is increasingly turning to India instead of the US or China. *CNBC*, March 15, 2018. https://www.cnbc.com/2018/03/15/southeast-asia-increasingly-turns-to-india-instead-of-the-us-or-china.html.

Charoenmuang, T. (2006). *Thailand: A Late Decentralising Country.* Chiang Mai, Thailand: Urban Development Institute Foundation.

Chellaney, B. (2015). Great powers surf to conquer. *The Hindustan Times.* https://chellaney.net/2015/03/12/great-powers-surf-to-conquer/.

Chellaney, B. (2018). China is stealthily waging a water war. *The Globe and Mail,* January 12, 2018. https://www.theglobeandmail.com/opinion/china-is-stealthily-waging-a-water-war/article37583969/.

Chhibber, N. K. & Shishodia, S. K. (2013). *India–Thailand Relations.* In Kumar, S. (ed.), *India–Thailand Bilateral Relations.* New Delhi, India: Mohit Publications.

Chinwanno, C. (2009). Sixty years of diplomatic relations between Thailand and India: From different perceptions to mutual benefit. In Phuangkasem, C. (ed.), *Thailand and India Relations: Partnership for Peace and Prosperity.* Bangkok, Thailand: Thammasat University and Embassy of India.

Chirathivat, S. (2010). Thailand's Greater Mekong Subregion: Role and potential linkages to Southwest China and Northeast India. *Millennial Asia,* 1(2), 171–195.

Chitrabongs, M. R. C. (2015). Omnipresence of the Ramayana in Thai Arts and Culture. *India Studies Journal,* Special Issue of the 2015 Conference, Thammasat University, Thailand.

Chong, J. I. (2013). China South East Asia relations since the cold war. In Andrew, T. H. T. (ed.), *East and Southeast Asia, International Relations and Security Perspectives.* London, UK: Routledge.

Chongkittwarn, K. (2018). Watch out for ASEAN's new Indo-Pacific. *The Bangkok Post,* December 4, 2018. https://www.bangkokpost.com/opinion/opinion/1587206/watch-out-for-aseans-new-indo-pacific.

Coedes, G. & Wright, H. M., (1966). *The Making of South East Asia/George Coedes*; translated by H. M. Wright Routledge & Kegan Paul, London.

Coedes, G. (1968). *The Indianized States of Southeast Asia/by G. Coedes* in (eds.), Walter F. Vella, translated by Susan Brown Cowing Australian National University Press Canberra.

Coedes, G. (1983). *The Making of Southeast Asia*. Los Angeles, CA: University of California Press.

Coedes, G. (1996). *The Indianized States of Southeast Asia*. Honolulu, HI: University of Hawaii Press.

Collins, E. F. (2013). Hinduism in South Asia. https://www.oxfordbibliographies. com/view/document/obo-9780195399318/obo-9780195399318-0112.xml.

Conrad Sangma, stated this at the Tenth Delhi Dialogue, New Delhi, July 19, 2018. https://economictimes.indiatimes.com/news/politics-and-nation/north-eastern-states-could-take-lead-in-promotion-of-act-east-policy-conrad-sangma/articleshow/65057287.cms

Das, R. U., Ratanakomut, S. M., & Sothitorn, A. (2002). Feasibility study on a free trade agreement between India and Thailand. Prepared for Joint Working Group on India-Thailand Free Trade Agreement (Ministry of Commerce, Govt. of India and Ministry of Commerce, Govt. of Thailand), Bangkok, Thailand: RIS and Chulalongkorn University.

de Casparis, J. G. & Mabbett, I. W. (1992). Religion and popular beliefs of Southeast Asia before c. 1500. In Tarling, N. (ed.), *The Cambridge History of Southeast Asia*. Volume 1. Cambridge, UK: University of Cambridge Press.

De, P. & Iyengar, K. (eds.) (2014). Developing economic corridors in South Asia. *Asian Development Bank*. https://www.adb.org/sites/default/files/publication/ 162073/developing-economic-corridors.pdf.

De, P. (ed.). (2014). ASEAN-India: Deepening Economic Partnership in Mekong Region. RIS, New Delhi.

De, P. (2018). *Assessing Economic Impacts of Connectivity Corridors: An Empirical Investigation*, New Delhi: RIS.

De, P & K. H. Singh. (2018). Look East to Act East: Connectivity Challenges to India's Northeast in Celebrating the Third Decade and Beyond: New Challenges to ASEAN-India Economic Partnership, (eds.), Prabir De, Suthiph and Chirathivat. London: Routledge.

De, P. (2018a). *Assessing Economic Impacts of Connectivity Corridors: An Empirical Investigation*. New Delhi: RIS.

De, P. (2018b). Shared values, common destiny: What we expect from the 16th ASEAN-India summit. *Economic Times*, November 11, 2018. https:// economictimes.indiatimes.com/blogs/et-commentary/shared-values-common-destiny-what-we-expect-from-the-16th-asean-india-summit/; accessed on November 12, 2018.

De, P. (ed.). (2014). *ASEAN-India: Deepening Economic Partnership in Mekong Region*. New Delhi: RIS.

De, P. & Iyengar, K. (eds.). (2014). *Developing Economic Corridors in South Asia.* Philippines: Asian Development Bank. https://www.adb.org/sites/default/files/publication/162073/developing-economic-corridors.pdf.

De, P. & Singh, P. K. H. (2018). Look East to Act East: Connectivity challenges to India's Northeast. In De, P. & Chirathivat, S. (eds.), *Celebrating the Third Decade and Beyond: New Challenges to ASEAN-India Economic Partnership.* London: Routledge.

De, P., Ghatak, S., & Kumarasamy, D. (2018). Assessing Economic Impacts of Connectivity Corridors: An Empirical Investigation. AIC, RIS.

De Prabir, Ghatak, S., & Kumaraswamy D. (2018). Assessing Economic Impacts of Connectivity Corridors: An Empirical Investigation with Special Focus on Northeast India, India: RIS and AIC.

Deloitte (2016). Global manufacturing competitiveness index. https://www2.deloitte.com/content/dam/Deloitte/global/Documents/Manufacturing/gx-global-mfg-competitiveness-index-2016.pdf.

Department of Foreign Affairs and Trade, Government of Australia. https://dfat.gov.au/international-relations/regional-architecture/eas/Pages/east-asia-summit-eas.aspx; accessed on December 7, 2018.

Department of Industrial Policy & Promotion (2018). FDI fact sheet 2018. http://dipp.nic.in/sites/default/files/FDI_FactSheet_29June2018.pdf.

Desai, S. (2017). ASEAN and India converge on connectivity. *The Diplomat,* December 19, 2017. https://thediplomat.com/2017/12/asean-and-india-converge-on-connectivity/.

Devare, S. (2005). *India and Southeast Asia: Towards Security Convergence.* Singapore: ISEAS-Yusof Ishak Institute.

DHL (2018). https://www.logistics.dhl/content/dam/dhl/global/core/documents/pdf/glo-core-dhl-gci-2018-ranking-overall-results-en.pdf.

DHL (2018). DHL global competitiveness index. https://www.logistics.dhl/content/dam/dhl/global/core/documents/pdf/glo-core-dhl-gci-2018-ranking-overall-results-en.pdf.

DNA (n.a.). India to link with Myanmar port to boost ASEAN connectivity. https://www.dnaindia.com/india/report-india-to-link-with-myanmar-port-to-boost-asean-connectivity-1873123; accessed on December 30, 2018.

Downie, E. (2015). Manipur and India's Act East policy. *The Diplomat,* February 25, 2015. https://thediplomat.com/2015/02/manipur-and-indias-act-east-policy.

Durai, S. (2019). Remarks by Ambassador at Coffee Seminar. https://embassyofindiabangkok.gov.in/mynews.php?nid=583.

Dutta, A. & Laskar, R. H (2018). Thai envoy lays stress on motor vehicles pact, *Hindustan Times*, December 14, 2018. https://www.hindustantimes.com/india-news/thai-envoy-lays-stress-on-motor-vehicles-pact/story-VMmI8k-SQ5DYcOztkxYffKI.html. accessed on December 18, 2018.

Economic Times (2018). Northeastern states could take lead in promotion of Act East policy: Conrad Sangma. *Economic Times*, July 19, 2018. https://economictimes.indiatimes.com/news/politics-and-nation/northeastern-states-could-take-lead-in-promotion-of-act-east-policy-conrad-sangma/articleshow/65057287.cms.

Eleanor, Albert (2017). ASEAN: The Association of Southeast Asian Nations, Council for Foreign Relations; https://www.cfr.org/backgrounder/asean-association-southeast-asian-nations.

Elizabeth, C. (2018). China's new revolution: The reign of Xi Jinping. *Foreign Affairs*, 97(3), 60–74.

Embree, A. & Gluck, C. (1997). *Asia in Western and World History: A Guide for Teaching*. London, UK: M. E. Sharpe.

European Colonialism (2019). Essential humanities. http://www.essential-humanities.net/history-supplementary/european-colonialism/.

Francisco, J. (1994). *From Ayodhya to Pulu Agamaniog: Rama's Journey to the Philippines*. Quezon City, Philippines: Asian Center, University of Philippines.

Gait, E.A. (1906). *A History of Assam 1863*. Calcutta, India: Thacker Spink & Co.

Gaughran, A. (2017). Rohingya fleeing Myanmar face difficulties in Thailand. *The Diplomat*, September 29, 2017. https://thediplomat.com/2017/09/rohingya-fleeing-myanmar-face-difficulties-in-thailand/.

Ghosh, L. (ed.) (2011). Connectivity and Beyond-Indo Thai Relations through ages, Kolkata: The Asiatic Society.

Ghosh, S. (2014). Viewing our shared past through Buddhist votive tablets across eastern India, Bangladesh and peninsular Thailand. In Singh, U. & Dhar, P. P. (eds.), *Asian Encounters*: *Exploring Connected Histories*. New Delhi, India: Oxford University Press.

Ghosh, L. (ed.) (2017). India-Thailand Cultural Interactions, Glimpses from the Past to Present, Springer.

Ghosh, S. (2017). Dvaravati votive tablets: Understanding their regional variations and Indian linkages, Chapter 2. In Ghosh, L. (ed.), *India-Thailand Cultural Interactions: Glimpses from the Past to Present*. Singapore: Springer.

Gnanasagaran, A. (2017). An important take on ASEAN centrality. *The ASEAN Post*, October 6, 2017. https://theaseanpost.com/article/important-take-asean-centrality.

Gnanasagaran, A. (2018). Strengthening ASEAN's labour force. *The ASEAN Post*, January 19, 2018. https://theaseanpost.com/article/strengthening-aseans-labour-force.

Gogoi, Hironmon iBorgohain, Tai Ahom Tradition and Culture *vis-a-vis* Thai Culture: an In-depth Analysis. http://icts13.chiangmai.cmu.ac.th/documents/FINAL_A-G_MAY_2018.pdf; pp. 348–358.

Government of India (2011). Census of India — 2011. https://www.census2011.co.in/census/state/assam.html.

Goyal, T. M & Mukherjee, A. (2018). FDI in Services and India, Working Papers id:12769, eSocialSciences.

Grant, T. (2017). *Food Processing Sector Challenges and Growth Enablers*, February 22, 2017. https://www.grantthornton.in/globalassets/1.-member-firms/india/assets/pdfs/food_processing_sector.pdf.

Grare, F. (2017). *India Turns East: International Engagement and US–China Rivalry*. India: Penguin, Random House.

Gupta, A. (2013). India's approach to Asia Pacific. Institute for Defense Studies and Analyses. https://idsa.in/policybrief/IndiasapproachtoAsiaPacific_agupta_190913.

Gupta, S. (1999). *Indians in Thailand*. New Delhi, India: Books India International, Kunming, China.

Hall, K. R. (1985). *Maritime Trade and State Development in Early Southeast Asia*. Honolulu: University of Hawaii Press.

Hie, L. H. (2016). *Can ASEAN Overcome the 'Consensus Dilemma' over the South China Sea? ISEAS Perspective*, October 24, 2016. https://www.iseas.edu.sg/images/pdf/ISEAS_Perspective_2016_58.pdf.

Hong, H. H. (2012). *Foreign Direct Investment in Southeast Asia: Determinants and Spatial Distribution*. France, Centre of Studies and Research on International Development, University of Auvergne, CNRS.

Hoontrakul, P. (2014). ASEAN 2.0: AEC and regional connectivity. In Hoontrakul P., Balding, C., & Marwah, R. (eds.), *The Global Rise of Asian Transformation*. USA: Palgrave Macmillan.

Hopkins, H. (1952). *New World Arising: A Journey of Discovery through the New Nations of Southeast Asia*. London, UK: H. Hamilton.

http://donlehmanjr.com/SEA/SEA5%20Chap/SEA5%20Ch2B.htm.

http://www.newindianexpress.com/nation/2018/jan/27/pm-modi-announces-1000-scholarships-at-iits-for-phd-students-from-ASEAN-countries-1764041.html.

https://asean.org/vision-statement-asean-india-commemorative-summit/; accessed on January 28, 2019.

https://embassyofindiabangkok.gov.in/mynews.php?nid=583; accessed on May 8, 2019.

https://www.globalsecurity.org/military/world/vietnam/vietnam-nguyen.htm; accessed on November 12, 2018.

https://www.india-briefing.com/news/indiamyanmarthailand-trilateral-highway-investment-opportunity-making-11535.html/.

https://www2.deloitte.com/content/dam/Deloitte/global/Documents/Manufacturing/gx-global-mfg-competitiveness-index-2016.pdf; accessed on November 5, 2018.

IBEF (2017). Huge potential for agriculture export from northeast: Study. *BusinessStandard*, September 7, 2017. https://www.ibef.org/news/huge-potential-for-agriculture-export-from-northeast-study.

INSSL (2019). Positioning India-ASEAN relations in a transformed Asian landscape. http://www.insssl.lk/preview.php?id=216; accessed on March 29, 2019.

Jacq-Hergoualc'h, M. (1991). Archaeological research in the Malay Peninsula. *Journal of the Siam Society*, 85(1 & 2), 21–31. http://www.siamese-heritage.org/jsspdf/1991/JSS_085_0j_JacqHergoualch_ArchaologialResearchInMalayPeninsula.pdf.

Jacq-Hergoualc'h M. (2002). The Malay Peninsula: Crossroads of the Maritime Silk Road (100 b.c.1300 a.d), transl. V Hobson. Leiden/Boston: Brill.

Jahan, S. H. (2012). Maritime Trade between Thailand and Bengal. *Journal of Fine Arts*, 3(2), 208–220. https://www.tci-thaijo.org/index.php/fineartsJournal/article/view/77665/62288.

Jamrisko, M. (2019). Singapore dethrones U.S. as world's most competitive economy. *Bloomberg*, May 28, 2019. https://www.bloomberg.com/news/articles/2019-05-28/singapore-dethrones-u-s-to-top-world-competitiveness-rankings.

Jangphanichkul, T. (1993). Brahma: God of Wealth and Prosperity. Bangkok, Thailand: Comma Publishing House.

Jany, G. (2017). Golf diplomacy: The Rohingya crisis challenges ASEAN's way. *The Politic*, October 13, 2017. http://thepolitic.org/golf-diplomacy-the-rohingya-crisis-challenges-aseans-way/.

Jaumotte, F. (2004). Foreign Direct Investment and Regional Trade Agreements: The Market Size Effect Revisited. IMF Working Paper, WP/04/206.

Johannes Gijsbertus (Hans) de Casparis, *India and Maritime South East Asia: A Lasting Relationship*, Kuala Lumpur. – Third Sri Lanka Endowment Fund Lecture, 10 August 1983.– "Sïgiri: rotsvesting of godenverblijf?" *VerreNaastenNaderbij* 17, 1: 1–10.– Foreword to: *Indonesian archaeological photographs on microfich*: photo collection of the National Research Centre of Archaeology of the Republic of Indonesia 1901–1956 at the Kern Institute, University of Leiden.

Kaplan, R. D. (2010). *Monsoon: The Indian Ocean and the Future of American Power*. London, UK: Random House.

Kaplan, R. D. (2011). *Monsoon: The Indian Ocean and the Future of American Power*. London, UK: Random House.

Kaplan, R. D. (2014). *Asia's Cauldron: The South China Sea and the End of a Stable Pacific*. Penguin Random House.

Kartik Bommakanti and Ameya Kelkar, "China's Military Modernisation: Recent Trends", ORF Issue Brief No. 286, March 2019, Observer Research.

Katoch, P. C. (2012). Existing Political and Economic Frameworks in the Asia Pacific- Have they fulfilled Regional Aspirations? In Maj Gen Y.K. Gera (eds.), *Peace and Stability in Asia Pacific Region: Assessment of the Security Architecture*, New Delhi: Vij Books India Pvt. Ltd.

Katoch, (2017). Dealing With Maoist Insurgency: Focused Approach Required. In Bajwa (ed.), *Indian Defence Review*, Lancer Publishers LLC. https://play. google.com/store/books/details/Indian_Defence_Review_Apr_Jun_2017? id=sqctDwAAQBAJ.

Kausikan, B. (2018). ASEAN: Agnostic on the free and open Indo-Pacific. *The Diplomat*. https://thediplomat.com/2018/05/asean-agnostic-on-the-free-and-open-indo-pacific/.

Kawai, M. & Wignaraja, G. (2009). *The Asian "Noodle Bowl": Is It Serious for Business?* ADBI Working Paper No. 136.

Kelegama, S. (2001).Bangkok Agreement and BIMSTEC: Crawling Regional Economic Groupings in Asia. *Journal of Asian Economics*, 12(1), 105–121.

Kershaw, R. (2000). *Monarchy in South East Asia: The Faces of Tradition in Transition*. UK: Routledge.

Koh, T. (2016). Standing together — A perspective on India-Singapore bilateral relations. In Bhattacharya, A. K. & Tan, T. Y. (eds.), *Looking Ahead: India and Singapore in the New Millennium — Celebrating 50 Years of Diplomatic Relations*. New Delhi, India: Lustra Print Process.

KPMG (2018). ASEAN business guide — Thailand. https://home.kpmg.com/ content/dam/kpmg/sg/pdf/2018/07/ASEAN-GUIDE-Thailand.pdf.

Kristof, N. D. & WuDunn, S. (2001). *Thunder from the East: Portrait of a Rising Asia*. New York: Random House.

Kulke, H. (2014). *Indian Colonies, Indianization or Cultural Convergence? Reflections on the Changing Image of India's Role in Southeast Asia*. In Singh, U. & Dhar, P. P. (eds.), Asian Encounters: Exploring Connected Histories. New Delhi, India: Oxford University Press.

Kumar, N., Rahul, S., & Mukul, A. (eds.). (2006). *India ASEAN Economic Relations: Meeting the Challenges of Globalization*. Singapore: RIS and ISEAS.

Kumar, P. (2014). India-Thailand Relations since 1990. Academic Discourse 3.1 59.

Kumar, S. (ed.) (2013). India-Thailand Bilateral Relations, Mohit Publications, New Delhi, India.

Kusalasaya, K. (2013). Buddhism in Thailand: Its past, and its present. *Access to Insight (BCBS Edition)*, November 30, 2013. http://www.accesstoinsight. org/lib/authors/kusalasaya/wheel085.html; accessed on November 20, 2018.

Laishram, R. S. (2011). Cultural links between Northeast India and East/ Southeast Asia. http://kanglaonline.com/2011/05/cultural-links-between-northeast-india-and-eastsoutheast-asia/; accessed on May 28, 2011.

Lambert, T. (2019). A brief history of Cambodia. http://www.localhistories.org/ cambodia.html.

Landon, M. (1944). Anna and the King of Siam. https://www.goodreads.com/ book/show/1284085.Anna_and_the_King_of_Siam.

Laplamwanit, N. (2018). A good look at the Thai financial crisis in 1997-98; fall 1999. http://www.columbia.edu/cu/thai/html/financial97_98.html; accessed on October 6, 2018.

Laude, J. (2018). Guidelines military air encounters adopted. *Philstar*, October 22, 2018. https://www.philstar.com/headlines/2018/10/22/1862056/guidelines-military-air-encounters-adopted#xBuhAeLmO4hrxS3s.99; accessed on January 11, 2019.

Lauridsen; Laurids S. (2019), *Drivers of China's Regional Infrastructure Diplomacy: The Case of the Sino-Thai Railway Project*; Journal of Contemporary Asia; Taylor and Francis; https://doi.org/10.1080/00472336.2 019.1603318.

Lefevre, A. (2014). Thai junta boosts spending on defence, education in draft budget, *Reuters*, https://mobile.reuters.com/article/amp/idUSL4N0QO1DS 20140818.

Lehman Jr., D. (2015). *The Rise & Fall of Southeast Asia's Empires*, Lulu, USA.

Lieberman, V. (2003). *Strange Parallels, Volume 1: Integration on the Mainland: Southeast Asia in Global Context, c.800-1830*. Edition 1, Cambridge.

Lintner, B. (2015). *Great Game East: India, China, and the Struggle for Asia's Most Volatile Frontier*. USA: Yale University Press.

Lintner, B. *Book Review — India ASEAN Economic Relations*. http://www. asiapacificms.com/articles/india_ASEAN_relations/; accessed on December 5, 2018.

Mabbett, I. W. (1977). The Indianization' of Southeast Asia: Reflections on the Historical Sources, *Journal of Southeast Asian Studies* 8(1): 143–161.

Macaes, B. (2019). *Belt and Road — A Chinese World Order*. India: Penguin, Random House.

Maini, T. S. (2017). The Rebirth of the Quad. *Hard News*, November 2017, 38–39.

Majumdar, R. C. (1927). *Ancient Indian Colonies in the Far East*. 2 Vols. Lahore, Pakistan: The Punjab Sanskrit Book Depot.

Manguin, P.-V., Mani, A., & Wade, G. (2011). *Early Interactions between South and Southeast Asia: Reflections on Cross-cultural Exchange*. Singapore: Institute of Southeast Asia Studies.

Mantraya Analysis#15 (2017). http://mantraya.org/analysis-chinas-new-game-in-indias-northeast/, accessed on December 30, 2018.

Marwah, R. (2019). Paper titled, *Bilateral* engagement: The Key to Navigating India's *interests* in BIMSTEC and ASEAN, at the International Workshop on the theme, Bilateral and Multilateral Matrix in South Asia organized by the School of Social Sciences and Internal Studies, Pondicherry University, on February 5–6.

Mason, C. (2000). *A Short History of Asia: Stone Age to 2000 AD*. London, UK: Macmillan, 247–253.

Matthew, P. (2018). Thailand in the Cold War. https://www.routledge.com/Thailand-in-the-Cold-War/Phillips/p/book/9781138014169.

Mehta, R. (2002). Potential of India's Bilateral Free Trade Arrangements: A Case Study of India and Thailand, RIS Discussion Paper 24, January 2002. http://ris.org.in/images/RIS_images/pdf/dp24_pap.pdf; accessed on October 6, 2018.

Mesangrutdharakul, W. (2015). Pali Sanskrit and Tamil words in South East Asia; A case study of the Thai, Lao, Malaysia Language. *Review of Integrative Business and Economics Research*, 4, 158–165.

Mesangrutdharakul; W. (2015). *Pali Sanskrit and Tamil words in South East Asia; A Case Study of the Thai, Lao, Malaysia Language*, Nakhon Ratchasima Rajabhat University, Review of Integrative Business and Economics Research, Volume 4 (NRRU). http://sibresearch.org/uploads/2/7/9/9/2799227/riber_s15-240_158-165.pdf.

Ministry of Tourism for India. UNWTO Barometer June 2018 for countries other than India. http://tourism.gov.in/sites/default/files/Other/ITS_Glance_2018_Eng_Version_for_Mail.pdf.

Moe, Thuzar, Rahul Mishra, Francis Hutchinson, Tin MaungMaung Than and TermsakChalermpalanupap, Yusof Ishak Institute. https://www.researchgate.

net/publication/305237012 Implementation challenges and coordination arrangements Chapter, January 2016.

Momin K. (2016). *India–Myanmar–Thailand Trilateral Highway: An Investment Opportunity in the Making*, India Briefing. https://www.india-briefing.com/news/indiamyanmarthailand-trilateral-highway-investment-opportunity-making-11535.html/; January 7, 2016.

Morey, S. (2008). *The Tai Languages of Assam*. The_Tai_Languages_of_Assam_2008.pdf.

Morey, S. & Post, M. W. (eds.). (2010). *North East Indian Linguistics*. Volume 2. Delhi, India: Cambridge University Press.

Morris, I. (2010). Why the West rules – for now. The patterns of history and what they reveal about the future, Profile Books Ltd., London 2010.

Moudgil, S. (2018). India-ASEAN Maritime Cooperation Prospects, 05-04-2018, Issue Brief, MaritimeIndia.org.

Mukherjee, A. & Goyal, T. M. (2015). Integrating South and Southeast Asia through services value chain: The case of India and Thailand, Working Paper No. 301, Indian Council for Research on International Economic Relations (ICRIER), New Delhi.

Mukerjee, A. & Tanu, M. G. (2018). Integrating South and Southeast Asia through services value chain: The case of India and Thailand. In Menon, J. & Srinivasan, T. N. (eds.), *Integrating South and Southeast Asia*. India: ADB and OUP.

Mun, S. C. (2016). Singapore's viewpoint on strategic engagement and regional cooperation. In Bhattacharya, A. K. & Tan, T. Y. (eds.), *Looking Ahead: India and Singapore in the New Millennium — Celebrating 50 Years of Diplomatic Relations*. New Delhi, India: Lustra Print Process.

Nanda, B. (2018). India and ASEAN @ 25, DPG Policy Brief. http://www.delhipolicygroup.org/uploads_dpg/publication_file/india-and-asean-25-1082.pdf.

Narayan, R. (2013). India to link with Myanmar port to boost ASEAN connectivity. *Yahoo Finance*. https://in.finance.yahoo.com/news/india-myanmar-port-boost-asean-102410266.html.

National Council for Applied Economic Research (2018). *The NCAER State Investment Potential Index as Cited in the NCAER Report*, p. xiv. India: National Council for Applied Economic Research.

NESDB Economic Report (2018). Macroeconomic Strategy and Planning Office Press Release. Thailand: NESDB.

Noor, F. A, (2009). What Your Teacher Didn't Tell You (The Annexe Lectures, Volume 1, Matahari Books, Petaling Jaya, Malaysia.

Nordea (n.a.). https://www.nordeatrade.com/en/explore-new-market/thailand/investment.

Nowell, C. (1936). The Discovery of Brazil-Accidental or Intentional? *The Hispanic American Historical Review*, 16(3), 311–338.

Oliver T., Jonathan, Ng & Matteo M. (2014). Understanding ASEAN: The Manufacturing Opportunity, McKinsey Productivity Sciences Center.

Panda, A. (2018). India poised to gain access to Indonesia's Sabang Island. *The Diplomat*, May 21, 2018. https://thediplomat.com/2018/05/india-poised-to-gain-access-to-indonesias-sabang-island/.

Panda, J. P. & Basu, T. (eds.). (2018). *China–India–Japan in the Indo-Pacific: Ideas, Interests and Infrastructure*. New Delhi: Pentagon Press.

Pant, H. V. (2018). The future of India's ties with ASEAN. *The Diplomat*, January 26, 2018. https://thediplomat.com/2018/01/the-future-of-indias-ties-with-ASEAN/.

Pant, H. & Deb, A. (2017). India-ASEAN partnership at 25. ORF Issue Brief No. 189, July 2017.

Panyaarvudh, J. (2019). Thailand's future sacrificed at the stake of China's BRI. *Nation Multimedia*. http://www.nationmultimedia.com/detail/your_say/30368821; accessed on May 4, 2019.

Parameswaran, P. (2018). What's in the new ASEAN air encounter code? *The Diplomat*, October 22, 2018. https://thediplomat.com/2018/10/whats-in-the-new-asean-air-encounter-code/.

Parashar, S. (2014). India and Thailand must battle terrorism and trafficking together: Harsh Vardhan Shringla. *The Times of India*, https://timesofindia.indiatimes.com/blogs/the-interviews-blog/28428/; accessed on October 29, 2014.

Parthasarathy, G. (2019). New security challenges in North-East. *The Hindu Business Line*, April 17, 2019. https://www.thehindubusinessline.com/opinion/new-security-challenges-in-north-east/article26866778.ece.

Patra, B. (2017). Kalinga and Siam: A study in ancient relations. *Odisha Review*, April 2017. http://magazines.odisha.gov.in/Orissareview/2017/April/engpdf/Kalinga_and_Siam.pdf.

Patranobis, S. (2018). Too Close for Comfort: China to Build Port in Myanmar, 3rd in India's Vicinity, *The Hindustan Times*, https://www.hindustantimes.com/india-news/china-myanmar-ink-deal-for-port-on-bay-of-bengal-third-in-india-s-vicinity/story-Lbm4IwOMuqrNvXGv4ewuYJ.html. accessed on December 30, 2018.

Pauker, G. J., Golay, F. H., & Enloe, C. H. (1977). Diversity and Development in Southeast Asia: The Coming Decade. New York: McGraw Hill.

Pham, T. & Newsham, G. (2018). China's worst nightmare: RIMPAC 2020 in the South China Sea? *The National Interest*, September 29, 2018. https://news.yahoo.com/china-apos-worst-nightmare-rimpac-080000842.html.

Phillips, M. (2018). *Thailand in the Cold War*. London, UK: Routledge.

Phukan, G. (1990). *Search for Tai-Ahom Identity in Assam: In Retrospect*. Proceedings of the 4th International Conference on Tai Studies, Volume 4, Kunming, China, p. 377.

Plummer, M. G. & Siow, C. Y. (eds.). (2009). *Realizing the ASEAN Economic Community: A Comprehensive Assessment*. Singapore: Institute of Southeast Asian Studies.

PM Modi speech. *Shangri-la Dialogue*, June 1, 2018. https://www.mea.gov.in/Speeches-Statements.htm?dtl/29943/Prime+Ministers+Keynote+Address+at+Shangri+La+Dialogue+June+01+2018.

Pollock, S. (1996). The Sanskrit cosmopolis, 300–1300: Transculturation, vernacularization, and the question of ideology. In Houben, J. E. M. (ed.), *Ideology and Status of Sanskrit: Contributions to the History of the Sanskrit Language*. Leiden, The Netherlands: Brill, 197–247.

Poolthupya, S. (2008). Indians in Thailand. In Kesavapany, K., Mani, A., & Ramasamy, P. (eds.), *Rising India and Indian Communities in East Asia*. Singapore: ISEAS-Yusof Ishak Institute. Retrieved July 15, 2019, from Project MUSE database.

Press statement by the Chairman of the ASEAN foreign ministers retreat, Chiang Mai, January 17–18, 2019. https://www.asean2019.go.th/en/news/press-statement-by-the-chairman-of-the-asean-foreign-ministers-retreat-chiang-mai-17-18-january-2019/.

PTI. https://economictimes.indiatimes.com/news/economy/foreign-trade/thai-companies-keen-to-invest-3-billion-in-indian-infrastructure; April 23, 2018.

Rachel C. (2019). https://timesofindia.indiatimes.com/companies/why-many-indians-are-moving-to-se-asia-to-launch-their-ventures/articleshow/68871835.cms; http://timesofindia.indiatimes.com/articleshow/68871835.cms?utm_source=contentofinterest&utm_medium=text&utm_campaign=cppst; accessed on May 8, 2019.

Rachman, G. (2016). *Easternisation: War and Peace in the Asian Century*. London, UK: The Bodley Head.

Rachman, G. (2016). *War and Peace in Asia*, August 5. https://www.ft.com/content/80122bbc-5985-11e6-8d05-4eaa66292c32.

Raghuramapatruni, R. (2018). India's Trade with the Bay of Bengal Initiative for Multi-Sectoral Technical and Economic-Cooperation (BIMSTEC) — A Study. *International Journal of Management Studies*, 5, 67–75.

Raje, S. (n.a.). The fatalism of architecture or architecture of fatalism? Aditi Dora. https://www.sawdust.online/expert-speak/the-fatalism-of-architecture-or-architecture-of-fatalism-aditi-dora/.

Ram, A. N. (2007). India-Thailand Relations: Evolving Convergences.' Dialogue: A Quarterly Journal of Astha Bharati 9.1.

Ram, A. N., Chakraborty T. & Chakraborty, M. (2018). Expanding Horizons of India's Southeast Asia Policy: Look, Move and Act East, Knowledge World.

Ram, V. (2018). India's defence diplomacy with Southeast Asia: An impetus to Act East. *Journal of Defence Studies*, 12(3), 55–78.

Ramerini, M. Portugese Malacca 1511–1641. https://www.colonialvoyage.com/portuguese-malacca-1511-1641/; accessed on November 20, 2018.

Rani, A. (2016). An Analysis of India's Trade Relations with Thailand. *International Journal of Research in Commerce, Economics and Management* VI.II.

Ray, R. K. (2017). India's economy to become 3rd largest, surpass Japan, Germany by 2030. *Hindustan Times*, April 28, 2017. https://www.hindustantimes.com/business-news/india-s-economy-will-become-third-largest-in-the-world-surpass-japan-germany-by-2030-us-agency/story-wBY2QOQ8YsYcrIK12A-4HuK.html; accessed on December 11, 2018.

Reid, A. (1993). (ed.) Southeast Asia in the Early Modern Era: Trade, Power, and Belief . Ithaca and London: Cornell University Press.

Reid, A. (1993). *Southeast Asia in the Age of Commerce, 1450–1680, Volume Two: Expansion and Crisis*. New Haven and London: Yale University Press.

Reid, A. (1988). *Southeast Asia in the Age of Commerce, 1450-1680: Volume One: The Lands below the Winds*. New Haven and London: Yale University Press.

RIS (2015). *ASEAN-India Economic Relations — Opportunities and Challenges*. New Delhi, India: AIC, RIS.

RIS (2017). *Mekong-Ganga Cooperation: Breaking Barriers and Scaling New Heights*. New Delhi, India: AIC, RIS.

Routray, B. P. (2017). *China's New Game in India's Northeast*.

SAARC Secretariat. Next steps to South Asian economic union: A study on regional economic integration (phase II). http://saarc-sec.org/download/downloads/Study_-_SAARC_Next_Steps_to_SAEU.pdf.

Sakhuja, Vijay (2017 November); Short sea shipping in Bay of Bengal takes baby steps; Eurasia Review, https://www.eurasiareview.com/04112017-short-sea-shipping-in-bay-of-bengal-takes-baby-steps-analysis/.

Sankalia, H. D. (1965). *Introduction to Archaeology*. India: Deccan College.

Sasi, A. https://indianexpress.com/article/business/govt-run-ports-higher-efficiency-benchmarks-production-turnaround-4670690/, New Delhi. Updated May 24, 2017.

Sastri, N. A. K. (1949) *South Indian Influence in the Far East*. Chennai: Tamil Arts Academy.

Sathip, N. & Ranoo, W. (1998). The State of Knowledge of Ahom History, in *Tai Culture, International Review on Tai Cultural Studies*, Volume 3, No. 1, SEACOM, Berlin, pp. 16–48.

Sengupta, J. (2017). *India's Cultural and Civilizational Influence on Southeast Asia, Observer Research Foundation, India*.

SCFI. (2019). Significance of Bihu festival. http://www.bihufestival.org/significance-of-bihu.html; accessed on April 18, 2019.

Sen, A. (2018). Thailand seeks India's partnership in pharma, bio-tech. *The Hindu Business Line*, January 12, 2018.

Sengupta, R. (2018). PM Modi announces 1000 scholarships at IIT's for PhD students from ASEAN countries. *Indian Express*, January 27, 2018.

Sharma, P. (n.a.). India's relations with Asian countries. http://www.historydiscussion.net/history-of-india/indias-relations-with-asian-countries/2253.

Shastri, S. V. (1982). *Ramayana in Southeast Asia — A Comparative Analysis. Studies in Sanskrit and Indian Culture in Thailand*. Delhi: Parimal Prakashan.

Sheel, K. (2014). Hu Shih and 'The Indianisation of China': Some comments on modern Chinese discourses on India. *China Report, 50*(3): 177–188. https://doi.org/10.1177/0009445514534119.

Shih, C. *et al.* (2019). *China and International Theory: The Balance of Relationships*. USA: Routledge.

Sidhartha, S. J. (2019). Going physical: Flipkart plans grocery stores. *The Times of India*, May 25, 2019. https://timesofindia.indiatimes.com/business/india-business/going-physical-flipkart-plans-grocery-stores/articleshow/69436682.cms.

Singh, S. (2001). The China factor in India's Look East Policy, In Frederic G. and Mattoo A. (eds.) *India and ASEAN: The politics of India's Look East Policy*, Delhi: Manohar.

Singh, A. (2018). The nautical dimension of India's Act East Policy. http://www.rsis.edu.sg/wp-content/uploads/2018/04/PR180409_The-Nautical-Dimension-of-Indias-Act-East-Policy.pdf.

Singh, A. R. (2017). Hydro-power potential of Northeast India and its development. *Eastern Panorama*. https://www.easternpanorama.in/index.php/movies/196-year-2017/december-2017-issue/3626-resources.

Singh, B. (2018). Advantage Assam Summit: Investment of Rs 1,00,000 crore committed. February 4, 2018. https://economictimes.indiatimes.com/news/economy/finance/advantage-assam-summit-investment-of-rs-100000-crore-committed/articleshow/62779498.cms.

Singh, D. K. (2017). *Proposed Export Promotion Strategy of APEDA Products*, APEDA, September 20, 2017, https://apeda.gov.in/apedawebsite/Announcements/FINALEXPORTSTRATEGY11.09.2017.pdf.

Singh, H. V. (2017). *India is an Average Low-Ttariff Economy, There are Misconceptions Otherwise.* https://www.brookings.edu/opinions/india-is-an-average-low-tariff-economy-there-are-misconceptions-otherwise.

Singh, D. (2001). Interconnection between South and Southeast Asia. In Frederic, G. & Mattoo, A. (eds.), *India and ASEAN: The Politics of India's Look East Policy.* New Delhi: Manohar.

Singh, S. (2001). *The China factor in India's Look East Policy. In India and ASEAN: The Politics of India's Look East Policy.* Frederic G. & Mattoo A. (eds.), New Delhi: Manohar.

Singh, U. & Dhar, P. P. (eds.). (2014). *Asian Encounters: Exploring Connected Histories.* New Delhi, India: Oxford University Press.

Smith, A. 1723–1790. (2000). *The Wealth of Nations/Adam Smith; Introduction by Robert Reich; Edited with Notes, Marginal Summary, and Enlarged Index by Edwin Cannan.* New York: Modern Library.

Smith, M. (1999). Indianization from the Indian point of ivew: Trade and cultural contacts with Southeast Asia in the early first millennium C.E. *Journal of the Economic and Social History of the Orient*, 42(1), 1–26.

South Asian History. http://www.gpmsdbaweb.com/memoir2/_supportdocs/European%20Domination%20Indian%20Ocean%20Trade%20Portuguese.htm; accessed on November 14, 2018.

Srichampa, S. (2014). *Hindus in the Globalized Thai Society.* Centre for Bharat Studies. Research Institute for Languages and Cultures of Asia, Mahidol University, Thailand.

Srichampa, S. (2015). *Hindu God Brahma in Thailand.* Centre for C Studies. Research Institute for Languages and Cultures of Asia, Mahidol University, Thailand.

Sridharan, K. (2001). Regional perceptions of India. In Frederic, G. & Mattoo, A. (eds.), *India and ASEAN: The Politics of India's Look East Policy.* New Delhi: Manohar.

Stark, M. T. & Allen, S. J. (1998). The transition to history in Southeast Asia: An introduction. *International Journal of Historical Archaeology*, 2(3), 163–175.

Sudhit, W. (2003). Historical ties India and Thailand. https://www.esamskriti.com/e/History/Indian-Influence-Abroad/Historical-Ties-India-and-Thailand-1.aspx.

Sugondhabhirom, A. (2018). "The Kings and I(ndia)": The Royal Thai family and the Siam-Bharat relations. http://newdelhi.thaiembassy.org/en/2018/07/kings-india-royal-thai-family-context-siam-bharat-relations.

Suryanaryan (2013). IPCS, India. http://www.ipcs.org/issue_briefs/issue_brief_pdf/SR139-SoutheastAsia-Suryanarayan.pdf.

Szczepanski, K. (2019). Indian Ocean Trade Routes. ThoughtCo. thoughtco.com/indian-ocean-trade-routes-195514; accessed on July 9, 2019.

Tan, A. T. H. (ed.). (2013). *East and South-East Asia: International Relations and Security Perspectives*. London, UK: Routledge.

Tan, K. S. & Bhaskaran, M. (2019). Rebuilding ASEAN's financial safety net. *East Asia Forum*, February 8, 2019. http://www.eastasiaforum.org/2019/02/08/rebuilding-ASEANs-financial-safety-net/.

Tarling, N. (2000). *The Cambridge History of Southeast Asia*. Cambridge, UK: Cambridge University Press.

Teo, S. (2017). The strengths and weaknesses of Asia's 2 major defense meetings. *The Diplomat*, March 21, 2017. https://thediplomat.com/2017/03/the-strengths-and-weaknesses-of-asias-2-major-defense-meetings/.

Thailand Board of Investment Report (2019). https://www.boi.go.th/upload/content/2019_year_of_investment_EN_5c5bfa4c544f1.pdf.

Thayer, C. A. (2014). New strategic uncertainty and security order in Southeast Asia. In Atanassova-Cornelis, E. & van der Putten, F. P. (eds.), *Changing Security Dynamics in East Asia*. UK: Palgrave Macmillan.

Dhwty (2015). The Majapahit Empire. The short life of an empire that once defeated the Mongols. https://www.ancient-origins.net/ancient-places-asia/majapahit-empire-short-life-empire-once-defeated-mongols-003623; accessed on November 14, 2018.

The ASEAN Post (2018). The ASEAN Post Team, January 1, 2018. https://theaseanpost.com/article/asean-2018-0.

The Economist (2019). *King Vajiralongkorn of Thailand is Crowned*. https://www.economist.com/asia/2019/05/04/king-vajiralongkorn-of-thailand-is-crowned.

The US Joins Anti-Piracy Organization (2014). *Sea Technology*, 55(11), 53.

The World Bank Press Release (2011). http://www.worldbank.org/en/news/press-release/2011/08/02/thailand-now-upper-middle-income-economy; accessed on October 5, 2018.

The World Bank Annual Report (2016). Washington DC, USA.

The World Bank. Current account balance. https://data.worldbank.org/indicator/BN.CAB.XOKA.CD?view=chart.

Thorton, G. & ASSOCHAM. (2017). Food processing sector: Challenges and growth enablers. https://www.grantthornton.in/globalassets/1.-member-firms/india/assets/pdfs/food_processing_sector.pdf; accessed on February 22, 2017.

Tonby, O., Jonathan, N., & Mancini, M. (2014). *Understanding ASEAN: The Manufacturing Opportunity*. Singapore: McKinsey Productivity Sciences Center.

UN News (2013). UN court rules for Cambodia in Preah Vihear temple dispute with Thailand. https://news.un.org/en/story/2013/11/455062-un-court-rules-cambodia-preah-vihear-temple-dispute-thailand.

UNWTO Barometer June 2018 for countries other than India. Ministry of Tourism for India, United Nations World Tourism Organization. http://tourism.gov.in/sites/default/files/Other/ITS_Glance_2018_Eng_Version_for_Mail.pdf. accessed on May 8, 2019.

Varadarajan, S. (2009). Asian integration process. *The Hindu*, 26 October 2009. https://www.thehindu.com/opinion/columns/siddharth-varadarajan/Asian-integration-process-an-lsquoact-of-foresightrsquo-India/article16855701.ece.

Vandenberg T. (2009). History of Ayutthaya: Foreign Settlements. https://www.ayutthaya-history.com/Settlements_Portuguese.html.

Vu, L. T. H. (2011). APEC 2011 and the future of regional architecture in Asia Pacific. *International Studies*, 24, 203–219. http://nghiencuuquocte.org/2014/05/28/apec-2011-and-the-future-of-regional-architecture-in-asia-pacific/; accessed on December 23, 2018.

Waddel, L. A. (2000). *The Tribes of the Brahmaputra Valley*, Reprint. New Delhi: Logos Press.

Wade, G. (2009). An early age of commerce in Southeast Asia, 900–1300 CE. *Journal of Southeast Asian Studies*, 40(2), 221–265.

Wales, H. G. Q. (1931). *Siamese State Ceremonies*. London, UK, Routledge.

Wang, G. (2010). Party and nation in Southeast Asia. *Millennial Asia*, 1(1): 41–57.

Watson, B. A. (2017). Introduction to Southeast Asia: History, geography, and livelihood. https://asiasociety.org/education/introduction-southeast-asia; accessed on September 20, 2017.

Wen, Z. (2017). Trans-border ethnic groups and interstate relations within ASEAN: A case study on Malaysia and Thailand's southern conflict. *International Relations of the Asia-Pacific*, 17(2), 301–327. https://doi.org/10.1093/irap/lcw011.

Westad, O. A. (2017). *The Cold War — A World History.* UK: Penguin, Random House.

Wheatley, P. (1961). *The Golden Khersonese,* University of Malaya, Kuala Lumpur, Malaysia.

Wheatley, R. (1982). Presidential address: India beyond the Ganges — Desultory reflections on the origins of civilization in Southeast Asia. *Journal of Asian Studies,* 42, 13–28.

Wheeler, A. (2018). Myanmar's role in shaping global shipping and logistics chains through China's Belt and Road dream. *Mizzima,* December 15, 2018. http://mizzima.com/article/myanmars-role-shaping-global-shipping-and-logistics-chains-through-chinas-belt-and-road.

Whelan, G. (2012). Does the ARF have a role in ASEAN's pursuit of regional security in the next decade? http://www.defence.gov.au/ADC/Publications/Commanders/2012/10_CDSS%20SAP.pdf.

Yahya, F. (2008). Brand India and East Asia. In Kesavapany, K., Mani, A. & Ramasamy, P. (eds.), *Rising India and Indian Communities in East Asia.* Singapore: ISEAS-Yusof Ishak Institute.

Yeonsik, J. (2011). The idea of kingship in Buddhist Cambodia. *Kyoto Review of Southeast Asia.* (11), 1–8. https://kyotoreview.org/issue-11/the-idea-of-kingship-in-buddhist-cambodia/.

Zachary, A. (2019). Thailand's stolen election: An illegitimate election risks prolonging the country's problems. *The Diplomat,* June 1, 2019. https://thediplomat.com/2019/05/thailands-stolen-election/; accessed on June 27, 2019.

Zoltan, B. (2018). Where Myanmar went wrong: From democratic awakening to ethnic cleansing. *Foreign Affairs,* 97(3), 141–154.

Primary Sources: Interviews of Officials and Experts

Visit to Chiang Mai, Rayong, and Bangkok, Thailand

May 20 to June 4, 2018

and

Visit to Chiang Mai, Bangkok in Thailand and Mandalay, Yangon in Myanmar

April 23 to May 3, 2019

Interviewees in Thailand and Myanmar

City	Name	Institutional affiliation	Issues of discussion
CHIANG MAI, April 24, 2019	**H.E.** H.E. Mrs. Suchitra Durai, India's Ambassador to Thailand and Mr. Akhilesh Mishra, DG, ICCR		**Launch of the ISC at CMU**
CHIANG MAI	Prof. Chayan Vaddhanuputi	Head of the Regional Center for Social Sciences and Sustainable Development, Chiang Mai University (CMU)	Issues of sustainable development and impacts on local communities
	Prof. Sampan Singharajwarapan	Vice-President, Chiang Mai University	Possibilities of educational exchanges and cooperation
	Prof. Yos Santasombat	Head of BIRD Department, Faculty of Social Sciences, CMU	Thailand border issues
	Prof. Thapin Phatcharanuruk	Dean, Chiang Mai University	Initiation of the India Study Centre at CMU
	Dr. Rangsima Wiwatwongwana	Head of Center of Research and Academic Services, CMU	Initiation of the India Study Centre at CMU and aspects of curriculum development of the ISC
	Mr. Bertil Lintner	Correspondent, Asia Pacific Media Services Limited; Swedish journalist and author of 17 books, including *China's India War*	Chinese influence in South and Southeast Asia — strategic issues
	Mr. Shirish Jain	Consular, Consulate of India in Chiang Mai, Thailand	Aspects of bilateral cooperation and importance of people-to-people contacts
	Mr. Ranjeet Singh	President, 2017–2019, Indian Community of Chiang Mai	Indians in Chiang Mai — their migration and interaction with the Thai community
	Mr. and Mrs. Frank Sethi	Lion's Club President in Chiang Mai	Indians in business in Thailand

RAYONG	Mr. Munish Rathi	Head of Chemicals, Aditya Birla Group	Investment in Thailand and potential for further Indian investment
	Mr. Rajeev Narang	SRF Industries	Issues of access to resources including labor and inputs for production
	Mr. Sandeep Kumar	Aditya Birla Group	Issues of costs and productivity
BANGKOK	Dr. Wisarn Pupphavesa	Thailand Development Research Institute	Prospects for the Thai Economy, Thailand's relations with USA and China, Integration with ASEAN; Linking with regional value chains
	Prof. Surat Horachaikul	Centre for Indian Studies, Chulalongkorn University	Activities of the India Study center for promoting India Thailand relations
	Prof. Suthipand Chirathivat	ASEAN Center, Chulalongkorn University	Economic cooperation including trade and investment issues
	Dr. Pitti Srisangnam	Director of Academic Affairs, ASEAN Studies Center	India–ASEAN economic cooperation
	Prof. Prapin Manomaiviboo	China expert, Asia Research Centre, Chulalongkorn University	China studies in Thailand
	Dr. Panitan Wattanayakorn, Chulalongkorn University	Advisor to the Deputy PM of Thailand for Security and Institute of Strategic and International Studies, Chulalongkorn University	Security issues in ASEAN and role of Thailand in maintaining peace and stability in the region
	Ms. R. Naruemon Thabchumpon	Institute of Asian Studies	Issues of ethnicity and migration, especially from Myanmar
	Prof. Srisurang Poolthupya	Professor Emeritus, Thammasat University	Historical linkages between India and Thailand

(Continued)

(Continued)

City	Name	Institutional affiliation	Issues of discussion
	Prof. Nonglucksana	Former Director, Centre for Indian Studies, Thammasat University	Language similarities, religious tourism and visits to India; India's soft power
	Prof. Chirapat Prapandvidya	Eminent Sanskrit scholar in Silpakorn University and President, Thai Bharat Cultural Lodge	Awareness of India's historical links through traders and missionaries and linkages through Hinduism and Buddhism
	Dr. Sanjay Kumar	Commercial representative, Indian Embassy in Bangkok, Thailand	Issues pertaining to the India–Thai FTA and RCEP
	Prof. Chulacheeb Chinwanno	Department of Political Science, Thammasat University	Trade and economic cooperation aspects of India–ASEAN and China–Thailand relations
	Mr. Sorendarpal Sachdev	Central Coordinator, Sri Sathya Sai Organization	Initiatives to bring together people of India and Thailand
	Mr. Sushil Dhanuka	Director, Mastex, and Secretary of the Thai Bharat Cultural Lodge	Teaching of Hindi at TBCL and yoga classes; initiatives to bring together people of both countries
	Associate Prof. Dr. Sophana Srichampa	Chair, Centre for Bharat Studies, Mahidol University	Activities of the Bharat Studies Center and initiatives undertaken
MANDALAY, MYANMAR	Mr. Nandan Singh Bhaisora	Consul General of India, Mandalay	India–Myanmar relations, trade and investment, and people-to-people relations
	Mr. Khin Maung Soe	Consultant, Analyst, and Political Scientist, University of Mandalay	Issues in India–Myanmar relations; Myanmar–China relations; border issues with Thailand
YANGON, MYANMAR	Prof. Khin Maung Nyo	Myanmar Institute of Strategic and International Studies	Issues in India–Myanmar relations; Myanmar–China relations; border issues with Thailand

Interviewed officials of the Thai Embassy in New Delhi, including H.E. Ambassador Gongsakdi, Mr. Apirat.
Interviewed Mr. Nanthapol Sudbanthad on August 20th at the Thai Consulate Office in Mumbai, India.

Index